Moving the Rock

Moving the Rock

Poverty and Faith in a Black Storefront Church

Mary E. Abrums

ALTAMIRA
PRESS

A Division of Rowman & Littlefield Publishers, Inc.
Lanham • New York • Toronto • Plymouth, UK

AltaMira Press
A division of Rowman & Littlefield Publishers, Inc.
A wholly owned subsidiary of The Rowman & Littlefield Publishing Group, Inc.
4501 Forbes Boulevard, Suite 200
Lanham, MD 20706
www.altamirapress.com

Estover Road
Plymouth PL6 7PY
United Kingdom

British Library Cataloguing in Publication Information Available

Library of Congress Cataloging-in-Publication Data

Abrums, Mary Elyeen.
Moving the rock : poverty and faith in a Black storefront church / Mary E. Abrums.
p. cm.
Includes bibliographical references and index.
ISBN 978-0-7591-1319-0 (cloth : alk. paper) — ISBN 978-0-7591-1321-3 (ebook)
1. African American women—Washington—Seattle—Religion. I. Title. BR563.
N4A27 2010
286.092'2797772—dc22 2009023041

Printed in the United States of America

∞ ™ The paper used in this publication meets the minimum requirements of American
National Standard for Information Sciences—Permanence of Paper for Printed Library
Materials, ANSI/NISO Z39.48–1992.

I want to thank my original editor and sister-friend, Janet Larson, who provided the help that brought the stories into being. More recently, my daughters, Maggie and Katie Hess, gave me the unwavering coaching, editing, and moral support that was needed to pull the final version of *Moving the Rock* together—it never would have happened without them. Finally, I especially want to acknowledge Reverend and Sister Kent and the women of Morning Sun Church for sharing their wisdom and their stories. Two of the women in *Moving the Rock*, Sister Kent and Mable Jackson, have "passed," but I hear their words of encouragement every day.

CONTENTS

CONTENTS

PREFACE

This is a book about a small group of poor and working-class African American women who live in Seattle, Washington, and the storefront church that sustains them. *Moving the Rock* describes the life experiences of the women and the long-term impact of poverty and racism on the women and their families. It is about the women's daily challenges and struggles, how they create contentment, and how they build a tenuous security that enables them to raise their children safely and successfully. It is also a book about my experience of participating in community-based research when differences in race and class between the researcher and the women were constant companions in the research process.

Although poverty remains an ever-present reality in the lives of one in four African Americans (U.S. Census 2005, 5), it is only in times of episodic crises like Hurricane Katrina that we glimpse into the lives of the poor. But these views quickly fade, leaving us with little information or context about the day-to-day realities of people who live in poverty through generations. The women in this book decided to share their lives and stories with the hope that they could make things better for poor black women. (The women self-identified as black and the terms *black* and *African American* will be used interchangeably.) They saw that I, as an anthropologist and nurse educator, would try to frame their stories in a way that would encourage others to listen; I have done my best to honor their wishes.

There are many people in the United States who are dedicated to making a difference in the lives of people who experience poverty and racism, and their work is invaluable. However, there is a sharp divide between those who live comfortable lives, including the professionals who work with the poor in schools, hospitals, and social-service programs, and the people who receive these services. There is an even sharper divide between policymakers, government officials, and private and public donors and poor people of color. Students in universities and colleges learn about race, class, and gender and study the problems of the poor from many different perspectives. Although many ultimately care for poor blacks and address the problems of poverty and race, white and middle-class students have often not had the opportunity to feel comfortable with and/or understand the complexities of the lives of poor people of color.

"Stereotypes abound when there is distance" (hooks 1995, 38). Stereotypes, when held by caregivers, educators, and policymakers, lead to poor care, inadequate educational opportunities for children, and the development of shortsighted policies and programs. These circumstances, often in spite of people's best intentions, create and maintain oppressive conditions. The word *oppression* comes from the word *press*. "Something pressed is something caught between or among forces and barriers which are so related to each other that jointly they restrain, restrict or prevent the thing's motion or mobility. Mold, immobilize, reduce" (Frye 2008, 364). Using the analogy of a birdcage, Frye (2008) notes that it is impossible to comprehend why a bird is confined when looking at just one wire of the cage. However, by stepping back, one sees the interrelationship of the wires or barriers and begins to understand how people's opportunities can be restricted by oppressive circumstances (365).

While theories of societal oppression help us to understand the complexity of the macro picture, it is the individual stories and the micro context that make this picture come alive. By studying a small environment carefully and thoroughly we can slow down and begin to see the day-to-day realities of racism and generational poverty. The stories, the women's voices, provide an insider's view into this reality, helping us to comprehend that the experiences of the poor are part of the overall picture of life in America.

Stories help us to examine how oppression influences our own stereotypes, personal interactions, and methods of problem solving as we work with poor people of color. Simultaneously, stories help us see people in poverty as knowing and active decision makers rather than victims. They illuminate the power and creativity of people as they persist in building opportunities for themselves and their children in spite of oppressive conditions. Without exposure to individuals and individual stories, we are often unable to adequately conceptualize the power, struggles, and challenges of the poor, and we have difficulty in serving them well.

Moving the Rock is written for readers who want to understand more about the realities of poor people's lives. It is written for students and professionals who provide health, educational, and social services to the poor. It is for readers who advocate for people who experience poverty and racism. It is for those who are interested in anthropological, African American, religious, and women's studies. It is for government workers who plan policy and create and manage programs that serve the poor. It is for churches, women's groups, and foundations. And most importantly, it is for the women of Morning Sun who want their stories to be told.

The Women of Morning Sun Missionary Baptist Church

Morning Sun Missionary Baptist Church (a pseudonym) is a small storefront church located in a residential area in the Central District of Seattle. The church's pastor defines a storefront as a church building originally intended for a different purpose, such as a store or a home. Many storefronts have fewer than fifty members who attend regularly. Morning Sun was originally a small white frame house resting on a large, grassy lot. The church has thirty-five registered members, consisting primarily of two extended families and a few elderly widowed women.

In this book, eight African American women from the church share the stories of their lives. The women have chosen Morning Sun because it is small enough for them to be actively involved, or it is close to home, or they feel connected to the pastor and his wife. Seven of the storytellers are from the two main church families, representing three generations; and one woman is an elderly widow now living alone. The women are between the ages of nineteen and eighty-two. They are all poor or working class, but their stories are very different. Some are on welfare or disability, and some have stable jobs. Some live in subsidized housing, and some own their homes. One woman has only a fourth-grade education; some have not been able to finish high school; some have their high-school diplomas or GEDs; and some have gone on for college or additional training. The pastor's wife, the most highly educated person in the church, is one quarter short of obtaining a graduate degree.

In their stories the women describe their kinship networks and demonstrate the interconnections of family, religious community, faith, and values in this small church environment. Their portraits teach us about the complexities of intergenerational poverty and about the intersection of poverty, race, and gender in the lives of the women.

The Research Process

The research that forms the basis for this book took place in Seattle in the 1990s. Although Seattle is seen as a progressive city, the poor, for the most part, are invisible. Little has been done to examine the lives of a relatively small, poor African American population in this city. With only 47,541 African Americans in Seattle (registered in the U.S. census as black or African American) (City of Seattle 2004), it is assumed that they have necessarily assimilated, but this is not necessarily true. The majority of African Americans currently live in both South and Central Seattle, but they have, like the families in this book, traditionally lived in the Central District ("the CD"). Small storefront churches dot the landscape—churches that maintain communities and traditions from an earlier Southern black lifestyle, churches that support their members as they go to work in a white world or send their children to schools, sometimes to schools across town that have predominantly white populations, where teachers, nurses, and social workers are primarily white, college educated, and middle class.

As a nurse anthropologist, I had the privilege of working with the church's women and their leaders for eighteen months. I spent time with the church members in formal services, during social times at church, and in their everyday lives. Feminist and black feminist theory integrated with critical reflexive anthropology provided the framework for the research. Ethnographic methods of anthropology, participant observations, and life history interviews were used to collect the data. These tools helped me to describe the women's everyday lives and realities in "an ethnography of the particular" (Abu-Lughod 2006, 162). Although few researchers are able to study with the poor for this extended period of time, they can learn how to communicate more sensitively and how to ask the right questions by "stepping into the space" of the women from Morning Sun Church.

When the study first began, I was interested in understanding more about variables that influenced the health status of African American women. I learned quickly that it was impossible to understand health issues without hearing the women's stories. It was like examining a piece of a puzzle without having a picture of the complete puzzle. I have previously written about how the women "make meaning" or interpret their health concerns and experiences (see Abrums 1995, 2000a, 2000b, 2004). The purpose of this book is to present the women's stories and the context of their lives as well as to describe the research process.

My position as a white woman and a member of the dominant society on multiple levels—race, class, and role as researcher—has inevitably influenced every aspect of this research. I cannot discount that I have been well socialized in a racist and classist society and by a patriarchal educational and health-care system. I agree with hooks (1981, 1989) that I can never be an authority on women of color. I can, however, speak to my experiences with the women of Morning Sun Church and provide the space for them to tell their stories. My representation of their views will necessarily be partial, and our combined views will change with time. In spite of these barriers, I think it is possible to portray the women and their church with integrity.

To depict the stories accurately, the questions must be asked: whose voices should be used, and whose goals should be addressed? Many authors have spoken to the difficulties black women have had, not in speaking, but in being heard (hooks 1989; Hurston 1935/1963; Collins 2000). Women of color, especially the poor, have been effectively silenced by the creation of stereotypical images of them, as well as by their absence in the ruling order, educationally, politically, and economically. Thus, I consider it critical to provide a space where the women of Morning Sun Church can have their say.

However, I am not a linguistic student and cannot accurately portray the beauty and the rich variation of black English. The women have lived in the South, the Midwest, the West, and the Northwest, and their language reflects both regional influences as well as family origins. I hope that the reader can hear the flavor of the language but recognize that nuances of dialect may have been lost or inadvertently misrepresented. I have sometimes summarized lengthy stories in my own words without sacrificing content, simply in order to make them easier to read. The women themselves have read and approved their stories as they have been written.

Because the women's stories speak for themselves, I have used very little analysis so as not to impose academic theories that may or may not represent the storytellers' views accurately. However, I agree with feminist and black feminist theorists that performing research with people who experience racism and poverty is political from the initial stages of conceptualization through its final application (Collins 2000, 2004; Haraway 2004; Harding 2004b; hooks 2004; Jaggar 2004). Research is an interactive process, and the self is always intimately involved in and changes every interaction (Rabinow 1977). Thus, it is important for readers to understand my politics and be able to situate my efforts. Feminism, anti-racism, and social justice ideologies have had a critical influence on my work. Although I attempt to present the church members' beliefs and their experiences through their lens alone, it is inevitable that my own beliefs and goals will influence the focus of the lens. Thus, this study realistically is a story of how the church members see their lives and how I see their lives within the context of our combined philosophies. My purpose in writing this book is ultimately to contribute to economic, social, and political justice for people who experience poverty and racism, as do the women of Morning Sun Church.

On Writing

The primary rule that I follow is to write so that anyone can read and learn from this book. This approach is modeled on hooks's (1994) stance that writing is for everyone to understand and that it is not solely for people in academics. This rule also acknowledges and respects Sister Kent's (the pastor's wife) theory that "the simplest is the most profound." She often notes that Jesus, the son of a carpenter, was the greatest teacher; and he always spoke simply and addressed everyone. For the women of Morning Sun, simplicity does not indicate lack of meaning or depth, but rather demonstrates the wisdom that comes from experience. The only exception to this rule of "writing simply" is found in the appendix: "Research Question, Theories, and Methods." This section gives credit to those who have worked and studied with people on the margins in multiple settings. Their knowledge and theoretical approaches frame the study and help to explicate its findings. However, this chapter may not be as accessible to readers as I would like, as the theoretical language remains somewhat academic.

Summary

There are three parts to this book. In Part One, the historical background, the church setting, and the core values and beliefs related to family and motherhood are described. Part Two presents the stories of the eight women who participated in the life history interviews. Part Three discusses my relationships with the women and the research process. Finally, the appendix presents the research question, theories, and methodology that provided the philosophy and the structure for the study.

My relationships with the women at Morning Sun changed over time. The pastor's wife initially introduced me to new people, saying, "This is Mary, she's here to learn about our mannerisms," or "She's here to study us black folks—it's *good* though!" As time went on, she changed her introduction to, "You know Mary. Isn't she lovely? She's just like us." This small degree of acceptance meant a lot to me. I had to work hard for it, overcoming much pain that had been generated historically and personally in each and every woman's life. And yet I know I am truly not "just like" them. I can imagine, but never fully experience, the lives that they lead, the struggles they face, the joys they know. In the end I am a reasonable authority on only one woman—myself—in relationship to a group of black women.

During this process, I have found that interweaving theory and practice is an ongoing challenge. I learned much during my time at Morning Sun that moved me from "ignorance to intelligence" (Abrums 2000b), but I struggle every day to enact my knowledge. The following example illustrates the complexity of this effort.

A group of Catholic sisters met with a diverse group of women from their community. The panel was scheduled from 9:00 a.m. until 3:15 p.m. The lone black participant said that she did not know much about

Catholic sisters and would just listen. She did so until 3:00 p.m., when she said the following:

> Well, I don't know if I can say it too good, 'cause you know I didn't go to school much. But in my heart I know. I'll just tell you a little story. Now all you nice ladies imagine that you lived in a house by a road on the top of a mountain. And there's a big rockslide and a big boulder came down right around the corner on this mountain. And every car that came round that corner hit that boulder and smashed up. Now I can understand what all you'd do. I heard you. You'd run right out and you'd take those people out of that car. You'd bandage them up, and you'd bring them in your house and feed them, and you'd pray with them. And when they got well, you'd send them home. Well, sister, what I think you ought to do is send somebody out to move the rock (Gifted with Hope 1985, 16).

In doing this research, I have moved myself and that is important, but it still does not move the rock. This book is dedicated to that effort.

INTRODUCTION
A Short History

All the members of Morning Sun Church have roots in the South,
but most have spent their lives in the Central District of Seattle,
a traditionally African American area in a city with a small black
population. Most of them, like approximately 25 percent of blacks nation-
wide, live below the poverty line. Their families and their small church
provide community and social support. When the women migrated to the
Pacific Northwest, they were required to adapt to a mostly white world
where it was cold and rainy and far away from home and family. While
this background is specific to the lives of these women, similar histories
and contexts can be found in multiple cities across the United States. What
were the factors that encouraged them to move, what did they find, and
how did they build churches and community? Did they escape racism and
poverty in Seattle? Did they fulfill their dreams of economic stability? To
better understand the histories of the women from Morning Sun Church,
this chapter reviews national and local contexts of migration, poverty, and
the influence of the church in the lives of African Americans.

Black Migration

Many blacks left the South in the late 1800s after Civil War emancipation
once the promises of reconstruction had died, leaving behind a series of laws
that effectively created a permanent powerless and landless working class.
These "Jim Crow" laws legally institutionalized racism and classism and re-
sulted in a nineteenth-century "exodus"—a term deliberately chosen at the

time for its biblical reference to the flight of the slaves from Egypt (Painter 1976/1986). By 1900, 335,000 African Americans had left the South to live in the northern and western United States (Gregory 2005, 12).

This early exodus set the stage for the even more extensive Great Migration, or Southern Diaspora, that occurred in two major waves during the twentieth century. Diasporas are described as "historically consequential population dispersions . . . inspired by opportunity as well as oppression" (Gregory 2005, 11). The initial wave began in the early 1900s with the hope of job opportunities created by World War I and slowed in the 1930s with the Depression, when most Americans, particularly rural Americans, stayed close to home. The older churchwomen in this book lived in the rural South at this time; and one of them, Betty Jones, says she did not even notice the Depression as a child in the 1930s in Louisiana because her family always had enough to eat on the farm. Another woman, Mabel Jackson, left her family farm in Louisiana in 1939, when she was nineteen, to join her new husband in Mississippi; but she returned alone two years later to be with her parents, who were sharecroppers. She knew that, even in the deteriorating conditions of the Depression in the rural South, she would not be hungry at home.

Orleck (2005) notes that it was the "poorest of the poor" who stayed behind following the first wave of the migration (9). Many of those who stayed were sharecropping families who experienced overwhelming poverty and hardship (Jones 1985, 86–87). When the sharecropping system was replaced with mechanical cotton pickers, things became even worse in the rural South, and the cruelties of poverty and racism, along with the hope of industrial jobs in the North created by World War II, helped many African Americans decide that it was time to go (Orleck 2005).

In this second wave of the Southern Diaspora, almost 7,500,000 African Americans were on the move from the 1940s to the 1970s (Gregory 2005, 15); and the women in *Moving the Rock* came to the Pacific Northwest during this period. Mable Jackson felt she had to leave, recalling, "Some was coming west, some was going north. . . . Everybody was leaving, going to different places."[1]

When African Americans left the South, most, like the families in this book, left for good. In this respect, they were unlike many white migrants who often returned to the South in a "revolving door" (Gregory 2005, 16). The two main motivations for black migration during this second wave were similar to those that had stimulated earlier movements—the poor labor market in the South and racism. Economic shifts in agriculture and industry had prompted both black and white migrations, but for blacks, "as long as Jim Crow ruled the South, that system of segregation, subordination and terror created powerful incentives for leaving and staying away" (23). Marie Jones Smith's narrative describes how her father "was getting out from down there and he said he wasn't going to stop until he did. . . . The south was not a place he wanted to be with his family—especially raising boys."

However, many blacks who had migrated north still thought of the South as their home. They maintained close ties with kin, returning frequently to visit or when times were hard. Parents often sent children to be raised by relatives away from the unsafe industrial urban areas while they worked long hours (Stack 1996). Betty Jones relates how she followed this back-and-forth pattern for several years, taking her children with her as she returned to Louisiana from Seattle to have her babies among kinfolk, often remaining for several months to pick cotton in order to support her family.

In the mid-1970s migration tapered off, and some blacks began to move back to the South. During World War II, migrants had found steady work in the industrial North, but the generation of young adults born between 1955 and the 1960s faced a different world. Everywhere they looked, they found "more squalor, sorry streets becoming sorrier by the day" (Stack 1996, 48). Factories were rapidly entering the global environment or moving from the North to southern states, where labor was less expensive. There were few jobs in the urban North for blacks with this decline of industry—available jobs were not reliable, and conditions were poor. Post–World War II mass firings and layoffs affected blacks disproportionately, and wages began to rapidly fall behind the cost of living (Jones 1985; Stack 1996). When jobs began to disappear in the North, about 50,000 blacks per year began to move back to the South, until by 1990 over a half-million African Americans had returned (Stack 1996, xiii).

By 1979 the Southern Diaspora was officially over, and, although some blacks returned to the South, the majority did not. The migration north and west had a tremendous impact on the country as millions of southern blacks settled in regions that had previously experienced little racial diversity (Gregory 2005, 20, 322). In 1970, 47 percent (10.6 million) of the total population of African Americans lived outside the South. The largest numbers of outward-bound southern blacks had gone to the industrial centers in the East, North Central, and Middle Atlantic states (i.e., Michigan, Ohio, New York, Pennsylvania, etc.); the Pacific states were the third most significant destination, with an estimated newly relocated 45,000 blacks in the Pacific Northwest (Gregory 2005, 17–18, 20, 322; Taylor 1994/2003, 159).[2]

The Central District

With the arrival of African Americans from the South, the black population quickly became Seattle's largest minority group, replacing the Asian population (who were being evacuated to World War II residential camps). The black population in the city increased dramatically in ten years, growing from 3,789 in 1940 to 15,666 in 1950 (Taylor 1994/2003, 159). With this influx of new arrivals, Seattle changed rapidly.

Newly migrating African American families moved to Seattle's Central District (also called "the CD" or the "Central Area"). Taylor (1994/2003) notes, "Black Seattle through much of the twentieth century was synonymous with the Central District, a four square mile section near the geographic center of the isthmus that constitutes the city" (5). The boundaries of the Central District vary somewhat, depending on the source; however, the City of Seattle (2006) defines the area by Madison Street on the north; South Judkins Street on the south; Lake Washington on the East; and 12th Avenue East curving into Rainier Avenue on the west. Realistically, any centrally located neighborhood that has been predominantly African American has been described as "part of the CD." (See "Map 1: The Central District" for locations of churchwomen's homes, church, hospitals, and so on, on p. 30.)

While the CD was predominantly African American in the 1940s, it was also a multicultural area where Chinese, Italian, German, Japanese, and Filipino immigrants and Native Americans lived, and it was considered to be "the center of Jewish life in the city" (Cross 2005, 17–18). In the 1940s and 1950s, with the rapid World War II and postwar population growth, housing shortages were exacerbated by neighborhood covenants that restricted African Americans to specific areas that were mostly in or near the CD (Taylor 1994/2003, 168–169). (Some of these covenants are still in existence—see Seattle Civil Rights and Labor History Project 2004–2009a.) Seattle was "a segregated city, as committed to white supremacy as any location in America. People of color were excluded from most jobs, most neighborhoods and schools and many stores, restaurants, hotels, and other commercial establishments, even hospitals" (Seattle Civil Rights and Labor History Project 2004–2009b).

Newly arrived black migrants necessarily tripled up in the oldest and most run-down houses of the city along Jackson, Madison, and Cherry streets. With the World War II evacuation of the Japanese population to residential camps, some African Americans moved into what had previously been Japanese hotels and took over small Japanese businesses. Yesler Terrace Apartments (where several of the women in the book have lived), Seattle's first public housing project, was built in 1940 to relieve a critical housing shortage, but allowed only 20 percent of its tenants to be black, due to the groundbreaking goal of integrating public housing. Until the late 1990s the Central District with its dilapidated craftsman and Victorian houses, public housing projects, run-down apartments, and high crime rate, was not seen as valuable residential property despite its proximity to downtown, the wharf, the International District, and the industrial areas (Taylor 1994/2003, 169–174).

Black Seattle was defined, however, not only by exclusion and territorial boundaries, but also by the development of a culture that maintained its roots in the South and built connections to the national black community. With the arrival of thousands of African American newcomers in the 1940s, the Central District's religious, cultural, political, and social institutions grew rapidly, and many are still in existence. The development of this environment ultimately led to the civil rights and black power struggles in Seattle in the 1960s. Garfield High School was host to Martin Luther King Jr. and Stokely Carmichael, and the CD became the center of protest for the Black Panthers as well as for community churches and political leaders fighting against segregation, poverty, poor housing, and inadequate education (Taylor 1994/2003; Cross 2005). These efforts continue in the CD today.[3]

In addition to consistent political efforts, the Central District has a rich cultural history. During the 1930s to the 1960s, it was the home of an extremely active nightclub district centered on Jackson Street. Illegal prostitution, gambling, and drinking, as well as nationally known jazz and blues entertainment, flourished under the unofficial "tolerance policy," in which police accepted bribes to ignore illegal practices (de Barros 1993; Zwerin 1994). The CD was home to many people who later became famous: it was there that Jimi Hendrix was brought up in poverty, at one point lived in Yesler Terrace, and acquired his first guitar with only one string (Cross 2005). In the 1940s the CD nurtured young musicians Ray Charles and Ernestine Anderson, as well as Quincy Jones, who played jazz in the Garfield High School Band (Cross 2005; Davila and Mayo 2001; de Barros 1993; Taylor 1994/2003).

Vestiges of a once active black community remain in the CD today— it retains its own newspapers and radio station, shops, restaurants, and churches. However, things have changed significantly since the 1970s. The Central District's black population has declined from 16,242 in 1970 to 9,542 in 2000 (counting black or African American alone, not including combinations of races) (U.S. Census Bureau 2000, cited in Davilo & Mayo 2001, A1; City of Seattle 2004). The highest concentrations of the city's overall African American population of 47,541 (8.4 percent of Seattle's total population of 563,374) are now spread out between the Central District and Southeast Seattle (City of Seattle 2004). In the 1990s, gentrification began to gradually erode the black population and culture of the CD as Seattle's white middle class sought affordable housing in an escalating real-estate market. Many poor and working-class black families were forced out of the area by the cost of housing. Some have held onto family homes, but most working-class black families have been unable to buy homes in the area, and the majority of middle-class blacks have gravitated to less centralized neighborhoods with better schools and more affordable and improved housing.

Today the CD is home to some middle- and working-class whites, working-class black families, and many poor African Americans who, at least for now, remain in subsidized housing. Although the area is becoming more integrated, bitter arguments over school busing and quality of education for black children continue unresolved in the CD and throughout the city. School problems compound residential issues and vice versa.[4] Taylor (1994/2003) sums up this dilemma, noting that Seattle has always manifested a conflict between the stated ideals of "racial toleration and egalitarianism" proclaimed by the majority of the city's population and "the private practice of discrimination" (p. 4).

As we listen to the stories in *Moving the Rock*, it is important to note that until the 1980s, African American women "suffered near-invisibility in western [and northwestern] history" (Riley, 2003, 22). Scholars have recently begun to unravel and document the specificity of black women's experiences and contributions to western and northwestern history. There have been notable black women leaders in Seattle's history, women such as labor activist Susie Cayton, who fought for better conditions for the working-class poor of Seattle, Anne Foy Baker, who founded Seattle's Mary Mahoney Registered Nurses Club, Odessa Brown, who created a children's health facility in the CD, and many others (Henry 2007; Peterson 1990; Spratlen 2001; Taylor and Moore 2003). *Moving the Rock* contributes to this history by adding the everyday stories of "ordinary" black women in Seattle, who for too long have been invisible in history but have made contributions every single day of their lives. These narratives, previously unknown to all but their families and small communities, add texture, richness, and meaning to African American history and the history of the Pacific Northwest.

National and Local Pictures of African American Poverty

Twenty-three percent of African Americans in Seattle live in poverty—a rate similar to that of blacks in the rest of the country (24.9 percent) (City of Seattle 2000; U.S. Census Bureau 2005, 5). The Central District harbors a large percentage of the city's poor, with 32.4 percent of its residents falling into the category of "official and hidden poverty" (City of Seattle 2004). The women from Morning Sun represent the diversity of the poor in the CD. Some are unemployed and dependent on disability or welfare payments. Some are the "working poor" and are or have been single working mothers with incomes far below the poverty line. Others are in stable relationships with both partners employed who remain in poverty on minimum-wage salaries. There are women with decent incomes and good jobs in two-partner families who periodically find themselves in stressful financial situations due to the needs of family members. There is often no resource other than family, and the sharing of scarce resources creates economic insecurity for all (Stack 1996).

In the nation as a whole, African Americans make up about 13 percent of the United States population, numbering 36.5 million in the 2000 U.S. Census. This number includes all who identify themselves as black or partially black (U.S. Census Bureau 2000). The real income (income after adjusting for inflation) of African Americans increased after World War II, and economic prospects continued to improve in the 1960s with the push for civil rights. Progress slowed in the 1970s and 1980s, and the economic gap between blacks and whites remains into the 2000s (Marger 2003).

Economic progress has gradually created a large black lower-middle and middle class, but there has been "little impact on blacks at the bottom of the economic scale" (Marger 2003, 278). In 2005, African Americans were still more than twice as likely to be in poverty as were whites, with almost one in four falling below the poverty line. The median black family income was 61 percent ($30,858) of a non-Hispanic white family's median income of $50,784—a greater difference than in 1970 (U.S. Census Bureau 2005, 5; Marger 2003, 278).

Although the majority of the poor in America are white (and have been since the 1930s), poverty "wears a black face" in America because of the visibility of the urban poor in segregated communities (Newman 2007, 304). However, proportionately, more African Americans live below the poverty line—with 24.9 percent of African Americans in poverty versus 8.3 percent of non-Hispanic whites (U.S. Census Bureau 2005, 5). The greatest numbers of poor people of all races are categorized as the "working poor": 8.7 percent of African Americans compared with 4.0 percent of whites (U.S. Department of Labor 2002).

Black Families and Poverty

Stereotypes about poor black families abound despite the concerted efforts of many scholars to carefully analyze the influences of class, race, ethnicity, geographical, and neighborhood environments. For the purposes of this book, current statistics and some of the related dynamics of black families in poverty will be presented. Although the narratives in *Moving the Rock* portray many dimensions of African American poverty, it is impossible to adequately cover the complex intersection of poverty, race, and the family; and readers are encouraged to review more extensive studies of black families in poverty.[5]

Research overall demonstrates the flexibility and resiliency of African American families against terrible odds; however, families in poverty today continue to face overwhelming challenges. The number of female-headed single-parent black families has increased steadily since the 1950s and constitutes 45 percent of all black families in the United States (U.S. Census Bureau 2002, cited in Marger 2003, 280). African American families supported by single working mothers are almost four times more likely to live in poverty than are families where the parents are married and at least one of them is employed (Newman 2007, 305).

A complex constellation of factors has contributed to a dearth of black marriageable working men, including the disappearance of jobs in the inner city, subsequent unemployment, and escalating incarceration rates as men become involved in drug-related crimes and try to survive in the underground economy (Collins 2000; Patillo-McCoy 2007; Marger 2003; Wilson 1996). Shifts in the mode of production and the decline of U.S. blue-collar jobs due to the global economy "relegate unskilled blacks to low wage, menial and dead-end jobs or push them out of the work-force altogether" (Patillo-McCoy 2007, 140). Incarceration rates (currently at 30 percent of non-college-educated black males—a risk that has increased threefold in the past twenty years) must be seen within an overriding framework of uneven and discriminatory sentencing practices in the criminal justice system as well as the devastating lack of employ-ment and educational opportunities in poor neighborhoods (Waller and Swisher 2006). Women, especially single parents struggling with everyday survival, do not want to marry men who are barely making it at best, and, at worst, are a drain on limited emotional and financial resources (Collins 2000; Tucker and James 2005).

Although poor black women often do carry the primary economic responsibility for their families, it should not be assumed that black men, including nonresidential fathers, are uninvolved. Research suggests that a minority of unmarried fathers fit the "absent father" stereotype (Waller and Swisher 2006, 393). Rather, many men who cannot financially sup-port their families have redefined "appropriate fathering behavior in order to both reflect their reality of limited resources and constrained hopes"

(Tucker and James 2005, 95). Even incarcerated men strive to remain involved with their families in spite of institutional barriers such as limited visitation (Braman 2004/2007; Petersilia 2003; Travis & Waul 2003; Waller & Swisher 2006).

Under circumstances of poverty, "traditional" family forms such as the nuclear family do not reflect the reality of nor offer the support needed by families. Instead, female-headed households may share responsibilities for children and elders with extended family who are blood and fictive kin (Stack 1974; Tucker and James 2005). These efforts do not, however, change the reality that many black women, including employed women, survive below the poverty line in the United States. The term *working poor* inadequately describes the everyday reality of women "whose earnings are so meager that despite their best efforts, they cannot afford decent housing, diets, health care, or child care . . ." (Newman 2007, 304). These issues are often even more difficult for the working poor than they are for the nonworking poor. Women working at low wage jobs often make slightly more than is needed to access the governmental safety nets that are available to the very poor—subsidized housing, medical care, and food stamps (Newman 2007).

In 1996 welfare reform replaced Aid to Financially Dependent Children (AFDC) with Temporary Aid to Needy Families (TANF), and the situation for women in poverty worsened. The intent of this reform was to "reduce welfare rolls and to move women toward economic self-sufficiency" (Burnham 2007, 414). Although thousands of women left the welfare rolls, many did not become economically independent. Most have been trapped "in low-paid, insecure jobs that do not lift their families above the poverty line" (414). Some have simply been pushed off welfare and have no reported income source whatsoever.

Important indicators that poverty has worsened include increases in housing insecurity, homelessness, food insecurity, and hunger. Requests for emergency shelter are at their highest since 1994. Many of the poor are unable to adequately feed their families. Burnham (2007) notes that the higher costs of working, along with reductions or elimination of food stamps, has meant that "women's access to adequate food became more precarious rather than less so as they moved from welfare to work" (416). Many former TANF recipients report cutting the size of meals or skipping meals, and half the mothers surveyed report that food sometimes does not last until the end of the month (Douglas and Michaels 2004). This situation is not new for poor families, as evidenced by similar stories in *Moving the Rock*. However, the fact that welfare reform has exacerbated this issue is particularly troubling.

Child care is another difficult problem for the working poor, as it frequently is for the churchwomen of Morning Sun, especially when young children are still at home or when older children are too sick to go to school. Many of the poor work at night, making child care especially difficult as mothers must often choose "between their jobs and the safety of their kids" (Douglas and Michaels 2004, 201).

Difficulty in paying for utilities is another measure of poverty that indicates inadequate shelter without heat and electricity, and is "often a prelude to inability to pay the rent" (Burnham 2007, 415). Forty-eight percent of former TANF recipients in one Illinois study are not able to pay their utilities (Work, Welfare and Families, cited in Burnham 2007, 415). In addition, mothers often go without health and dental care for themselves—only 23 percent of women who have gone off welfare through TANF receive health insurance through work (200). Some of the women in *Moving the Rock* must constantly prioritize—asking themselves whether they should buy food or see the doctor or pay the electric bill.

In addition to income, employment, child care, health, hunger, and shelter data, wealth or assets owned is a revealing determinant of socioeconomic class position. Accumulated wealth determines the ability to buy a house, pay for higher education, provide a safety net for family members in trouble, and pass down property, thus providing security and opportunities for future generations (Oliver and Shapiro 2006). In the United States "the typical white family has assets about ten times those of the typical black household" (Marger 2003, 280). This lack of accumulated assets reveals the relatively recent arrival and tenuous position of many lower-middle- and middle-class African Americans. The churchwomen's stories in this volume reveal varying success in this struggle, especially as related to home ownership, and many of the women have not yet been able to build a savings or a safety net of any kind.

The Church and the African American Community

The importance of the black church in the heritage, culture, and education of many African Americans cannot be underestimated. While it is beyond the scope of this book to analyze the depth and meaning of the black church, the reader is referred to scholars who have studied this influence extensively.[6] This section briefly describes some of the historical, cultural, philosophical, spiritual, and instrumental dimensions of the black church on African American life.

The church's significance began during the years of slavery and continues to the present day. Christianity was originally introduced to blacks to promote black subservience and white domination. However, it was in the meetings after church services that blacks developed the social cohesion that created a unique Christianity specific to their historical and social concerns as an oppressed people. A distinctive religious expression arose that incorporated both African spiritual beliefs and adaptations to white Christianity (Blassingame 1972/1979; Cone 1970; Du Bois 1903/1989; Karenga 1989).

African Americans have never accepted the idea that slavery or any type of oppression was "meant to be." Instead, they have employed a hermeneutic reading of the Bible, weighing the contradictions observed in Christian behavior and what they themselves experienced against what has been manifested in the Bible. For example, one slave woman stated that when she learned to read, she would not read the part of the Bible that supported slavery (Wiggins 2005, 62). Sojourner Truth emphasized that the Bible's teaching must be compared "with the witness," that is, evaluated within one's own experience. Fannie Barrier Williams admonished others not to "open the Bible too wide" (Grant 1989, 216–217).

Warren (1997) notes that the music created in the black church has reflected this struggle against oppression as well:

> Out of the bondage of enslavement came the spiritual. Out of the Depression of the 1930s came the great gospel songs. Out of the Civil Rights Movement of the second half of the twentieth century have come the bold and beautiful freedom songs and contemporary gospel and praise songs. Those songs that have become part of the black Christian tradition give praise and thanksgiving to God in all circumstances, expressing confidence in His loving care, no matter what the situation . . .

expressing the viewpoint that "God is on the side of the oppressed." (Du Bois, cited in Warren 1997, 9)

Today over 89 percent of African Americans self-identify as religious, and the majority of those who go to church attend predominantly black churches. The black church has developed independently from white mainstream Christianity, and for the past two centuries, Sunday in America has been the most segregated day of the week, with the majority of blacks and whites attending separate services. This separation evolved as a result of both white discrimination in the Christian church and a desire for black congregational independence (Wiggins 2005).

This context has enabled the black church to function as the center of power and social life within the black community. It has offered sanctuary and comfort to its members and has been essential in supporting the self-worth of African Americans. The church has a unique liberatory philosophy that is based on serving the needs of its population in a racist and classist society. It has been a center for activism and social change and has provided guidance to families as well as given direct instrumental support to its members when needed (Karenga 1989; Wiggins 2005).

Black Women and Their Church

The story of the black church is the story of women who are "at the core of the black church which could not exist without them" (Wiggins 2005, 2). Many congregations are predominantly made up of women. Black women have developed their organizational and leadership skills and have found a supportive haven in the church (Hine and Thompson 1998; Mattis 2005).

> For black women, developing spiritual practices and getting involved at church have provided significant resources for coping with the challenges of being black and female—for managing the myths, negative stereotypes, and discrimination of the outside world. For many African American women, the church has been crucial for their very survival. (Jones and Shorter-Gooden 2004, 259–260)

Black women have defined their relationship with Jesus as central to their self-understanding and their faith. Grant (1989) elaborates on the meaning of Jesus to black Christian women, seeing that they relate to Jesus as a co-sufferer who identifies with them and stands beside them—Jesus "identifies with the 'little people' . . . where they are; he affirms the basic humanity of these 'the least' and he inspires active hope in the struggle for a resurrected liberated experience" (221). He condemns oppression in all its forms, empowers the weak, and fights for justice and freedom for all who experience oppression.[7] Mattis (2005) supports the idea that black women strongly identify with Jesus but argues that many mainstream religious black women see Jesus more as "triumphant Lord, comforter and enabler rather than co-sufferer" (176). This belief in Jesus stresses the power to be found in Jesus and in the women themselves.

In addition to the centrality of Jesus in their lives, black Christian women see biblical Scripture as a major source of wisdom. The women's experiences and use of the Bible determine the questions that apply to them and to all who are oppressed. Thus the source of their understanding is from both God's revelation to them through the Bible and how this content is heard and interpreted through their own experiences (Grant 1989, 215).

Faith in Jesus and the Bible sustains black women on a day-to-day basis; however, other beliefs have influenced and inspired them as well. During the civil rights movement of the 1960s, Dr. Martin Luther King Jr. was a strong proponent of creating social justice through love, unity, and nonviolent persistence. Black liberation theology simultaneously developed during this time and proposes more radical actions for social justice than did Dr. King's message of nonviolent unity. This theology, like its third-world Latin American counterpart, critiques the idea of "turning the other cheek" and encourages an active struggle against the social evil of white racism that creates and maintains poverty (Cone 1989, 191). Liberation theology measures the work of the black church by how well it addresses and relieves the oppression of the black poor (Cone 1989). (Refer to note 6 for theorists who more adequately describe the complex resistance philosophies in Dr. King's teaching, as well as a more in-depth analysis of black liberation theology.)

The black church was the center of protest for the civil rights movement. Dr. King's dream that all people, especially all children, deserve the same chance for success in the world motivated women to become the backbone of the movement. The women had no problems "connecting spiritual with earthly forms of salvation" (Jones 1985, 280–282). Due to their work in the church, they knew how to organize and create a feeling of kinship with those outside their immediate families, and through these channels, they built a strong resistance community (Hine and Thompson 1998).

The black church was highly visible during this time of national protest, and an important focus within congregations was "the eradication of racism and amelioration of its effects" (Wiggins 2005, 13). The church today continues to provide rest and renewal from the complexities of racism and the stress of day-to-day life for blacks in a dominant white culture. However, this anti-racist work is only one of the many strengths of the black church. It also offers a "surrogate world for its members and the community" (13) where members find cultural comfort, similar experiences, a shared theology, and a collective religious commitment.

Everyday Church Life

In a pivotal study of black women's religious commitment, Wiggins (2005) has studied with women from two of the largest denominations of the black church in a metropolitan city of Georgia. The women consistently cite five mandatory elements as essential to their dedication: prayer, praise, personal associations, preaching, and pastoral leadership (38). These dimensions help church members bridge the chasm between their everyday lives and allow them to move into the realm of the sacred. The women see the collective prayer at the beginning of the service as a time to refocus on the spiritual realm. It is personal time to seek out God and give Him their burdens. "Praise" time is a ritual space where the members transcend the everyday as the Spirit moves collectively through the congregation, usually through the power of singing and release. Members of Morning Sun note that this time of praise is "medicine" that can take away physical and emotional pain.

"Personal associations" are connections that make church members feel they have a social support system that values them—their absence is noted, and it is common to have members ask, "Where were you?" (Wiggins 2005, 37). Black churches typically serve as extended families through both kinship and fictive kinship relationships. These networks "demonstrate care and concern" (37). At Morning Sun, the pastor's wife adopts the responsibility of building community by checking on her members during the week and making sure that her "sisters" know that their presence and participation are important to her on a personal level. The terms *church mother, Sister Last Name* or *Brother Last Name, church family,* and *church home* are all indicators of this familial community (Mattis 2005, 194–199). Some members value this close intimacy more than others, but all see church as a safe place where mutual beliefs and caring bind them to one another in a surrogate family (Abrums 1995; Wiggins 2005).

The women in Wiggins's study note that the pastor's job is to provide careful leadership and teach the gospel with strength and wisdom. They value good preaching, preaching that moves them and demonstrates how to apply biblical Scripture in their lives. Some women want preaching to include a political message about racism, whereas others feel that this is out of place and prefer a more universal and inclusive philosophy. This difference in emphasis often illustrates core beliefs held by a specific church. For example, there are churches that support political activism and those, like Morning Sun, that see prayer as the most powerful agent of change (Abrums 1995; Wiggins 2005).

In addition to preaching style and philosophy, "pastoral leadership" is evidenced by the minister's sincerity, honesty, perseverance, and approachability. The women in Wiggins's (2005) study want someone to lead them into a deeper knowledge of Scripture, but they do not always believe that the preacher should have the last word. They see that ministers (predominantly male) do not always understand the problems, especially related to marriage, that women face. Although they listen to ministerial guidance, it, like their reading of the Bible, is subject to their critical hermeneutic interpretation as they compare the pastor's advice and applicability to their own experience. They see that their minister is human and thus subject to missteps and human frailty, and they must sometimes allow necessary forgiveness for his failings.

The black church offers its members several types of assistance when needed: practical or instrumental assistance, emotional help, and appraisal assistance. These forms of assistance are often intertwined: when elderly members need help getting around or doing yard work, church members come to their aid, and when someone is sick, visits from members include gifts of food, moral support, and prayer. There is often direct financial assistance given to members if the need arises and the church is financially able to help (Wiggins 2005).

Emotional assistance comes in many forms. Support often comes from the church in times of illness and crises. The church is very involved in the raising of all its children. Leaders and other involved adults influence parenting by acting as role models and lending "extended family" support to single mothers; by encouraging members to take in foster children; by supporting grandparents raising children when their grown children are in trouble or unavailable; by teaching disciplinary skills; by supporting parental advocacy efforts with schools and health care; and by active guidance in youth development regarding "worldly temptations." Religious texts give families guidance in resolving conflicts, in grieving, and in understanding their responsibilities in taking care of elderly parents, children, and youth in trouble. Churches protect families by insulating them and individual members from external assaults such as unemployment, underemployment, and incarceration. A key component of this emotional assistance is seen in the many prayers that help members deal with adversity in their families (Abrums 1995; Mattis 2005, 194–199; Wiggins 2005).

Another form of assistance is "appraisal assistance," where members give credit to God and the church when they experience the successes or even the challenges of life (Wiggins 2005, 80). For example, they give God recognition for employment or educational opportunities; or if they lose a job, they try to see that it might be God's way of letting them know they need to change direction. Black women often confront painfully oppressive circumstances on a daily level and are routinely denigrated in multiple ways. As they try to understand or "appraise" their experiences, the women in Wiggins's study relate that faith in God helps with a transformative process that heals both physical and emotional wounds. They see that church helps them be more positive or shift to a dependence on God when burdens overwhelm them. Some women credit the church with helping them through a drug habit or an addiction, or assistance in learning to trust again when they have been betrayed. The women relate that when a transformation takes place, they no longer feel lonely, afraid, or depressed, because they realize that God is with them. They learn how to survive, how to be spiritually transformed, and how to stay sane in the face of incredible stresses and challenges. The power that women find within their faith and through the shelter of the church cannot be underestimated. As Molly Lake Lander in *Moving the Rock* states, "I am somebody because I am a child of God!" This statement recognizes that all persons are loved by God and have dignity no matter what their circumstances (Abrums 1995; Wiggins 2005).

The mission of the black church is to help its members worship God and provide assistance due to the multiple social, political, and economic assaults that African Americans experience. Members see it as a refuge, a "hospital" for healing, a community, and a place to build strong families. It is a space where members prepare for eternity and where they find transformation that they hope leads to spiritual, emotional, and sometimes physical comfort. The church's mission to "save souls" is not separate from its task of helping people survive their worldly challenges. Helping one another and the poor and troubled are seen as Christian responsibilities. Thus the role of the black church is both "individual empowerment" and "community uplift" (Wiggins 2005, 106).

The black church has been the foundation of the African American community in Seattle, as it has been in many cities that experienced intense growth from migration (Drake and Cayton 1945/1993; Du Bois 1903/1989; Taylor 1994/2003). During the 1940s and 1950s, churches in the Central District assisted new migrants with finding housing and employment. Although most of the churches were struggling financially, they often instituted charitable organizations to address the needs of the impoverished in the area. In addition, churches provided an active social life for the area's residents by sponsoring picnics, dances, and sports teams, and by offering activities to help their members grow culturally and educationally (Taylor 1994/2003, 137–140).

There were and still are many large churches in the Central District, such as First African Methodist Episcopal and Mount Zion Baptist. But there are also many small "storefront" churches, like Morning Sun, with fewer than fifty members. Fellowship with other small black churches adds to an active community network where church members connect with a much larger group of friends and neighbors.

The first part of this book describes the work and beliefs of the people of Morning Sun Missionary Baptist Church. The church provides the context for its members' life stories and for the women's descriptions of how their faith and their church sustain them.

Part One
MORNING SUN MISSIONARY BAPTIST CHURCH

CHAPTER ONE

MORNING SUN CHURCH
AND ITS LEADERS

T he morning sun shines weakly against the February cold as I cross
the invisible line that marks the area of Seattle known as the Central District. Early morning walkers and joggers, mostly white,
are replaced by black women shepherding their children along sidewalks
or waiting patiently at bus stops on their way to Sunday services. The children are bundled against the cold, but bright dresses and neatly pressed
dark slacks are visible underneath their everyday parkas. The women
march stoically along in high-heeled shoes, wearing warm woolen dress
coats, some in fine hats that proclaim the Sunday morning. Small groups
of women, serene and smiling, their dark faces framed by spotless white
veils, seem to float by as their veils drift behind them. Periodically, a full-
suited man accompanies women and children, or a casually dressed young
man walks carefully groomed children to their grandmother's Sunday services. A few small groups of men cluster together in their everyday clothes
at the news corner, where a man wearing a gray apron under his coat, his
head covered by a woolen cap with soft earflaps, sells the Sunday paper.

Some of the women and children, or others like them, are on their way
to Morning Sun Missionary Baptist Church. The church was once a home,
and today it is a lovely little white storefront church with a cross at the top
and a sign in front that lists the church name, the name of the pastor, the
times of the services, and a quote from John 3:16: "For God so loved the
world that He gave His only begotten Son, that whosoever believeth in
Him should not perish but have everlasting life." The immaculate church
sits on a wide, well-maintained yard, surrounded by a white wire fence

and gate. In the early spring, purple irises bloom by the church door, and later roses and chrysanthemums brighten the garden. The church stands out from its neighbors in its neatness; most of the surrounding homes are run down, some deserted with boarded up windows, others with iron bars over doors and windows. Signs of regeneration intermingle with symbols of decay on this street, as on many streets in the Central District. Four young men at one end of the street throw rocks at a rat, trying to corner it under a car, while other men hammer into the morning quiet as they re-build a house across from Morning Sun Church. Reminders of last night's fracas—two suitcases and two television sets—sit woefully in the front yard of a tired home, juxtaposed against the tidiness of a neighbor, recently renovated and transplanted from another location, its owner attracted to the area by reasonable prices, large lot sizes, and good access to the city.

The interior of the church, like the exterior, is beautiful in its sim-plicity, well loved and cared for. The main floor of the "church house" is freshly painted, and sunlight streams through the windows onto six newly upholstered, mauve-colored pews on each side of a carpeted aisle. The aisle leads to a simple altar, furnished with the pastor's wooden pulpit with an engraved cross on the front and three formal chairs for the pas-tor and occasional guest ministers. To the right of the pulpit, facing the congregation, rest the piano and two pews for the choir. To the left are a small pulpit for nonordained speakers and three metal folding chairs for the women to lean on as they kneel to pray at the altar.

On the wall behind the altar is a large velvet tapestry of Jesus and His disciples at the Last Supper. The remaining three walls are bare of decoration except for a large frosted glass window on each, tightly closed against the February chill. On milder days the windows are open, allowing a gentle breeze to cool the church while parents keep a watchful eye on restless children playing in the churchyard.

On this particular February morning, eight members of the Morning Sun Church family are present—five women, one man, and two small children. These people form the core group of the Morning Sun Church family and are the most regular attendees. They, like the women and chil-dren on their way to church on the street, have put away their work-weary clothes from the week and are carefully dressed in their Sunday best.

As Reverend Kent speaks softly to his congregation, he repeats the gentle, sustaining words that are central to his belief system, the words this church has heard time and again: "Jesus is a way-maker, and a heart-fixer, He's a mind-regulator. . . ." As he speaks, his wife, Sister Kent, begins to play the piano softly, and the church family echoes Reverend Kent's words. The women sing quietly at first and then in rich, clear voices as the piano music becomes louder and the pastor's words fade into the words of the song.

The Pastor

Reverend and Sister Kent have been shepherding the little flock of Morning Sun Church for the past twenty years. As a young minister, the Reverend did evangelistic work "out in the field," assisting frequently at Morning Sun Church, at that time located in a rented building. When the pastor of Morning Sun died, the members asked Reverend Kent to keep the congregation together. He says, "How can you go when they ask you to stay?" In 1974 he and Sister Kent found a permanent home for the church, making the original down payment on the small church. Today, twenty years later, Morning Sun Church is completely paid for, and its future is secure. Reverend Kent notes, "We wasn't used to no storefront, but they call you to a place and you put in the money." Sister Kent brought all of her skills and abilities as an accomplished pianist and educator to her new position. As the daughter of a minister, she settled into her role as "pastor's wife" with expertise.

Reverend and Sister Kent are the central pillars of Morning Sun, contributing their energy to the church and its members on a daily basis. It is largely through their efforts that the little church is maintained. They sometimes donate almost half of the church's small income and are in charge of all day-to-day upkeep. In the summer, Reverend and Sister Kent wear their canvas gardening hats and work in the churchyard. In the winter Reverend Kent, who does not drive, walks several miles to the church on Saturday to turn on the heat so that it will be cozy on Sunday. The couple comes early on Sunday morning so that the pastor can sweep and tidy up while Sister Kent practices her piano selections.

Although Morning Sun is called "Morning Sun Missionary Baptist Church," it is an organized church and not a mission. Reverend Kent believes it is better to have his own church than to work for a larger church, but he acknowledges with disappointment, "I always thought it would grow and grow! It's been so many years now!"

A small, wiry man in his seventies, Reverend Kent is always impeccably dressed, usually wearing a dark suit, a white shirt, and a dark tie. On cold days he tops his suit with a dark wool dress coat and a dark gray fedora hat on his head. Occasionally he wears a brown suit or a sports jacket to a more casual evening service such as Bible study, but he always apologizes for his informality. He admits that on a hot day he sometimes wears shorts at home but feels he cannot even go out to the garbage because someone might see him—he is a preacher and he is supposed to have his pants on!

Reverend Joseph Kent has a basic goodness and sincerity about him. His ways are quiet, gentle, and honest; and he is dedicated to the Lord and to his calling. Every morning he starts his day by reading the Scriptures and praying, "because then, no matter what happens, everything will be all right."

Joseph Kent was originally raised on a farm in Louisiana along with ten other children. He "came up through the church" and was taught, "First religious education, then the other." His parents gave their children "the basic foundation: If you didn't work, you didn't eat. If you didn't work, you didn't sleep. If you borrow, you pay back. Someone don't own you if you got your basic five senses."

Farm life did not suit Joseph. At age fourteen, in the middle of the Depression, he left home and started working as a janitor at Woolworth's in a nearby town. In 1943 he married Bessie Freeman (Kent), a history teacher in his town. He says, "She's got a lot more meat upstairs than I do." A year after marrying, they separated. In 1949 Joseph moved to Seattle, and today he believes that God sent him there for a purpose.

In Seattle, Joseph got a job operating heavy equipment for the City Parks Department. In 1951 he bought a small well-maintained home with a beautiful view of Madison Valley in the northern part of the Central District. He sent for Bessie, and they remarried in 1955. They paid off the house in 1965 and have continued to live there.

Joseph was not happy with his work, and he began to study for the ministry with the Moody Bible Institute. In 1967 he was badly injured in an accident involving a large grass-cutting machine and was unable to work any longer. Since then, Reverend and Sister Kent have lived on his "pension" and sporadic donations from "pastor's aid."

When Reverend Kent first told Sister Kent that he planned to become a minister, she worried because he had always been so quiet. She asked him, "What will you say?" When he first got up to preach, she was nervous, but he surprised her and did well. She told herself, "We in it now!" As a minister's daughter, Sister Kent had not wanted to marry a minister because it was hard to live up to people's expectations. However, once Reverend Kent began to speak, she believed in him. He told her, "Jesus will take care of me—He'll tell me what to say." Both feel that Reverend Kent has the "gift" of preaching.

Reverend Kent often says that the Lord "do the preaching—He just use me as the instrument." He carefully prepares for every sermon, commenting, "A loaded wagon don't make too much noise but an empty one make a lot of noise." He preaches from the Bible to help his congregation use its messages in everyday life. Each Sunday he passes out small scraps of paper with the Scriptures of the day in the hope that members will study the readings at home. Once he gave out a typed list offering Scriptural readings for particular problems:

When in sorrow, read John 14
When men fail you, read Psalm 27
When you have the blues, read Psalm 34. . . .
(How to Use the Bible in Everyday Life n.d.)

Although Reverend Kent studies the Scripture carefully and opens himself to act as God's instrument, he also feels that the congregation must do its part to actively receive the message. A period of "devotion" precedes the sermon, with a woman member leading the fervent and personal devotional prayer aloud. Then the choir begins to sing with the definite purpose of raising the Spirit. If the proper level has not been reached by the time the sermon is about to begin, Reverend Kent waits, urging Sister Kent to play another song for the choir to sing, and he pushes them to "pick it up a little" so that the "Power" can come in.

When Reverend Kent begins to preach, the usher keeps latecomers in the back or outside. Sometimes Reverend Kent will stop (somewhat grievously) and wait—very effective in a small church—for the transgressors to enter and settle into their pews.

Reverend Kent's sermons are generally well spoken and scholarly, gradually building in intensity. He is not a "yelling preacher" but is a gifted storyteller, a comedian, and a mimic. Sometimes when the Spirit moves him, he bounces or "dances," as Sister Kent calls it, and once he jumped straight up about twelve inches. His preaching styles entertain as well as teach the congregation. Members are accepting and supportive of his different approaches, attributing his actions and words to "the power of the Spirit."

Reverend Kent believes that "everybody who preach ain't been called and ain't no pastor," and that "there's all that hollering but when it comes to lead, they can't do it." He notes that God has His own way of choosing:

> God say, "Are you able?" He's telling us—there's a big price tag. Are you ready for it or do you just think you is? . . . A lot of things, if it'd been left up to me that I wanted to do, but all that ain't left up to me. I made a promise—something like a contract and I can't break it. . . . Jesus did not choose His disciples . . . because maybe they was good-looking, talked real good, say a whole lot. . . . He didn't choose them because they were brighter or nicer than other folks. . . . God tried [Abraham] all kinds of ways. . . . He found out. . . . "Here's a man I can trust."

One of the most difficult aspects of Reverend Kent's job is dealing with people's problems. He tries to help people with their worries, saying, "He'll work it out if you let Him." He advises people to pray, do their part, and then let go, and God will take over. He emphasizes that Jesus said, "I'm with you always, but if you leave me, then you on your own!" He points out that God is always available to them, saying, "You know, sometimes you dialing the phone and can't get through . . . sometimes we not on the right channel and can't get through. . . . Jesus is on the main line, tell Him what you want!"

Reverend Kent counsels his church members both privately and from the pulpit. When Molly Lake Lander's husband came home after a separation, Reverend Kent announced, "Brother Lander, it's nice to see you here. I know you had some hard times but you through it now. The wife, she so happy; the children so glad to have their daddy back. . . . You had some close calls but the Lord brought you back for a purpose." He often asks to speak to members privately after services, saying, "Christ told me to do this." After Brother Lander found a job, Reverend Kent encouraged Molly Lander to thank Jesus but also to thank the people who helped, reminding her, "The Lord works through people."

Reverend Kent sees himself first and foremost as a shepherd who is responsible for the souls of his flock. He tells them, "When I go, I have to give an accounting for me and for you." He notes, "You ain't s'posed to lead them wrong; you s'posed to lead them right."

The Pastor's Wife

Bessie Freeman Kent was raised in Shreveport, Louisiana. When her parents married, her father was a seventeen-year-old Baptist preacher and her mother was just fourteen. Twenty-one children were born to the couple, but twelve died of childhood illnesses. Her father took good care of his family, and they always had enough to eat and were happy. The girls were encouraged to get an education, but, unlike the boys, they were not allowed to work—they were needed at home.

All the children in Bessie's family finished high school, and some went on to college. Bessie graduated from high school at age sixteen and went to Leland College in Baker, Louisiana, on a scholarship. She majored in history and took education classes. She then taught high-school history and studied for a graduate degree in library science at Bishop College. Sister Kent values education highly and sees it as a way to overcome discrimination.

Like many other African Americans, Sister Kent learned black history thoroughly in the southern black schools. As far as she knows, none of her relatives were slaves. Her father's "mother's father" was an African minister, "the preacher in the family." Her grandfather on her mother's side was "Irish and Indian" and owned property in Louisiana that his father "must have secured for him." Her parents never rented a home but always owned property.

Sister Bessie Kent is Reverend Kent's partner in life and in work. The couple agrees about the proper roles of husband and wife. Sister Kent says frequently, "My husband takes good care of me." They both believe that "the man is the head . . . that's the way it's supposed to be." Reverend Kent realizes he is on tenuous ground with this statement in his congregation, where the women tend to both work and raise the children, stating, "The problem is, the man is not taking his role. The man s'posed to lead! Take a look around—it's sad. . . . Man should take your stand! You s'posed to be one! . . . I don't want to go on with this, I'll get all tangled up. . . ."

Sister Kent is a slight woman with soft, light brown curls framing her face. She loves to look nice, and her position demands it. She arrives at church in sturdy walking shoes but quickly changes into high-heeled pumps that match her outfit. She compliments members, guests, and children, always finding something nice to say to everyone.

As an accomplished musician who has studied voice and music, Sister Kent is confident of her abilities and knows that she has an important role to play. She directs the choir, plays piano for the services, and is in charge of celebrations and fund-raising efforts. She guides all efforts with different committees that are always made up of the same few members, assigning tasks and special readings to various members, asking members' families to help out with many details.

Sister Kent is actively involved in the Women's Mission, which helps the women of Morning Sun to "go forward" to live out their lives as Christian women. During the summer the mission meets on a weekly basis, but during the winter the women are afraid to meet after dark, so they read assigned work at home. The weekly Sunday school before services draws two or three women participants and is led by Sister Bessie Kent (formally addressed in class as "Superintendent") and Missionary Mahalia Lake ("Madame Teacher").

Sister Kent is also involved in mothering young children and in teaching the young girls about proper behavior and personal development as they grow into womanhood. In this way she functions as "othermother" to the young people of the church (Collins 2000, 178–183). She often urges the young women to become more involved in the church: "Think about your commitment. . . . Academically, I want you to go to school and everything, but you better put God first in your lives."

In addition to acting as spiritual advisor and "othermother," Sister Kent serves as sister, counselor, and friend to the older church members. She often spends long hours on the phone with members working through problems. She urges them, "Let's pray up for each other!" One of the members relates, "She talks to me and my nieces . . . like she is on our level. We're real open with her. . . . Some people you feel you can talk to and trust . . . and some you just feel like you can't. . . . She feels like a person you can really talk to if you're down."

There are inevitably conflicts and differences in value systems among the women in this small church. Although the women accept Sister Kent in her sister and counselor roles, they also mother her and see her as naïve, sheltered, and somewhat "spoiled" by her good and loving husband. Some of the women imply that they know the ways of the world and can take care of themselves; and that Sister Kent does not and is in need of protection. Although Sister Kent may be in her seventies (she won't say), she frequently remembers that she was the baby in her family; and in some ways this "baby sister" role continues as women of the church, far younger than Sister Kent, mature and have children, experience divorces, and endure other worldly difficulties. Sister Kent remains untouched by the everyday demands of children, of finding enough food, and of paying for shelter.

In her study of black church-going women, Peterson (1990) finds that there are several requirements for reaching maturity and "the age of wisdom": raising children, keeping the family history, and acting as church leader and educator. Although Sister Kent fulfills two of these criteria, the other women, all mothers, grandmothers, and great-grandmothers, possibly see that she has missed out on the maturational experience of child rearing.

Sister Kent helps all the women in her congregation, and she made a special attempt to help me in my work. She refused to be formally interviewed, but she encouraged other women in the church to participate. She did this both because she wanted to assist me with my study and because she worried I might develop a limited view and make generalizations from working primarily with the poorest members of the church family.

In an example of Sister Kent's teaching, she asked me what I thought about the pastor and herself. I responded that they were "proud, hardworking, took care of themselves, and owned their own home," and that Reverend Kent was an interesting combination of "pride and humility." She repeated this exactly several times so that she could tell her husband. She continued to press me—What did I mean that it was "admirable" that she and her husband worked hard, owned their own home, and had pride? She asked, "How does this relate to you and your husband?" until I finally said, unsure of her point and myself, "Well, you are like us." She then pointed out that when she was growing up there was no welfare and that the people she knew all owned their own homes. She was surprised when she learned that this was not true for everybody. Thus she gently led me to confront my own stereotypes and prejudices about black people. Why was their lifestyle, so like my own, surprising and worthy of remark? I will never forget her soft persistence against my ignorance and her investment in my growth as she led me to examine my own racism.

Sister Kent supported me in my research, but she also made it clear that curiosity could be negative. In one discussion she noted that some people are curious and enter a situation only to criticize the people and discover the negative. She felt that when the "upper crust" is curious about people, as they were about Jesus (who was only a carpenter), there are often bad results. She demonstrated that the most effective lessons—as any good preacher or preacher's wife knows—are those that "hit the mark" intentionally or unintentionally. Even as I write this, I stop once again to think about whether my words demonstrate or will create a negative form of "curiosity."

This was not the only time I worried about my role as researcher in this community. However, when I asked Sister Kent her opinion, she reassured me, saying, "God put this work in your heart," and urged me to continue. She quoted Martin Luther King Jr., saying, "'There's a time and a place for everything.' This is in your heart." Sister Kent accepted that my intentions were good but knew that I needed her wisdom.

Beliefs on Race: "We Are All Out of One Blood"

In a small church with a number of the members living below the poverty line, Reverend and Sister Kent are unable to address the constant and ongoing issues of need. However, they try to inspire pride and a positive attitude. They encourage people "to live better, to do better, and to work." They try to help people "have a look-up." Reverend Kent notes proudly, "If I was hungry, I wouldn't tell nobody about it."

Just as they cannot "fix" the problems of poverty that plague many of their members, Reverend and Sister Kent cannot change the fact that their church members experience discrimination. However, the Kents steadfastly refuse to see their members as objects or victims. They try to inspire their people to ignore and overcome the obstacles they face every day. Their goal is to keep their members going, not to fight the system that holds them back. As one member says, "As a small church, we just mostly try to hold it together."

The often-stated church philosophies about equality and justice are rooted in both the physical concept of "blood" and the spiritual knowledge that God cares for all equally. Reverend Kent frequently points out, "We all out of one blood!" Sister Kent says vehemently, showing the vein in her arm, "We all bleed the same!" Quoting Scripture, Reverend Kent says, "'God so loved the world, He give His only Son.' He didn't leave nobody out—no age, color, nothing because He loves us all." Reverend Kent feels that it is important to accept that God knows what He is doing: "I'm just like God made me to be and I'm not going to worry about what somebody else thinks—I'm just going to love everybody."

Reverend Kent believes, "We have to live by the rules . . . we might not get justice all the time, but that's the reason we have God . . . violence begets violence . . . hate begets hate." Several church members respond in unison, "That's a hard one to learn." They quote Scripture together, repeating, "If you stand still, I'll fight your battles—they that wait upon the Lord shall renew thy strength." Reverend Kent believes that, whatever happens, if we pray and wait, "Jesus will take care of the situation. . . . He'll do it so sweet." He acknowledges that "turning the other cheek ain't so easy—call you 'chicken' . . . but it's best to be a live chicken than a dead hero. That's what's killing this generation."

Reverend Kent reminds the congregation frequently to "count their blessings," and "put forth an effort," not to "complain or be sensitive," and not to "blame somebody else." He sees that injustice is a reality, but he is "not a marcher." He does admire Dr. Martin Luther King Jr. because of his nonviolent beliefs and because "he was for everyone together." However, Reverend Kent believes strongly that prayer and loving others are the keys to change. The church members often reiterate that if anyone can do it, God can.

I once asked Sister Kent what she thought of the phrase "Prayer is the opiate of the masses." She answered without hesitation, "Jesus changed the world more than anyone else."

CHAPTER TWO
THE FAMILY

The Church Family

Reverend and Sister Kent are the leaders of the Morning Sun Church family, which is a part of "God's family." One member testified to the strength of her family identification with God: "There ain't no love like His love. He's closer than my brothers, my mother." The philosophy of Morning Sun Church is that all people on earth are members of God's family. However, in this conservative Baptist church, the official belief is that only those who are "saved" by "accepting Christ as their personal Savior" through baptism and by leading a Christian life are assured of "going home" to God in heaven.

Some church members have more liberal views: one member believes that no one knows what another person is doing to "get right with God" and that one cannot always tell from the outside what is going on inside; another feels that as long as she reads her Bible and has a good heart, she will go to heaven. Most members, including the church leaders, try not to judge others, noting that "Jesus can wash us whiter than snow in a minute."

The "Morning Sun family" is made up of church members who are seen as "family" in the sense that they have a communal life together, celebrate and cry together, love one another, and help one another in times of trouble. Their common goal is to keep their small church community alive and prospering, both spiritually and in the material world. Similarly to other African American churches, the "church family" or "church home" offers a sheltering "homeplace" for individuals and families that "provide[s] crucial material, financial, social, intellectual and emotional support in times of need" (Mattis 2005, 199–200).

One becomes an official member of the Morning Sun Church family by bringing a letter of reference from his or her former pastor to transfer membership. Sometimes a minister refuses to write a letter if there has been a conflict or if there is a question of character. When Reverend Kent left his former position, the pastor resented his leaving and at first would not give Sister Kent "her letter" so that she could officially transfer with her husband.

Grown children of participating members who were "dedicated" as children at Morning Sun are still carried on the membership roll, even if they no longer attend regularly. They may not go to church at all anymore, or they may attend another church but have not yet obtained their "letter" from Reverend Kent. The official church membership of Morning Sun consists of thirty-five members, but in reality there are six adults, in addition to Reverend and Sister Kent, who come every week.

There are other semipermanent visitors, supporting members, and "patrons" who are considered to be part of the church family. They contribute to the church's financial support and take an active part in special events. One elderly woman, Betty Jones, has attended Morning Sun regularly for fifty years but has never transferred her membership from her home church in Louisiana. Her daughter also comes frequently but also attends other churches and is not committed to Morning Sun. But both women are considered part of the Morning Sun family—triply connected as longtime guests/supporters, as blood relations of official members, and as "some kind of blood kin" to the pastor and his wife.

The idea of family goes far beyond the usual meanings of church membership, or even of "God's family." Church members often become "fictive kin" for one another. In a church, members become part of a kinship network when they "assume recognized responsibilities of kinship"(Stack 1974, 60). Although not as reliable as blood kin, these relationships extend the number of people who can be counted on, and they are necessary for survival in some poor black communities. Often, the family cannot remember exactly how a particular kinship relationship started. Some members of the church have lost their parents and now see Reverend and Sister Kent in this role. One young woman "adopted" Reverend Kent, asking him to be her father, telling him "I couldn't ask for anyone better." One member's son/nephew went everywhere with Reverend and Sister Kent for years, and she says, "They raised him right behind me."

References to church family as kin are frequent. On Mother's Day, one prominent member announces that she feels like a mother to everyone in the church; another woman gives a bouquet of flowers to an elderly widow, saying that the woman is now her mother since her biological mother has "passed."

The church family members often pray, "Bind us together so close that one can't fall without the other." When a church member has a crisis, the Morning Sun family becomes distressed, with all members worrying and praying and helping out as is possible. Reverend and Sister Kent become especially overworked, spending many of their days visiting, counseling, praying, and supporting the family or church member. When one "church mother" was gravely ill, Sister Kent explained the turmoil in the church to me, saying, "It's just like when your dad died to you." When this member "passed," Reverend Kent thanked the congregation, stating, "It's a family—you went as far as you could go. . . . One of our family has crossed over so there's one chain missing. . . ."

Included in this idea of church family is the notion that all church members have a "family" title. Reverend Kent is seen as the father of the family, addressed as "Reverend" or "Pastor" or "Preacher," and sometimes more informally: "Hey, Rev!" Sister Kent's role is more ambiguous—as seen by her title of "Sister." She is an equal to the other women in the church but is also their leader and role model and is addressed as "Superintendent" when teaching. In general, women and men are addressed as "Sister Last Name" or "Brother Last Name" when at church functions. Formal introductions demand titles, so a mother will introduce her own daughter who is the speaker as "Sister Last Name." Children are addressed by their first names until they become "Sister First Name" during adolescence.

The Extended Family within the Church Family

Several extended families of church members, as well as a few solitary women living alone, make up the Morning Sun Church family. The extended family structure is a strength of black families, providing "extra hands, added wisdom, as well as auxiliary shoulders to lean and cry on" (Jones and Shorter-Gooden 2004, 257). The concept of extended family within the black community has been well developed elsewhere and will not be reiterated here.[1] In Morning Sun, the "extended family" fits the following description:

> The black extended family means a multigenerational, interdependent durable kinship system, which may include kin and non-kin, and is welded together by a sense of obligation to one another. It consists of members who interact daily, providing for the domestic needs of children, adults and elderly, assuring their survival and care. The family network is diffused over several kin-based households and extends across geographical boundaries. It has a built-in mutual-aid system for the welfare of its members and the maintenance of the family as a whole. Fluctuations in household composition do not significantly affect cooperative familial arrangements. (Adapted from Martin and Martin 1978, 1; and Stack 1974, 31)

Caretaking in the Morning Sun family extends to adults and the elderly rather than being organized solely around care of the children. In the extended families with blood kinship ties, power appears to be shared, with members readily flowing in and out of one another's homes. Each individual woman has her "own place" (a "homeplace") that offers privacy and a refuge for immediate family, but all homes are simultaneously shared spaces, with all equally "at home" in one another's houses (Burton and Clark 2005, 170; Stack 1974). However, in the church extended family, relationships with fictive kin are more formal, and visiting requires a phone call and an invitation.

The Generations

Within this idea of the extended family is the concept of the "generational family." The term *generations* has an obvious meaning—that of biological great-grandparents, grandparents, parents, and children—but there are other meanings as well that the people of Morning Sun attribute to the concept of "generations."

The members of Morning Sun identify strongly with preceding and succeeding generations. Children are recognized as being "just like Aunt

Marie" or as having "all of my sister's ways." If someone is seen as having a particular quality, such as energy or perseverance, she is compared with another family member who has that quality.

The idea of "generations" is also used to explain expectations or disappointments in the family. Reverend Kent frequently mourns over children who put their parents in a rest home and do not return to visit, saying that this is no way to treat "the generations." When one member disagrees with her daughters, she merely shrugs and says, "That's the generations," as if this explains it all.

"Generations" is used in yet another way besides comparing traits and referring to differences in family values. Reverend Kent frequently talks about "the seed," saying that "you can't change the seed—handed down through third and fourth generations." This seed can be from "something somebody did way back in generations and you'll have to pay for it":

> We'll see people in a certain condition and we say, "He's in that condition because he sinned" . . . It's handed down from generation to generation. Sometimes it don't get you, it'll get your children. . . . In our family . . . I know one niece out of the whole family who says she ain't supposed to work. . . . You got to watch that seed—that seed is there—a lot of people don't like to talk about that seed.

When someone "messes up" after a lot of chances, Reverend Kent philosophically notes, "It might be in the seed." Sister Kent states, "If things not improved by the fourth generation, they really debased, ignorant," acknowledging that sometimes no one can change what is in the seed.

But the seed can be good, too. Reverend Kent says, "If the seed is there, it's just there . . . education can bring out what's there. If there ain't nothing there, can't. But way back, if there's a good seed somewhere, it'll come out." This idea of a generational seed gives families an explanation when someone "goes bad." It also enables a person to have hope that long after he or she is gone a "good seed" may prosper. It allows Reverend Kent to remain hopeful, seeing that his words, like generational seeds, may come to fruition in a way that he cannot know right now; and it is a method of giving credit—as well as blame—to generations that have gone before, acknowledging previous contributions as well as earlier sins.

CHAPTER THREE
MOTHERHOOD
"Somebody Prayed for Me"

I t is Mother's Day, the most important day of the year at Morning Sun Church. Church members and extended families are gathered to honor their mothers, and the church is colorful with bright dresses, dark suits, and flashing smiles. Joyful at being together and proud of their families, the members of Morning Sun are at their most beautiful. It is impossible to reconcile this picture with the many stereotypes that are held about black people, especially poor black people. At times, some of the church members have been unemployed or on welfare or were pregnant as teenagers. Some are the working poor, and some live in the projects. Some have suffered from alcoholism or have family members in jail or daughters who have been involved with gang members or drug addicts. Several of the elderly survive on permanent disability from poor health, work-related stress, or injury. Three children are developmentally delayed, with one suffering from possible fetal alcohol syndrome. Some children do not always have enough food or the right foods to eat.

All of the church members have been touched in some way by the crimes of poverty and oppression. However, these descriptions do not describe the fullness of the church members' lives. The adults are also the laborers, the teachers, the domestic servants, the child-care workers, the middle-class homeowners, the loving and strict parents, the music makers, the God-fearing peace lovers, the computer operators, and the foster mothers. The children are the quick, bright-eyed, leaning-forward-hands-raised-high-in-class kind of students, the drill team marchers, the athletes, and the children in the orchestra. Some church members have had more material success than others, some are more educated, and perhaps some are more spiritual. But all are here together as members of God's family and the Morning Sun family.

On the right side of the church sit Missionary Mahalia Lake and her daughter, Sister Molly Lander, her husband, Will, and their two lively little children. Molly's two older girls, Caren and Roberta, sit with their cousin Robert Junior (raised by Mahalia Lake) and Caren's children. Caren, pregnant with her fourth child at age twenty, carries a baby and manages two toddlers. She is a blooming young mother—her hair prettily pulled back in a bun, wearing a matching orange T-shirt and shoes and a short black skirt. Roberta, a high-school senior with an athletic build and her grandmother's bright smile, struggles to help her sister with the three babies. They are giggling together like sisters do.

Even though their mother, Molly, has been working for several years, the family continuously struggles below the poverty line and has lived in the housing projects for many years. Today, Molly has on a new black dress with white collar and cuffs, and her oldest daughter, Caren, fixed her hair for church. Her husband, Will, wears a blue pinstriped suit and an open-collared dark shirt. With Molly's job as a child-care worker and his new job as a maintenance man, they once again have hope that the future will be brighter for their family.

Molly's younger daughters are pristinely dressed, with tiny plaits and ribbons in their hair. Shani, wearing a white suit with a pleated skirt, sits in the pew, her little purse at her side, writing briskly on scraps of paper. Bebe shows off her new shoes and dress—black on top with a flowered skirt that flares out when she spins. Their grandmother, Mahalia, beams proudly at her offspring. She is dressed for "her day" in a white suit with a pleated skirt that waves softly as she moves to the music. Her bright red blouse sets off a necklace with a heart locket, a Mother's Day gift from her children, and her hair, also the result of Caren's efforts, curls softly about her face.

When Molly and Mahalia, the sole choir members, get up to perform, a transformation takes place as they smile and sway and lift up their voices in praise to the God who supports them. While Mahalia sings she closes her eyes and rocks to the music. Occasionally she raises her hand and waves in time to the music or reaches out to touch Molly. Mother's Day—

today is their day. Molly and Mahalia have made up their minds not to let sorrow or their worries touch them today, and they ignore the jumping of thirteen-year-old Robert Junior, who has behavior problems and cannot sit still in the pew. They steadfastly sing about their blessings.

On the other side of the church is the Jones family, also out in full force. Old Mr. Martin Jones is in church for the first time all year, dressed in a black suit and white shirt, wearing a dapper tie and hat that belies his eighty-two years. In spite of the unexpected pleasure of his presence, it is clear that it is Mrs. Betty Jones's day, and she is beaming. Five of her six adult children are present for Mother's Day. John flew in from California, and Jeremy brought his son, a college student at the University of Washington. Anne and four of her children, along with assorted great-grandchildren, are sitting together, spread out over three pews. Marie is, as always, with her partner Sam Peters, and Mrs. Jones is so glad she found a nice man after all those hard years. Marie's "three little girls"—now "three little women"—have also come with their five children. Mrs. Jones's youngest, Joann, her husband, and their two children arrive late, as usual. Eighty-year-old Mrs. Jones greets people and chuckles delightedly as she shows off her family. Every girl is a beauty, each boy handsome in a dark suit.

Sister Mable Jackson sits in the back, alone, and watches the goings-on around her. She can barely move due to her arthritis, but she does not want to miss out, so she has walked from her house around the corner. She is dressed beautifully in a peach suit with her "usher" pin displayed prominently on her ample breast. She has not been forgotten—a younger churchwoman, who lost her own mother, brings her flowers and claims her as her mother. Both women are in tears, and Sister Jackson buries her face in her bouquet so that no one will see her cry.

As Sister Kent sits down at the piano, she adjusts her white suit jacket over her pastel pink dress. Her white high heels find the pedals, and she begins to play and sing. It is easy to see the wisp of a girl she once was, comfortably singing out as she gets her small congregation on track, preparing for the Spirit to come alive in the church. Reverend Kent sits at the front, listening to the women's devotions and to the music as he meditates quietly on God's word, waiting for the "message" to bring to his people.

The Church and Motherhood

The subject of the sermon, of course, is mothers, and the words and the music are carefully chosen to reflect the theme. According to Collins (2000), black motherhood is often "sanctified" in the black church. This "superstrong black mother" image has been a difficult one for black women in that it presents an unrealistic picture that is difficult for women to live up to (174). However, Reverend Kent takes a down-to-earth approach. He starts the service by referring to his mother and his religious home, saying, "My mother never whupped me much. She whupped me with 'The Word.' She read the Bible to me and then she read it some more!" He then uses biblical stories to describe mothers who are not images of perfection but rather, like the women in church, have faced overwhelming odds and prevailed. These biblical mothers are sympathetic sister images—women who, if they were alive today, would know, understand, and empathize with the conditions that the women of Morning Sun experience. In rapid-fire succession Reverend Kent expertly compares contemporary problems and the women's experiences to biblical mothers Eve, Hagar (the mother of Moses), and Mary, emphasizing "lessons" for his congregation of struggling mothers. He includes the story of the mother of Moses:

> It's all about another mother who came to her wit's end. The children of her people were being killed. A lot of mothers have their children being killed today and they forget to go to Who can help. They had a wretched government! She had a three-month-old child, she was working on a basket. She put the basket in the reeds. The baby's sister watched over him at a distance. You know the story: how the daughters of Pharaoh come down to bathe and saw the basket—See, God have a way of working things out! . . . [Later on] she was working in the Pharaoh's house, still taking care of her own baby, and she got paid for it! That's the reason I love the Lord so much!

By using these familiar Bible stories, he makes the following points: these mothers were "up against it," too, and worried and grieved for their children; oppression has been going on for a long time; it is necessary to turn one's back on wealth and cast one's lot with the poor and oppressed; and

God has a way of working things out for the oppressed and downtrodden, but first a person must let the peace of Christ enter her heart.

Biblical mothers provide the women of Morning Sun with role models and sister support as they make their way in the world. These images of mothers are not of superstrong mothers or mammies or matriarchs or dependent welfare mothers (Collins 2000). They are images of women who persevere. They are women who teach their children "The Word" and live by it in their everyday lives. These biblical women and their children survived and in some cases prospered, not because they were strong, but because the Lord came to their assistance at critical times. They knew how to put themselves in the hands of the Lord and never stood alone—they had support in carrying their burdens and in facing their challenges.

Reverend Kent states that he does not deal with politics, but he clearly has his own brand of social justice. He works with his congregation to both motivate them to help others and "hang on" when they are "up against the wall," reassuring them that Christ will help them both with their immediate concerns (as He helped Moses' mother) and by bringing peace into their hearts.

Reverend Kent acknowledges that economic concerns have changed the structure of the family, noting that men often don't have jobs, and women must work and are less available to their children. He alludes to the "system" that creates this reality: "It ain't supposed to be that way! Bible says men supposed to . . . it's a sick society. Women don't have time for that now, got to go to work"—to which the congregation responds, "Men won't!"

The pastor preaches a strong role for men in family life and in the transmission of values, but he knows his members' situations well; he tries to "work with what I have"—the women, the mothers. He emphasizes, "A good mother makes all the difference."

Reverend Kent finishes his sermon urging his congregation to treat their mothers well. "We should remember our mother. Someday [she] won't be there and [we'll] miss her so. [We'll] be sorry [we] didn't do more." He prays: "Help those who miss their mother. Enable them to realize if they [are] saved, they'll see their mother again. We making preparation for another home—one not made with human hands, where there will be no more sorrow, no more goodbye."

In addition to the formal teachings on motherhood, Morning Sun uses many songs that refer to "mother." Mother is seen as a helper, a friend here on earth in the quest to make it "home." She is somebody who prays for her children, always has them on her mind, guides them to the Lord, and is there for them no matter what.

The members of the congregation respond strongly and positively to the sermons, stories, advice, and music. They show their appreciation and agreement with enthusiastic call and response, heartfelt "Amens!" and ongoing discussion after the service. This agreement demonstrates that the value systems and beliefs on motherhood represent their own beliefs. Their work as Christian mothers, othermothers, and community mothers is thus reinforced and honored in church on Mother's Day.

The Community and Motherhood

Collins (2000), Jones and Shorter-Gooden (2004), hooks (1989), and Hine and Thompson (1998) note that many theories and stereotypes about African American mothers, especially poor black mothers, have evolved. Collins (2000) critiques these theories and the images of black women as mothers—the mammy who takes care of white children at the expense of her own; the matriarch who dominates her children, creating dysfunctional families; the lazy welfare mother; and the "superstrong black mother," often used as an exemplar in the black church. This final image is one of strength and resilience but also fosters an almost impossible ideal for black women to live up to—especially when many are, in fact, overworked, exhausted, and without enough money to feed their children (174).

As a counter to these stereotypes of black motherhood, Collins (2000) cautions that women in the black community demonstrate great diversity in how they shape and define motherhood, and that this process is always "dynamic and dialectical," developing at least in part as a response to the forces of race, class, and gender oppression (176). The particular expressions that black women's relationships take with their children, one another, and the community depend on the specific dialectic that occurs between "the severity of oppression" and the actions taken "in resisting that oppression"(177).

Othermothers, Community, and Activism

Consistent practices at Morning Sun Church that demonstrate Collins's theory are the meaning of "othermother" and how this role relates to community activism and power, and the socialization of black children under conditions of oppression. In Collins's theory of "othermothers," biological mothers are expected to care for their children, but othermothers (grandmothers, sisters, and aunts) also share responsibilities with blood mothers (Collins 2000, 178–183). These arrangements can become long term or turn into informal adoption (Stack 1974; Gutman 1976). Neighbors and unrelated "fictive kin" as well as relatives traditionally care for one another's children, even to the point of disciplining them, thus challenging the notion of children as "property" of a parent or parental unit. Often othermothers form a network, a supportive community as they care cooperatively for one another's children (Collins 2000).

This concept of othermother is a reality in the Morning Sun community, as the women support one another in multiple ways as they raise their children. Sister Kent advises the young women in the church. Mable Jackson, with the help of the Kents, raised two of her nephew's children. Marie Jones Smith and Molly Lake Lander mother multiple children in their jobs as child-care workers, and they also care for grandchildren, nieces, and nephews, while Marie takes in foster children as well. When Marie had young children of her own, "Grandma," a neighbor, along with the children's aunt, helped care for the children while Marie worked two jobs to support them. Mahalia Lake helps raise her grandchildren and great-grandchildren, especially her grandson, the boy's mother having died from an overdose and his father, her son, in prison. In the Jones family, grandmother Betty and her three daughters work together to fulfill mothering responsibilities for all of the Jones offspring.

A further refinement of this idea of othermother can be seen in the concept of "church mothers." The women of Morning Sun do not define themselves as "church mothers," saying they are "too young" or "not better" than the other members. However, women in the early years of Morning Sun fit the historical meaning of church mother as clarified by a woman speaker on Women's Day:

> You don't hear me talk much about "mothers" because we don't have mothers in church like we used to have. . . . The mothers and the pastors ran the churches fifty years ago . . . and I tell you those mothers meant something to that pastor! They meant something to that church. . . . If you were there, in church, your mother didn't have to say a word to you—that [church] mother could knock you down. . . . Now days the mother better not say nothing to your child. . . . So we rarely can do the things we should . . . things that God want us to do. . . . Your best is the worst to somebody else . . .
>
> "Mother" is over the women in the church. . . . That's not the pastor's job, that's the mother's job: she teach 'em how to dress; she teach 'em how to act; she teach 'em how to be good wives; she teach 'em how to be good mothers. . . . The pastor's overseeing the whole church . . . but the mothers take care of the women.

As women care for one another's children as well as their own, they begin to see all black children as "our children." They often define their roles and become involved politically in the community as they fight for their own children. They then push the limits of the narrow traditional meaning of the word *mother* by fighting for social justice for all "our children" (Collins 2000). When Marie Smith talks about problems in the black community, she refers to "our kids, by that I mean black kids," signifying ownership of the community's problems and her relationship as othermother to all black children. Hine and Thompson (1998) note that for black women,

> Strength comes from being part of a community. . . . Service is not sacrifice but part of the fullness of life. The busiest most successful woman is expected to take in her brother's child, and her cousin's too, if necessary. The most powerful woman is the one who finds a way to feed, clothe, and educate others. The history of black women teaches that every life belongs to the community. (308)

Although we again see the challenging image of the "superstrong black women" in this description, the ideal that "all children must be cared for" remains a community value. "Motherhood" in Morning Sun Church is presented and enacted as both a site of self-definition and a starting point for political activism. Inevitably the women fight for their children as they struggle to feed and educate them and as they teach them how to handle themselves in a racist society. In their narratives, Linda Wilson and Mable

Jackson describe how they have worked with school principals, teachers, and school boards to make sure their children receive good educations. Molly Lander and Mahalia Lake tell about standing up to health professionals to ensure that their children are well cared for (Abrums 2000b). Joann Newton and Marie Smith "come out fighting" when they see that their children or foster children are mistreated by anyone or any system. Caren Lake, although only twenty years old, is rapidly learning how to advocate for shelter, food, and health care for her children.

As in Collins's theory (2000), the meaning of "motherhood" as community activism for the women at Morning Sun is specifically a black Christian women's standpoint, one that has developed under the joint oppressions of racism and poverty and within the support of the community and philosophies of the church. While there is not a distinct dialogue at Morning Sun about fighting the injustices of discrimination, there is much conversation, music, prayer, and "preaching" about surviving, growing, and finding peace in spite of the conditions that oppression creates. The women pray for Jesus to help them as they stand up for their children.

Socialization of Black Children

A second theme in Collins's (2000) theory on black motherhood that applies to the women of Morning Sun relates to the socialization of black children by mothers. This includes both protecting children and helping them learn the "skills of independence and self reliance" (186). Children must learn how to survive and prosper under conditions of race, class, and gender oppression. Jones and Shorter-Gooden (2004) note that black mothers must "prepare their children to live in a racially charged America. Racial socialization means raising a child to like herself, to have positive feelings about and connections with the black community, and to be competent and successful in the broader society while carefully navigating bigotry and discrimination" (239):

> [Black mothers] spend significant energy shifting emotionally and psychologically, constantly anticipating and coping with the assaults that their children encounter. They buffer, filter, deflect, defend, bolster, fortify, and embrace—even as they wrestle with their own sadness, fear,

and anger about what their children must endure as black people in this society. . . . Black mothers must constantly decide whether the challenges and disappointments their children face are race specific. (237)

The majority of black mothers, including the women from Morning Sun, have raised healthy and productive children in spite of the challenges of oppression and poverty. The women of the church speak with great pride and love for their mothers and grandmothers and for their children. They know they have a hard job as mothers and feel good about the work they are doing; but they simultaneously acknowledge legitimate fears and concerns about raising black children to be safe and healthy. The women's stories in *Moving the Rock* reflect the complex demands of socializing black children. Underlying these stories is the consistent theme that Jesus and their Christian faith provide the support they need for this life's work.

Part Two

THE WOMEN OF
MORNING SUN CHURCH

Table I.   Church Families in the Study

Family	Members
Pastor and His Wife	*Reverend Joseph Kent* and *Sister Bessie Kent*
Now Living Alone	*Sister Mable Jackson* (71 years old)
	Timmy (23) (nephew-son)
The Jones Family	Martin (82) and *Betty Jones* (80)
	Marie Smith (48)
	Linda Wilson (30)
	Natalie (12)
	Charmian (8)
	Angela (4)
	Simon (2)
	Caroline (29)
	Alice (10)
	Patricia (28), pregnant
	Jimmy and *Joann Newton* (37)
	Christine (15)
	Jimmy Junior (18 months)
	Anne (55)
	3 daughters and 3 sons
	John (53)
	1 daughter and 1 son
	Martin Junior (50)
	1 daughter and 1 son
	Jeremy (46)
	1 daughter and 1 son
The Lake Family	*Mahalia Lake* (59)
	Will and *Molly Lander* (41)
	Caren Lake (19)
	Derrick Junior (3)
	Dameon (18 months)
	Daniel (newborn)
	Pregnant with Ciara
	Roberta Lake (16)
	Shani Lander (6)
	Bebe Lander (4)
	Harry (40)
	Robert (36)
	Robert Junior (13) (raised by Mahalia)

* Names in italics indicate those who shared their stories in *Moving the Rock*.

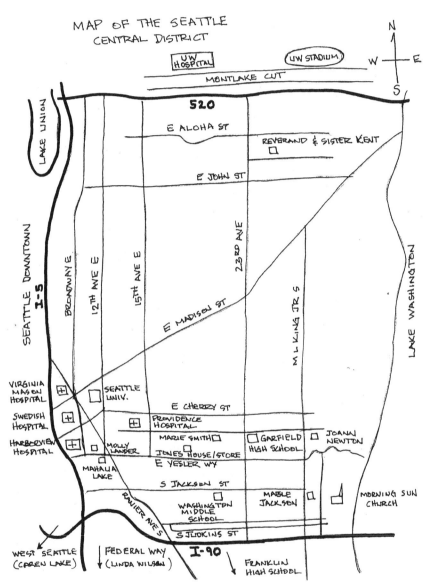

Map 1. The Central District

THE LAKE FAMILY

MOLLY LAKE LANDER
"I Guess I Have to Go to Jesus"

Mahalia Lake had just returned from grocery and Christmas shopping. As she struggled to carry her packages into her low-income apartment she saw Molly Lander, her forty-one-year-old daughter, coming home from work. Molly, dressed in a stained, oversized beige down parka that went almost to her feet, trudged up the steep hill from the bus stop to meet her mother. She carried two overfull bags, one a bright pink Mickey Mouse backpack that had been "handed down" to her for her children. Her hair had escaped from its headband and was sticking out all over. Molly barely greeted her mother as she wearily made her way to where she waited. She sat down on a nearby bench, huffing, wheezing, and coughing. Mahalia softly urged her to come inside and "rest a while." Molly came into her mother's house and threw herself prone on the sofa, murmuring that she did not feel too good but still had to go downtown. Mahalia silently went to the tape recorder and started her new tape, "Nat King Cole's Christmas Hits." As the music played, Molly slowly revived enough to stand and jerk the parka, stuck with a broken zipper, over her head, revealing a black T-shirt and black leggings. She sat down heavily on the sofa again.

In a few minutes Molly needed to meet her six-year-old child at the school bus; collect her four-year-old from day care; find something to eat for dinner, which entailed a trip to the grocery or fast-food place; take the city bus downtown to do her errands; help with her children's homework; supervise her sixteen-year-old daughter Roberta; and check on her pregnant daughter, nineteen-year-old Caren with two babies in West Seattle.

It would be another night alone. Her husband had gone to California almost a year earlier for a family funeral and had not yet returned. The day's work was over, and the evening's work was about to begin.

As Nat King Cole's rich voice poured into the room, singing, "Chestnuts roasting on an open fire," both women began to sing softly. Mahalia stood looking out the window onto the busy street and rocked softly while she sang. Molly stayed seated, but as she sang she slowly put more and more of herself into her song. The words to the song painted a picture ironically at odds from the reality of the dingy apartment. But the music fed the women's souls. As Molly listened and as her mother cared for her without touching her, Molly slowly started to come to life—the hope of the Christmas season reaching out to her.

The stories of Mahalia and Molly are deeply intertwined. When Mahalia was nineteen she had Molly, her first child and a girl. Since that time, the two of them have made it together in the world. Of course there have been and still are others—husbands and brothers and children—but they are not to be counted on in the same way. Caren, Molly's first daughter, is "coming up," and "she tries" but she is not any real help yet—she has her hands full with her own babies and still needs more than she can give.

With Molly and Mahalia, one thinks of the prayer cited frequently in Morning Sun Church, "Bind us so close together that one can't fall for the others," and fall they do when any family member falls. Their security is fragile with little or no reserve, no safety net to help them except what the government provides. But they always climb back up again and make their way forward, attributing their persistence to the help of Jesus.

Molly and Mahalia are the most reliable, and often the only, choir members at the church. Dressed up on Sundays and somewhat rested from Saturday off, Molly and Mahalia are beautiful together. They smile and sing, closing their eyes and swaying to the music. Wearing bright colors, or both in black and white, they touch each other, fuss with each other's hair, and laugh together as something tickles them both. Although Mahalia is tall and Molly is short, both are imposing in size and look alike with the same bright smile. Occasionally six-year-old Shani joins them in the choir, and the three generations proudly sing out together.

The family works as hard and is as determined as most families. Yet the labor of sheer survival keeps them running only to stay in one place.

Living in low-income housing projects, they are easily stereotyped as "welfare." More accurately, they are "the working poor." Mahalia, now in her late fifties, is a single parent who raised three children and worked as a nurse's aide in a nursing home until she became ill from stress and fatigue. Molly says, "It was like she was here but she was so tired and she worked so hard. . . . She got to a certain point and everybody said, 'Okay. No more.'" She qualifies for disability income, receiving $450 per month (this has increased slightly since the time of the study). One-third of her income is for rent, and then she pays her utilities, phone, and life insurance. She receives $67 in food stamps and her health care through Medicare. Sometimes she supplements her food allowance with free food from the housing project office. She takes advantage of senior citizen discounts and says life is "getting easier" with her bus pass and senior discount cards for fast-food restaurants.

Molly is a child-care worker for Head Start. Before taxes she makes $1,300 per month, taking home $1,000, but is employed only nine months of the year. Her $9,000 supports a family of five—sometimes nine when Caren, her boyfriend, and their children are "in between." At this income level, Molly and her family are well below the federal government's definition of poverty, which, at the time of the study, was $17,416 or less for a family of five. Head Start teachers are laid off during the summer and rehired every fall. Each summer Molly applies for unemployment, and about halfway through the summer she begins receiving approximately half of her usual salary. She says, "It's a struggle." To receive unemployment she must look for jobs, and every two weeks she takes the bus to the unemployment office to drop off her "job search" form.

During the school year Molly has health insurance through her job but has to pay $5 per visit to her HMO. To insure her children, she would have to pay $90 per month per child, so she hopes that welfare will cover major expenses for them. Molly says that her children "do not get sick." Some health concerns have to wait. For instance, Roberta, who is sixteen, had a tooth knocked out by a softball; and although this bothers Roberta, there is nothing Molly can do about it, and she says Roberta will have to learn to live with it. Molly's husband, Will, employed off and on, has no insurance.

Both younger children are in day care—six-year-old Shani goes after school, and four-year-old Bebe goes all day while Molly works. Welfare supplements this $500 expense so that Molly pays $71. She tries to keep them in day care in the summer as the children love "Ms. Star's" and there is no place for them to play and little to do at the housing projects.

Caren, Molly's oldest daughter, is the only "welfare" (as people generally conceive of it) recipient in the group. She receives Aid to Families with Dependent children (AFDC) (now known as TANF, or Temporary Aid for Needy Families). Caren receives $800 per month for herself and two children, including food stamps. She uses the Women, Infant and Children (WIC) Nutrition Program to help feed the children and herself when pregnant. She pays about $130 per month in rent for her apartment in the West Seattle Housing Project, which she shares with the father of her children. Although Derrick does as much as he can for Caren and the babies, he has conflicting demands. His mother is living in a motel with his seven brothers and sisters and has a drug abuse problem. When his mother asks him for money, he has to help her—"She's my mother." He has been looking for a job for several years, but with a police record he has not been successful.

The Lake family contends daily with the intersecting challenges of racism, sexism, and poverty. Mahalia has been married and has two adult sons, Molly is married, and Caren has a partner; but the women are the center of the family and have provided the stable incomes with sporadic help from the men when they can find work. Heavy and dark skinned, Mahalia and Molly are on the lowest rung of the African American caste system. They are poor and they look poor. They experience discrimination from both whites and more well-to-do blacks alike.

A study of the Lake family is a study of day-to-day survival and life on the edge. None of them has ever been able to buy property, nor have they ever received even a small inheritance. The family has no "accumulated wealth," savings, or assets. Molly and Mahalia own life insurance policies, with the hope that they can leave their children a better start than they have had. They do the best they can, seeing that the children are cared for, serving God, and trusting in a heavenly reward.

"Molly Was My Mother's Day Present"

Molly is at church services, as she is every Sunday, with her two youngest children, four-year-old Bebe and six-year-old Shani. The girls bump and wiggle for the entire two hours. Bored, they play with scraps of paper and Bebe plays with her toes, pulling them through the holes in her tights until her tights are no longer tights at all but raggedy holes partly covering her legs. Midway through the service, the child determinedly marches down the aisle in the remainder of her tights to go downstairs to the bathroom. Shani is right behind her, her single pointer finger high in the air, indicating their mission. After a few minutes the adults can hear whoops and hollers, and Molly gets up with a sigh to attend to her children.

Molly's children are the only young people who attend Morning Sun regularly. They are often sick, with runny noses and hacking coughs, whimpering or sleeping soundly in the pews from the effects of the over-the-counter antihistamines Molly gives them, or crying in frustration from the whacks they receive when they can no longer contain themselves. Shani and Bebe wear well-worn tights under their dresses, stained jackets, and ill-fitting dress-up shoes. When they leave the house, they are pristinely groomed, but Bebe is apt to be filthy (somehow) by the end of the service.

However, the children look sparkly and perky with their hair well groomed in little plaits all over their heads, the plaits fastened with bright hair clips. They are friendly and sit by me for weeks on end, imitating me by writing busily on scraps of paper or trying to learn their ABCs as I write them out for them. They quickly learn that I have no power over them and that my mild chastisements are not followed by physical discipline. As long as they sit with me, they are out of the reach of their mother and grandmother, who can only give them "that look" from across the aisle. They are my first and most loyal friends.

As I make friends with the children over the weeks, I slowly learn their mother's and grandmother's stories. Molly was born in a West Chicago tenement apartment. Her mother Mahalia was raised in Georgia and migrated to Chicago with her mother (Big Mama) as a young woman. There she met and married her husband, and they lived in the same apartment building with Big Mama. In 1951 Mahalia's first child, Molly, was born on Mother's Day with the help of Big Mama and a midwife. Mahalia says, "Molly was my Mother's Day present. Guess that's why we so close." Molly weighed only 6 pounds 4 ounces, so her grandmother "used the oven for an incubator," holding the baby in front of the oven to warm her. Molly's younger brothers Harry and Robert tease her about her dark skin, saying she was "burnt in the oven."

When Molly was a child in Chicago, her father supported them. He "did junking, did painting" and was an iceman for a time. When Molly was five years old, a taxi skidded on the ice and hit Mahalia, breaking her leg. During her mother's recovery, Molly climbed on the stove to do the cooking while Mahalia took care of the two boys.

Mahalia and her husband did not get along, and with a small settlement from the taxi accident, she moved the family to Seattle. Molly was taught by her mother and grandmother to be independent of men, and she did not find the separation from her father particularly hard. She understood that Mahalia, like Big Mama who had migrated from the South, left Chicago to start a new and better life and to provide more for her children.

Growing Up in Seattle

Molly was nine when Mahalia brought the three children and her mother to Seattle, where Big Mama's sister lived. Big Mama joined Mt. Zion Church, and, without bus service, the family walked four miles to and from church: "It took us all morning, but it was just the fact that we couldn't do anything 'til we went in that direction." In Seattle, unlike in Chicago, where everything was near by, the Lakes rode the bus or walked long distances to get anywhere.

The family moved several times within the Central District in Seattle. They tried to buy a house, but the loan fell through; they had to move to make room for the freeway; they had to move again when their rental house was sold.

Although Mahalia was sick for a time, the family got by with Big Mama's help. Molly remembers that the family never had to buy fruit because the neighbors let them pick apples, pears, and blackberries, and Big Mama canned fruit and jam. Molly states:

> We had a pretty carefree childhood . . . we always had something to eat. It wasn't always maybe what we wanted but we always had something to eat. And so basically we didn't worry about it too much. 'Cause my mom didn't make it our responsibility to take care of the house and stuff . . . I guess she tried to keep as much of it as possible off of us. . . . She sheltered a lot of it from us . . . we had rough times, but . . . we didn't

worry about being thrown out on the streets or stuff like that . . . she told us to always pay your rent so at least you'll have a place to stay. So we just figured she always paid the rent. . . .

Molly was a tomboy, but she developed early, started her period at age ten, and "had more chest than anybody." Her mother cautioned her, "Be extra careful. . . . It's a different thing now. There's times that you can't be climbing all over boys. . . ." This was hard on Molly because "people would think I should act a certain way."

No one talked with Molly specifically about sex, but she remembers her grandmother telling her to pull her dress down and cross her legs. By the eighth grade she knew what this meant, but "birth control was like something you didn't have and you just didn't talk about it." Molly was the last in her group to have a boyfriend at age fifteen. One of Molly's friends was "on her own" with an alcoholic mother, and she urged Molly to "try it [sex]," but at first Molly refused. Most of her friends already had babies when Molly became pregnant at sixteen.

Molly did not have to tell her mother she was pregnant because "she knew . . . she told me . . . she looked at me, told me." Mahalia identified Molly's pregnancy because Molly's eyes looked "glassy." Mahalia was "a little disappointed" with the pregnancy, but Big Mama was supportive. Molly then attended the alternative school at the YWCA and received her best grades with the individual attention there. Molly's boyfriend was a year older, and he continued in regular school. His parents had known Molly "since elementary school," and they were tolerant of the pregnancy. The boy's mother wanted them to marry, but Molly was not interested.

Molly went to Harborview Medical Center, an inner-city university hospital, for prenatal care when she was three months pregnant. However, the presence of medical students embarrassed her, and she did not know how to refuse to have them in the room. (Molly has recently had good experiences there with nurse practitioners and relies on them for her children's care.) When Molly was about seven months pregnant, the baby was stillborn, weighing only three pounds. Molly felt she was too young to handle seeing the baby, and she was put to sleep and her labor induced.

Molly and her boyfriend eventually broke up and she continued to go to school and began to work in summer youth programs in day care. Back in regular high school, Molly could not pass English and became "tired of high school." She left without graduating and worked full time in child care until she was twenty.

As a young girl, Molly missed her prom, and she brings this up frequently, saying, "Most people say, 'Did you miss your prom?' No, I didn't miss going to the prom because I just didn't have . . . the stuff I needed to go to the prom, so I just didn't. And I didn't dance so it didn't interest me, really, you know." Later she lamented that Caren did not go to prom either. In Roberta's junior year, Molly planned to save enough money so that Roberta could buy a dress, but Roberta turned down the chance. Molly has two daughters left, and she hopes that one of them will go.

Having Children

Even though Molly was sexually active after the birth of her baby, she did not become pregnant again for four years, saying she was "blessed." She tried birth control pills after her first pregnancy, but she stopped after a couple of months, stating, "I wasn't a birth control person, 'cause half the time I would forget it anyway. So it was like, 'Okay, three days done passed and you ain't took it so that month's shot,' and then the next month's shot, so it was like remembering what day to start on after your period and. . . .'Pshew! Hang this stuff.'" She then tried various other forms of birth control but found none of them worked well for her, and she experienced two miscarriages. After the birth of her last baby, Bebe, Molly had her tubes tied. She does not completely trust this method, saying, "I'm trying to hurry up and get through my midlife period. . . . At my age; I *pray* I be through menopause. If I have a baby going through the change of life, talk about cry! Oooo, Mary, you have to visit me at the insane asylum because that's exactly where I'd be! . . . I'm *tired* of it!"

When Molly was twenty, she became involved with the father of her two older children, Caren and Roberta. Her pregnancies were normal, but both births were difficult, and Molly was unhappy with her health care. She continued to see the father for several years, but she did not want to marry him, noting, "That way, I didn't have to take no lip. I didn't encourage him [to see the kids]. I didn't really ask, see, 'cause then if he says something to me, I could slap him down. . . . I just didn't want to be bothered by that time . . . we just didn't click anyway." The man was divorced, and Molly felt he would divorce again. She did not want her girls to be exposed to several fathers, saying that she knew too many welfare kids with too many fathers. She wanted her children to know only one man as their father—the man she married. The meaning of "father" for her was based on the man's permanent commitment of marriage to the woman and her children, rather than on biological fatherhood alone.

Molly stayed home with Caren and Roberta for several years. She was on Aid to Financially Dependent Children (AFDC), and when the girls started preschool at Head Start, Molly volunteered there and finished her GED as well. She enjoyed her years at home with her daughters and spent time at their schools: "It was really important; it was nice for them."

Molly has never moved far from her mother, but having her own space is very important to her: "Girls move out and get their own place and boys stay with their families." Molly, Mahalia, and Caren all live in low-income housing projects. Molly and Mahalia are in Yesler Terrace Low Income Housing in the Central District, and Caren is in low-income housing in West Seattle. Mahalia's son Harry lives with her, and until recently, her grandson, thirteen-year-old Robert Junior, did as well. He is now in a group home. Molly lives with her children Roberta, Shani, and Bebe, and her husband, Will, when he is in Seattle. Caren is with her two babies (later four) and her boyfriend Derrick in their own apartment. Later Caren's family moves several times to be with both extended families in Seattle and California.

In spite of each woman "having her own space," it is often difficult to understand just who is living where and when. Questions about living arrangements receive vague replies. There is always a lot of back-and-forth with all of the spaces shared by family members. Mahalia eats dinner and watches TV almost every night at Molly's apartment. She and Molly often take food on the bus in the late afternoon to Caren's apartment to cook dinner there. The Lake family network, like that of many poor black families, "is diffused over several kin-based households" (Stack 1974, 31).

Molly and the Family

Molly's brothers have not finished high school. Harry dropped out because he was bored but was accepted into the Marines in his late twenties because "they said his IQ was so high." He earned his GED in the Marines but was discharged in less than a year because he had trouble conforming to the rules and regulations. Today Harry is a writer working "off and on."

Molly and Mahalia speak proudly of Robert, the youngest son. Robert is in prison, but he always helps Mahalia financially when he is able to work. (Robert's son, Robert Junior, lived with Mahalia from the time he was eighteen months old until he was thirteen years old.) On explaining Robert's imprisonment, Molly merely states that Robert did "something stupid," hanging out with the wrong people. She adds, "He's a male Lake. He took more after his father . . . he never resolved any of the problems [of] his youth . . . he needed some early counseling . . . so he could share his disappointments about not having a dad. . . ." Molly does not worry about Robert in jail—"Why worry about it? He ain't going nowhere. Lessen he loses his temper and hits one of them guards. . . . When he told me he got convicted I told him, 'You wanta see me, you stay on the outside. I'm not going behind them jail bars.'"

The family has always expected a lot of Molly. The pastor's wife, Sister Kent, says, "Everything falls on Molly." Molly says,

> [Everyone thinks I should] always be strong. . . . If I get sad and depressed, it's like everyone else is going down the toilet—so, "Hah, sorry Charlie, you don't have time to feel sorry for yourself" . . . If something bothers Mom, she's going to bring it to me. If something bothers Harry, Robert . . . Caren, everybody bring it to me. . . . So it's like, "Excuse me, you guys" . . . I guess I have to go to Jesus 'cause everyone else is coming at me . . . if something really bugs me and I need to talk, I talk to my husband most of the time. . . . I have to hear everybody tell me how to live my life—"I don't think so. I'm forty-one here, you guys, I got gray hair that I can see now. I can make my own mistakes."

There are things that she cannot discuss with her mother and will not put on Caren, such as issues regarding her marriage:

> I try not to talk to [Caren] too much about the bad things that go on. I try to spare her 'cause I know how, being the oldest. . . . She worries about her younger sisters. . . . And she's got her own [children] and . . . I don't think there's too much [she] can do with [her] sisters. . . . Caren wants to move to California. . . . She needs to get out on her own and be independent and see if she can make it without the family.

Molly seeks outside help when she has troubles. When she and Will separated, she worked with the counselor at the housing project community center and was involved with a black women's support group. She attended Al-Anon, but found that its white middle-class participants had issues that were vastly different from hers. She mainly depends on her faith, on her gospel music, and on Jesus.

Daughter-Sister-Mother-Friend

When Caren and Roberta were young and Molly was unmarried, she and Mahalia worked together, functioning as "othermothers" as they raised the children together. When Roberta was four and Caren six, Mahalia took over the care of her son's boy, Robert Junior, who was eighteen months old. Robert Junior's mother was a drug addict and an alcoholic, and he was abused. He is now thirteen and has a variety of behavioral problems that have been difficult to diagnose.

Raising their children as siblings, the two women have been sisterfriends and peers as well as mother and daughter. Mahalia maintains a close relationship with Molly's older girls, Caren and Roberta. They talk on the telephone or see each other every day. Robert Junior, after many difficulties, has moved to a group home but comes to visit the family often.

Today Molly and her daughter Caren raise Molly's "second set" of girls and Caren's two boys together, much as Molly and Mahalia once did with the older children. Watching them manage four children (later six) who are under six years old is a study in grandmotherhood/motherhood/sisterhood/friendship. If a child has trouble with one "mother," he appeals to the other. Similarly, if one "mother" is lax about discipline or has her hands full, the other simply takes over without question.

Mahalia declares firmly that she refuses to babysit for the "younger set," Shani and Bebe, and that Molly no longer asks her, and "I love her dearly for it." In spite of this statement, Mahalia is still very involved with her youngest grandchildren. When Molly's schedule demands it, Shani goes to "grandma's" early in the morning, and Mahalia walks her to the bus and picks her up in the afternoon. Mahalia keeps Bebe and Shani with her when they are ill or tired, watching them at her place or Molly's and taking them on her errands. She actively disciplines the children and often has the final say in decisions about them. For instance, when Shani has surgery for kidney problems, Mahalia states firmly, "She'll go back to school when I say she's ready!"

This involvement on Mahalia's part is not a one-sided arrangement. She provides child care for Molly, but she expects repayment. When shopping together, she frequently asks Molly to buy her something, saying, "Buy your babysitter some chocolate ice cream. School is out all week at one p.m."

Death of a Baby

When Caren was five and Roberta three, Molly became involved again with the father of her first baby who was stillborn. Molly then had a second baby, Ruth, with this father, but Ruth died when six weeks old. Molly tells the story, beginning with, "It was a beautiful day and I was out mowing the lawn." When she went inside to check on the baby, she found that Ruth had died. She remembers:

> I freaked out. . . . The only way I could deal with it was to get rid of all her stuff right away so I wouldn't get too attached. Otherwise, I was afraid I'd hang on forever. . . . That was a hard time; but some things you just have to accept because no matter how mad or how angry or upset you get, you just can't change some things. And we're all born dying, so . . . she just wasn't meant to be; and my mind was gone, but still I thought of Violet [her friend]. . . . She helped me clean out the baby room. . . . I cleaned it all out in one day right away. When she died, I had no more use for the stuff. I took it all to another girlfriend who was having a baby. Took it all away. . . . It was like those people that linger and mourn, y'know, feel sorry for theirselves—I didn't want to go through that.
>
> So then it was crib death, then after [the autopsy], they found out she had leukemia. To me that could've answered why the first baby didn't live any longer than it did. I wasn't strong enough to sustain her. . . . So, it was like God sent me an answer to questions that had been bugging me for a while—cleared them up. So that's when I went back to church. I went back to my faith. And sometimes God does things to make you look at your life or to answer questions. . . . As far as health care, I used to say different fathers was the difference.

For Molly, the sacred and the scientific answers intertwine, offering a reasonable explanation that has helped her find meaning in her babies' deaths. With the death of the second baby, God has helped her resolve the questions that followed the birth of her first stillborn baby, showing her that both babies had problems—possibly due to having the same father—and that she could not have prevented either death.

Marriage

When Caren was eleven and Roberta was nine, Molly met Will Lander at Morning Sun Missionary Baptist Church, and they decided to marry: "I wasn't planning on being married. . . . It's not something I just said, 'I want to be married' or 'I have to be married before I die' . . . It's just something I never really concentrated on. . . . Single was fine. . . . My thing was, 'If God wants me to be married, He'll send somebody to church.' So, He did. . . ."

Will is a small, handsome, wiry forty-four-year-old man. He has a kind, usually unshaven face, and he speaks in a deeply rural Louisiana Cajun dialect. Molly feels she "got caught up in his excitement 'cause he wanted to get married. . . ."

> I had never been married, but one thing I knew, I wasn't staying with nobody unless'n I did get married, so shacking was out! I don't go that route . . . I don't see the benefits in it, myself. . . . I told him, "I'll marry you." So if he ever inherit anything or die and leave me anything I can get it! [*laugh*] . . . "I don't want to live all my life with you—you die and I be broke."

When they were first married Will worked as a maintenance man at a downtown government building and shared his money generously. Molly says, "He's not going to stay in my house without giving me some money!" The family qualifies as low income and remains in the apartment.

Will's background is "drastically different" from Molly's, and this creates conflicts. He was raised in the segregated South on a farm "where his mother and father worked for the white man," while Molly was brought up in a more "mixed community" in the Central District of Seattle. Will is more wary about the children's white playmates, and his upbringing adds to fears that

Molly does not share. When their daughter Shani has surgery at Children's Hospital, Will is afraid to spend the night with her because he often restlessly walks outside at night—but he is hesitant to walk in the hospital's white neighborhood and fears he will not be allowed to reenter the hospital because workers will not believe he is a parent. When Molly teases him, saying "Scared of the dark?" he answers, "Scared of what's in the dark."

Molly was able to stay home for a year after each of the births of Shani and Bebe since Will was working, but then she returned to work. Molly often thinks about how nice her life would be, now that her two older girls are almost grown, if she had not had the two youngest children. Her mother and brothers have little energy left for "the second set"; and, when Will is gone (as he has been for many months), she feels the stress of truly being on her own as a single parent: "The last two [children] are, I wouldn't say, in the way; but nobody really expected the last two. . . . It's not that they don't love 'em but, like, everybody's up in age and kinda tired. . . ."

"You're Here and I Need and You Have"

When Will and Molly married, things changed between Molly and Mahalia. Molly says:

> I guess when you spend so much time with your family unmarried and then you get married, it's like, "Okay, he stole my daughter," or the whole picture changes. . . . Sometimes you realize why people move . . . to other states, to escape the ties, 'cause if you're there, they just, they want. It's like: "Well, you're here and I need and you have" . . . But everything's not just mine anymore—it's me and my husband's. . . . And then I have two more kids. . . . It wouldn't have mattered if he was a millionaire. . . . Just that I was her only daughter and for thirty years it'd been . . . a team.

When Molly was a child there were no men—"Grandma was in charge of decisions and that was that with no conflict." But marriage complicates this picture. Tension occurs when Mahalia, who has always shared Molly's life and belongings, can no longer do so.

> When you have a man in the house and he's bringing in part of the money then you just can't give away everything. They [the wife's family]

just can't come in and go through the refrigerator like they used to. And they get mad 'cause you say, "That's not mine. That's his" . . . Sometimes people buy stuff when they have money. They put it up to save it so when they don't have no money, they have it when they want it, they can have it . . . [but] everybody wants to eat it up. . . . That's why I keep my own house. So when she gets mad at me, I just stay over here in my house 'til she cools down.

When Will lives temporarily in California, Molly and Mahalia slip back into their old comfortable pattern, with Mahalia coming to dinner every night and treating Molly's house like her own and vice versa. When they shop, Mahalia buys this and Molly buys that, to be shared. Or if Mahalia is broke, she will borrow two dollars from Molly for candy (if Mahalia will share the toilet paper she bought last week!), or Molly will automatically pay for two Christmas trees, knowing her mother's situation at the time. They borrow clothes from each other and treat each other's homes as their own, with Mahalia casually cleaning Molly's yard or house, or putting her feet up to read a magazine, or turning on her favorite TV show. But after Will's return, when Mahalia cautiously asks Molly whether she can come over after supper to watch her gospel hour on cable TV, Molly gently tells her, "I don't have any idea of what's going on at my house."

The constant sharing and negotiations over money and goods is related to privacy but must also be understood within the context of scarcity. The sharing relationship between the two women, which often includes Caren as well, enables them all to get by. Molly's refrigerator is often almost empty. When the children squabble about dinner, Molly tells them that there are hot dogs and that it is better than some people have. Mahalia often goes without breakfast and then quickly eats fast food when she is out because she is starving. Caren does the same, even when pregnant: she skips meals to feed the kids and then, on her errands, buys a bag of cookies to eat. Molly often complains that she has not eaten all day because every time she has tried, the kids "got the food out of me."

The children do not look undernourished, but it is clear that the family never has enough to eat. The children are frequently sick and whining throughout the day. When meals are served at church, they eat everything and beg for the salad and broccoli. Molly and her family are typical of a family in poverty: they often run out of money to buy food to make a meal; the adults skip meals because there is not enough money for food or to feed both the children and the adults; and they rely on a limited number of foods to feed their children, rarely buying products like fresh produce (Wehler 1995).

Molly and Mahalia are overweight, and this is related to their hunger and food insecurity. They are hungry because they skip meals and there is no food at home. When they have a chance to eat, they often overeat, choosing foods heavy in fat and sugar because these foods feel satisfying. When food is available, they eat more than they should in anticipation of the times when there will not be enough, demonstrating starve-and-hoard behaviors.

Food is an ongoing issue, not just because there is not always enough money for food, but also because of the difficulty, both financially and practically, of buying large quantities of food at a time. There are no large grocery stores near their homes, but only small expensive mom-and-pop stores. Each shopping trip involves careful calculations of how much money will be left until the next payday and whether there is the time or the energy for a lengthy bus ride carrying bags of groceries. When they have access to my car, Molly and Mahalia ask to go to specific grocery stores. There, armed with their carefully clipped coupons and knowledge of the newspaper-advertised sales, they buy large, heavy items or purchase more groceries than usual. Forays out to fast-food places, such as McDonald's, Kentucky Fried Chicken, or Taco Time, are frequently more convenient and seem to fit the budget better, as they spend a little money at a time, even if in the long run eating out is more costly.

Occasionally Molly borrows twenty dollars from a friend to "make it until payday" or tells the children to "ask Uncle Harry" for help. But more often than not, Molly tries to help family members either by protecting them from the daily drain of constant small demands—as she does with Will when she encourages the kids to "let up on him" for a while so that he can buy his Christmas presents; or she gives family members what little money she has when there is a need. When Caren moves to California, Molly frets that she can no longer help when Caren is "short." When Caren is upset and wants to move back, Molly hurries to finish her tax return to have enough cash to get Caren and her children home to Seattle. She speaks often about giving Caren money to rent an apartment or to buy her a car. Mahalia's requests for assistance are small and fairly constant, but Caren's are episodic and tend to deplete the family's limited resources rapidly and thoroughly.

Molly's life is fragmented and disorganized, and it is difficult to get ahead financially. There is no way to budget systematically when a family lives continually on the edge with wages below subsistence level. There is no way to save money for emergencies or for special purchases or even to plan ahead for meals. It is a constant process of skimping on one necessity to pay for another. Molly and Mahalia often make jokes about their situation, deciding whether to buy the dress and sit in the dark for a month; or laughingly saying, "The bill collectors can wait."

Charitable organizations are available, and the family takes advantage of them. They utilize the housing project community center Christmas giveaway to pick out some of their gifts for one another. One year Molly was thrilled to get new school clothes for her children at a radio station's school giveaway.

Buying new school clothes is a priority for Molly every autumn, and one year I go shopping with her. She directs me to drive to a discount store in West Seattle, usually three bus transfers away for her, because it is one of the few stores that has "layaway." Molly picks out an outfit for each of her younger children and a shirt for Roberta. The wait in the layaway line takes forty minutes, and several parents lose patience with recalcitrant children, smacking them harshly or sending older siblings to wander around the store, jerking their toddler brothers or sisters after them. When it is her turn, Molly gives the clerk the clothes and pays five dollars to hold the outfits for two more weeks. For the next three months, twice a month, she takes the three buses to West Seattle and returns to patiently wait in line to pay $8.41 each time.

Molly and Mahalia complain that layaway has gone out of favor in many places because of credit cards but hope that it is "coming back." They do not usually qualify for credit, but Mahalia does have one card that she uses infrequently because she is afraid of going into debt. They do not have checking accounts but use money orders to pay bills.

One of the most striking things about Molly's and Mahalia's lives is how much time everything takes. Saving money, when one has barely enough, requires a tremendous investment of time and energy. The layaway lines at the discount store are long; the wait for the bus is long, there are several transfers, and the bus is slow; it takes time to get food daily or to go to a remote store to save money; the wait at the health clinic is lengthy. Everything takes more time.

The Children

Although the relationship between Molly and Mahalia is important, there are equally strong ties that bind Molly to her husband and children. Since Molly often says that she has told Will that he comes seventh in line, after her children and grandchildren, the stories about the relationships will be told in that order.

At the beginning of the study, Caren is nineteen; Roberta, sixteen; Shani, six; and Bebe, four. Caren is pregnant and has two little boys: Derrick, three, and Dameon, eighteen months. Molly talks often about the different personalities of her children and grandchildren and her hopes and dreams for each of them. She sees Caren as bright, industrious, neat, and tidy—she is always "cleaning up and throwing out." Caren helps with her younger sisters and is a good mother to her babies. Molly bails out Caren time after time when she makes mistakes, saying, "Her grandmother spoiled her"; or she is learning through experience, gaining "bought sense." When Caren first became pregnant at age fifteen, Molly was disappointed but accepting, relieved that Caren had made it to "some kind of maturity." Although Molly hopes Caren will finish high school one day, she sees that Caren's most important job is to take good care of her children.

Molly compares her second daughter, sixteen-year-old Roberta, to her brother Harry, and says she is "the lazy, intelligent one." Roberta is athletic and plays on softball and basketball teams in high school. Molly has never seen Roberta play, as she is unable to arrange the necessary transportation or child care to attend the distant games at night. She dreams that Roberta will someday go to a black college in the South. Molly frequently says that she feels Roberta is "over the hump" and will not get pregnant for a while, if at all. (Roberta will be the first Lake in all the generations to graduate from high school and go on to community college.)

Shani is a tiny but solid little six-year-old. She charms adults and loves to sing out in the choir. Molly believes she could be a gospel singer or perhaps a writer because she loves to read. She has chronic kidney problems from a defective ureter and is hospitalized periodically. Bebe is a mischievous four-year-old who knows no bounds. She never accepts "no" for an answer, and Molly says that she has to be prepared to immediately back up her words physically. Bebe often leaves chaos in her wake, like the time she jumped in Caren's car outside of church, shifting the car out of park and sending it rolling into the neighbor's yard with herself and Shani in the car. Shani got scared and jumped out midway. Caren spanked both girls, and the whole church was in an uproar. Molly feels that Bebe and Caren's mischievous son Dameon are difficult but intriguing children. She gets angry with them but protects them by keeping them with her as much as possible.

Roberta and Shani go to Summit—a kindergarten-through-grade-twelve alternative school in primarily white and middle-class north Seattle. They travel about forty-five minutes to school each way on the bus every day, but Molly chooses this option over a brand new school across the street from her apartment because she feels the children will get more attention at a smaller alternative school. Bebe goes to "Ms. Star's," a day care that picks her up and brings her home every day. Shani joins her there after school and during the summer months. Caren's boys attend Head Start.

Molly states adamantly that she is "not a feminist," but she has strong ideas about raising her girls to be independent women. She believes that girls need self-esteem to protect themselves from dependence on a man for their self-image and for their livelihood. Her mother was able to leave her husband because a woman had raised her, and Molly herself is not dependent on Will. When she and her husband disagree over raising the children, Molly listens, then says her "piece" or says, "Uh-huh!" and leaves the room, implying she will do what she wants.

Molly believes that "a house is for children" and that they come before housekeeping. She makes no attempt to protect her sparse and battered furniture but allows the children to eat, spill, climb, jump, and use colored markers or glue at will. Realistically, there is not a lot of space for them to play otherwise. There is likely to be food or garbage on the floor, clutter on every surface, and dirty dishes from last night in the sink.

Molly seems strict with her children, slapping their legs or hands or telling them, "I'm looking for a tree [a switch]," when they are misbehaving, but in reality she is indulgent, even tempered, and patient with them. Because of Molly's relaxed attitude, the children are not on a particular schedule and often take midday naps or stay up late. Occasionally they miss naps, go to bed early, and get up at four a.m. to watch cartoons.

Molly sees that life is hard, and children ought to be allowed to be children. In this way she is like her mother who sheltered her children from knowing too much about their situation, thus allowing them to have a carefree childhood.

"A Working Man"

Molly and Will have been married for eight years when Will goes to California for his nephew's funeral and ends up staying almost a year. Molly follows "the Bible's advice," that if a couple can't get along, they should separate until they can work out their differences. She believes that she and Will may have a permanent separation, but not a divorce—there are financial as well as religious reasons to stay married. Molly states that she comes from a line of strong women, but once Will is gone, she wants him back. Her prayers are finally answered, and Will reenters Molly's life as easily as he left. Molly seems happier, but their lives are not trouble free.

Molly says that Will is a "working man," and he is employed off and on, but there are barriers to his maintaining a permanent position—he is uneducated and speaks a Cajun dialect that is hard to understand. When he is unemployed, resources are scarce, and there are conflicts. As Stack (1974) notes, a relationship with a nonworking man saps potential resources of the kin network, and often the family wants that man gone. At one point Will is hired for a janitorial job with full benefits, with the understanding that he will learn to drive in order to run small loading equipment. For the following weeks, Will tries to figure out how he can get a driver's license. He cannot take driving lessons as they cost four hundred dollars, and he cannot teach himself, as he does not have access to a car. He badly needs glasses in order to drive safely, and the family has no money for this. The company allows him to stay on without driving, albeit with a decreased salary; and for a time, things seem to be going well. Molly is excited and full of plans for her home. The job lasts almost a full year, but he is then let go and Molly is not sure why. She feels that things went downhill after the manager who hired him transferred to another store.

"And a White Picket Fence . . ."

Molly has dreamed of owning an old house with a white picket fence and a big porch where she can sit and rock when she is old, but she now believes that this dream is unlikely to come true. Occasionally she still says she wants "an old-fashioned house" if her husband wins the lottery or if she inherits a lot of money [*laughter*]. She rationalizes that even if the children buy a house for her, they will want to live with her; and now she looks forward to the day when they are all out of the house. When she speaks nostalgically about her dream house or of her children buying a house for her, Mahalia says, "Dream on!" or "You were born in the wrong family!"

While Molly is always careful to pay her rent, she is sometimes late with her payment because she carries the money order around in her purse, saying laughingly, "I like to pretend I'm not broke." Molly feels secure in her low-income project apartment. She is a long-term resident and knows that even if she loses her job, the city will allow her more time to pay.

The apartment complex recently underwent exterior renovation, and Molly appreciates the changes. However, she is somewhat frustrated because the residents were not consulted and there are many problems. Roberta's room leaks when it rains, and the workers replaced the wooden baseboards with plastic that mice can chew through to come into the house from the basement. The exteriors have been repaired (which makes everyone who sees the projects feel good), while the interiors "where we live" are still very depressing. The walls and flooring are stained, the paint is gray, the linoleum is torn, the appliances old, and the furniture sparse, raggedy, and stained beyond cleaning. Molly wants to fix up her home, but the tenants are not allowed to paint the units or replace the linoleum themselves. They are told that if they do paint or put down linoleum, they must scrape the paint off when they leave and take up the flooring. In the meantime, they are advised to vacuum up (neither Molly nor Mahalia has a vacuum) any small chips of the flaking old lead-based paint, as it presents a serious health hazard for children. Molly routinely spends time on her hands and knees picking up paint chips to safeguard her creeping grandchildren. Mahalia, with serious hypertension, is unable to bend over without dizziness, so her paint chips stay where they are—in spite of the presence of children.

When Will has his janitorial job, Molly is able to clean and decorate the house. She covers the dirty and torn linoleum with a rug, finds a nice used sofa, and puts up new blue curtains for fifteen dollars. She now has a hand-me-down kitchen table with three chairs, a sofa, a tattered loveseat, and a new TV for her living/dining area. A large picture of Jesus is on the wall, and the house is cluttered with kids' belongings, laundry, and items of everyday living. The children sleep on mattresses on the floors of the bedrooms, and cardboard boxes function as bureaus; but Will and Molly have a double bed. While nothing can disguise the general dinginess of the walls and atmosphere, Molly does the best she can.

One of the most difficult moments in my research is when Molly and Shani visit my comfortable house. Shani bounces around, looking in every nook and cranny, and then cheerfully announces, "I want you for my mother." She points to the extra bedroom and calmly says, "I could sleep right here."

Molly is resigned to living in her apartment and has exchanged her dreams of a house for the small measure of security the apartment provides. However, things are changing rapidly in the Central District. Her housing project is on premier city property, and there is a plan to develop "mixed-income" housing. If this happens, many of the current tenants will be displaced and may never be able to afford the newly developed units and houses. This is an ever-present worry for Molly and Mahalia. But with faith and prayer, they continue to hope for the security of their homes.

CHAPTER FIVE
CAREN LAKE
"Having a Dream"

aren is a beautiful young woman, the pride and joy of the Lake family. Small and of medium build, with light eyes, hair, and skin, she fits the dominant societal definition of beauty more readily than do her sisters, mother, and grandmother, with their dark skin and large frames. As Caren tells the story of her life at age nineteen, she has not yet had the experiences of the other women that lead to maturity and wisdom. But Caren is friendly and articulate and chatters away like the hopeful young woman she is, relating the story of her growing-up years.

Her mother, Molly, and grandmother Mahalia raised Caren alongside her sister Roberta and her cousin Robert Junior. She attended local public schools and was involved with church activities like most young people in her social circle. When she was fifteen she met and fell in love with Derrick, and her life began to change. It is Molly who provides the framework for how things went after Caren and Derrick became involved.

When Caren first got pregnant, she called Molly at work, saying, "Mom, what if I told you I was pregnant?" Molly said, "Girl, I'm at work, leave me alone." Caren answered, "Mom, I am," and Molly, shaking her head, just said, "Caren." Molly relates:

> Actually I was surprised [that she had made it to age fifteen]. I just said if my kids make it past into the teens into some kind of understanding about what they're doing. Too many kids having babies. . . . I see twelve- and thirteen-year-olds. . . . Maybe there's not enough explanation or, I don't know, too much interest in sex. . . . I said, "You know when you

start having children, you don't have no life no more" . . . so she had Derrick [Junior] and thought she had no life—she had half a life. Then she had Dameon and now she had no life, less'n I decide to babysit 'em. . . . I was strapped down at that age, but . . . I see me settling down into the mold easier than Caren. Staying in the house works on her nerves . . . not being able to keep up with her friends, which I don't know why, they all have babies anyway. . . . One of her group is going to college—thank you, Jesus!

Caren had prenatal care throughout her pregnancy. Molly attended childbirth classes with her and was her coach at the birth. Molly says, "Who else? She didn't holler 'Derrick,' she hollered 'Mama!'" Caren had a healthy pregnancy and an easy labor. Molly had breastfed her babies and tried to talk Caren into doing so, but Caren said, "How can I be nursing in the streets?" Molly told her, "Girl, stay at home then. . . ."

After the baby's birth, Caren and Derrick and Derrick Junior moved to Los Angeles to live with Derrick's father and stepmother. Caren missed her family and came back with the baby after one year. When Caren returned she was pregnant with her second child, Dameon. This time she did not have an easy pregnancy. Playing in the snow with her little sisters, she fell and "started bleeding and bleeding." Her grandmother Mahalia called an ambulance, and Caren stayed at the University of Washington Medical Center for four months until the baby was born by cesarean section. Hospitalized over Christmas, she missed baby Derrick Junior terribly. During this time she worked on her GED and passed all but two parts of the test.

Caren is currently nineteen years old and pregnant with her third baby. Caren, Derrick, and their two toddlers, ages three and eighteen months, live in low-income housing in West Seattle. Her grandmother Mahalia allows me to take Caren to the doctor for her checkups, saying that Caren likes to be "babied." When I suggest that I ride the bus with her from West Seattle "for the experience," Mahalia makes it clear that my purpose is not to do my research but to help take care of Caren by giving her a ride in her last month of pregnancy.

It is a sunny fall Tuesday when I pick up Caren for her doctor's appointment, and the housing projects are quiet, empty, and clean at ten a.m. Caren lives across from a playground and has a clothesline behind her unit. The apartments overlook a valley with a colorful autumn view, and bright flowers grow in some of the yards.

At the knock on her door, Caren carefully asks, "Who is it?" before opening. The house is clean and tidy, and Caren hurriedly feeds Derrick Junior some cereal, complaining that she is late because her mother did not call to wake her. Caren is carefully groomed, her hair slicked back into a bun. She does not look eight months pregnant, wearing her regular jeans unzipped with a sweatshirt pulled down over her belly. She runs quickly up the stairs with a bottle for baby Daemon, who is still sleeping with his father, turns on the cartoons for Derrick Junior, and warns him three times not to open the door. She carefully locks the door before leaving.

Even though Caren says she is shy, she is interested in the study, and on the drive to the clinic she laughingly agrees to help because, "I'm not doing anything anyhow." She feels "stuck way out" in West Seattle and is unhappy with her living situation—the apartment is too small and she does not like the floor plan with the kitchen and living room in one room. She wants to be near her mother and grandmother but likes "a quiet house." If she is in the Central District, she is afraid that too many friends will stop by to visit and party.

Caren hopes to get a house through Section 8 and does not care where it is, as long as it is nice. If she qualifies, and if a house is available, the Section 8 government subsidy will pay two-thirds of the rent, and Caren will pay one-third. With a third baby on the way, she wants a three-bedroom house with a yard for the boys and hopes to pay about $130 a month. Caren is a "low priority" for a Section 8 because she already has a low-income apartment. To qualify, she would have to move out of her apartment for two months into unsubsidized housing or stay with family, and she is reluctant to give up her situation. But Caren is adamantly seeking a better life and does not want to stay in a housing project, no matter how much "sense" it makes. Mahalia's often repeated words, "That's what it's all about—having a dream," are important to Caren.

Direct Encounters in Health Care

Caren is eager to go to her prenatal visit, and she is grateful to have a ride. It takes her two hours each way on the bus from West Seattle. Providing the transportation gives me a chance to talk to Caren and to understand more about her health care. Caren (and sometimes her children) and I go to several clinic appointments over time. Two of these visits are described below: one visit at the Women's Clinic in University Medical Center when Caren is eight months pregnant with her third child; and one visit several weeks later when we go for a routine clinic checkup for Caren's new baby Daniel and her toddler Dameon at Harborview Pediatric Clinic, an inner-city university hospital clinic.

When we first arrive at the Women's Clinic at about 10:30 a.m., Caren says she has not had time to eat and is hungry. We go to the hospital cafeteria, where she buys a doughnut, a cookie, and an apple. As we wait Caren tells me that the worst part of the clinic visit is the *wait*. We arrive early and wait forty-five minutes before we are put in an examining room. In five minutes, an Asian nurse comes in and takes Caren's blood pressure, gives her a cup to urinate in, and sends her to the bathroom. The nurse does not do an assessment or any teaching. When Caren returns, the nurse is gone. Caren pulls open a drawer and begins reading through a packet on pregnancy and birth. She has the material at home but says she likes reading about the baby's development at thirty-four weeks. She looks at a brochure describing birthing rooms and says wistfully that she would like to have her baby in one of these rooms because "it is just like a nice bedroom," but she does not think construction of the units will be finished in time.

A young white social worker enters after about fifteen more minutes. Caren does not remember her name, although she knows her from when she was hospitalized for her high-risk pregnancy with Dameon. The social worker asks Caren whether she is still working on her GED. Caren says she wants to wait until after the pregnancy, and the social worker asks, "Why will it be any easier after the pregnancy?" Caren explains that she will have more energy and that her day-care fees and her twenty-five-dollar application fee will be paid for if she waits—she does not have the necessary funds. Caren, who was chatting happily with me in the waiting room, has clearly withdrawn. She keeps her eyes averted from the social worker and speaks briefly. The social worker asks her whether Derrick, the baby's father, lives with her, and Caren says, "No," somewhat shortly. She complains that she is not getting enough rest because her kids are up late and wake up early—she has no energy for a GED.

The attending (faculty) M.D. enters, and the social worker leaves quickly. The doctor, an East Indian, explains to Caren that a physician on the faculty sees each patient for one visit during her pregnancy. He asks who Caren's doctor is, but she has had so many residents that she does not know. On the way to the clinic she had mentioned that seeing the same person was not important to her, but that it was important to go for prenatal care—"I don't want nothing to go wrong with this baby. I want them to be checking to be sure everything is all right."

The doctor stands with his back to Caren and speaks to her while he browses through her chart. He never looks at her. He asks whether she's had any problems. She complains of cramps in her thighs. He does not address this but tells her to get on the examining table. He fumbles around with the sheet that he ultimately does not use. He adjusts the lower part of the table with a loud "thump!" He tells her to pull her "panties—pants down" and "unzip." He feels the position of the baby. He then, without any warning or explanation, puts a cold "glop of goo" on her belly, listens to the baby's heartbeat, and says it is good. The rest of the conversation (with his back to us as he continues to study the chart) goes as follows:

Caren: How many weeks am I?
Doctor: I have you plotted out at thirty-six weeks.
Caren: That's even better!
Doctor: Are you going to attempt a trial of labor and delivery from below?
Caren: Um hmm. They said I could.
Doctor: Your firstborn was seven pounds, three ounces, so there's no reason—the reason for your [previous] cesarean was the placenta previa.
Caren: Um hmm. [*listening, waiting, drumming her fingers*]
Doctor: Did they discuss with you that we'll take a look at your cervix after your delivery? [Caren has abnormal cells due to estrogen influence during pregnancy.]
Caren: They done checked me so many times.
Doctor: Are you drinking milk?
Caren: I don't drink milk.
Doctor: Why not? It makes you sick?
Caren: Yes.
Doctor: Ahhh.

59

The doctor then asks whether we have any questions, smiling at me with a little bow, but still not looking at Caren. I do not doubt that my presence changed things, but I cannot know how he would have acted if I were not present.

Later, when I ask Caren what she thought of this doctor, she says, "He was the nicest one I've had. He asked some questions. None of the other ones have done that."

When the doctor leaves, the nurse returns and says that the social worker has not finished with Caren. The doctor needs the room, so the social worker takes us to a corner of the waiting room. She asks Caren about childbirth classes, but Caren says she missed two, so they told her not to come to the rest of the classes. The social worker asks her about transportation to the clinic and says there are cab vouchers, but you have to call twenty-four hours ahead. "For example, if your appointment is on Tuesday, call on Friday to set it up." She then offers Caren some suggestions on getting her boys to bed early, saying, "Put them down one-half hour earlier each night even if you have to go to bed with them." Caren listens up to a point but is clearly offended when the social worker suggests a parenting class. She says, no, she is not going. As the social worker leaves, looking uncomfortable, Caren murmurs to me, "I ain't going to no parenting class. . . . I don't think I need that. My mama and my granny never had that and I think I turned out okay. I don't want no one telling me how to raise my kids." About the boys' sleep habits, she says, "I know she's right. I just got to start doing it. I *know* what to do." She adds that it is hard to wake them from their late and long naps because this is the only time she has alone. She generally sleeps with her children, loves the feel of their warm bodies next to hers, and believes that they are safer sleeping with her.

We then go to the desk to make an appointment for Caren. We wait in a fairly long line and are told that "her" doctor is not available for two weeks. Since Caren is in her last month, she now comes in every week, so she is given an appointment "with one of the other ones you've seen" for the following week and an appointment with "her" doctor in two weeks.

When we return for Caren's follow-up appointment, the same social worker checks with Caren about the boys' sleep patterns. Caren describes how she has implemented some of the social worker's suggestions by putting the boys in their room at eleven p.m. and letting them play or sleep but stay in their room. Caren often goes to bed at this time. The social worker responds, "That's good. So they don't roam around the house or anything? Little kids can get into all kinds of trouble. I want you to get your rest and yet make sure they're safe." On the way out Caren mumbles, "I guess [social workers are] okay if you need help. I just don't need help right now. . . . I ain't gonna hurt [the boys] or nothing."

During these appointments, the doctor, the nurse, and the social worker seem uncomfortable and unsure of how to approach Caren. Caren is reticent and evasive, although she was cheerful and talkative minutes before her appointment. She is eager for teaching, as evidenced by her obvious interest in brochures and parenting magazines in the waiting room, but no one really tries to offer her information about her pregnancy or birth. In this routine event, the health providers seem to make several assumptions about Caren: that she is not interested in learning about her pregnancy and growing baby; that she does not want to finish school (in her last month of pregnancy with two active boys to care for); that her boyfriend might be living with her even though she is on welfare; that she might be a careless mother, possibly neglectful or abusive of her children; that it is easier to look at the chart than to try to interact with her. But Caren thought this was a good visit—the doctor had talked to her.

Sister Kent says, "People in certain circumstances have to put up with some things." As a nurse, I question this assumption and am happy to see a different model a few weeks later when Caren has a well-child pediatric appointment with "Dr. Margaret" for her new baby Daniel and her toddler Dameon. Dr. Margaret is a nurse practitioner who takes care of Molly's two youngest children as well as Caren's children. Although Molly and Caren insist Dr. Margaret is a doctor, they are not uncomfortable when they realize she is a nurse practitioner. They just like and trust her.

Molly and four-year-old Bebe meet us at the clinic so that Molly can help Caren manage the children. The baby has a rash Caren is worried about, and she tells me, "That's the reason I ain't going to miss this appointment!" Her friend has advised her, "Don't let people be kissing his cheeks. That's the reason he got that rash." Caren says, "I know it!" Molly and Caren look over Daniel's rash and whisper together, trying to hide it from me, until Dr. Margaret comes in.

When Dr. Margaret enters the room, it is clear that she knows the family well, and they are happy to see her. Dr. Margaret is a slight white woman in her mid-forties who is gentle, soft spoken, respectful, and thorough. Caren calls her "Margaret" and is very open, receptive, and eager with her, leaning up close against her as they look at the children together. As Dr. Margaret tells her how to take care of cradle cap, Caren speaks gently to baby Daniel, "My baby, I so sorry I been putting oil on you."

The rash is diagnosed as diaper rash from loose stools, possibly from the Carnation formula. Molly says, "Similac works best for black babies, I've found." Dr. Margaret agrees to write a note to WIC so that Caren can receive Similac for Daniel. Molly tells Caren, "If you'd breast-feed like I told you, you wouldn't be having all these problems with formula." The baby is gaining weight well and looks good. Dr. Margaret then turns her attention to Dameon, and she and Caren lean together, touching shoulders as she assesses Dameon's development. Dameon is very frightened, and Molly helps Caren hold him during the exam. Dr. Margaret looks in Dameon's ears and they are infected, as they often are. The women debate whether to send him to see an ENT doctor or treat him again with antibiotics. Molly and Caren explain to me that Dameon is afraid because he has had a bad experience with health-care workers. Last summer he had a bump on his head, and the doctors had to rule out child abuse at the clinic. Molly and Caren say they understand that the doctors have to follow this procedure at City Hospital—this is how Robert Junior, Caren's cousin, was diagnosed as an abused child.

Both Bebe and Dameon misbehave during the exams and receive several whacks from their mother and grandmother. Dr. Margaret does not seem concerned. Caren says, "I've got boys. I'm gonna whack them, or later on they'll hit me, steal my money. I'm not having any Robert Juniors [her cousin who is troubled] at my house!" Her partner Derrick tells her that boys will hit their mothers if discipline is not established early.

Caren's children receive immunizations, and then we take the children to the lab for Daniel's PKU test. Finally, after two hours, we are finished. Dr. Margaret has remembered everything, and Caren leaves with a prescription for a formula change, advice on cradle cap, sleep advice (wake them earlier in the morning versus the social worker's advice of putting them in the rooms earlier at night), and antibiotics for Dameon's ear infection. Dr. Margaret is compassionate, tactful, and thorough. She is confident that Caren is a good mother, giving excellent loving care to her children. There are no negative judgments about Caren's youth, no assumptions that she might hurt her children or that she cannot understand instructions or is not interested. Caren is friendly, talkative, receptive, affectionate, and intimate with Dr. Margaret.

Everyday Life for a Young Mother

Caren attended Washington Middle School in the Central District and later took the bus to Ballard High School in the north end. When she became pregnant with Derrick Junior, she tried the alternative school but quit to take care of her baby. She currently works off and on to finish her GED, but she says she learns best by having someone show her and then by doing it herself. She wants to get a job so that she can be off welfare as soon as possible, saying that welfare is simply not enough money to live on. She hopes to be in college by the time she is twenty-one and dreams of being a registered nurse or a legal secretary. She is good with children and "good with hair," and her mother wants her to be a child-care worker or a beautician. She says she has to get an education "for my kids." She feels her children, who will be nine, ten, and twelve by the time she is twenty-eight, will "be grown" and she wants to be doing her own thing.

Caren shares the story of her days. She and the children usually sleep late, and then the children watch "Sesame Street" and "Nickelodeon." At about one p.m. she or Derrick takes the boys outside to the playground for a couple of hours. Caren often goes to the Central District to do her errands while Derrick watches the children. Dameon naps from three to six p.m., and Derrick Junior plays quietly or watches TV. During this time, Caren, who likes a clean house, tidies up. The house is spotless because, as she says, "There's nothing in it." After naptime, Caren fixes dinner and puts the children to bed at about eleven p.m., sometimes midnight. After the children are in bed, she and Derrick sit outside on the front steps and eat ice cream with the teenage couple next door.

The Support of Women

Caren is very close to her mother, her grandmother, and her sister Roberta. She visits them often, and they visit her. They talk on the telephone several times each day. The women, in spite of the distance between homes, often share everyday meals. Molly and Mahalia find a ride or take the bus to West Seattle, carrying supplies to cook.

Caren frequently asks to be dropped off at "Granny's house" after her doctor's appointments. Mahalia waits for her, and they go downtown to do their errands together. Caren needs Mahalia to cosign and cash her welfare checks because Mahalia has a bank account and Caren does not. If Caren has to go to Check Mart, she is charged twenty-two dollars to cash her check.

As Caren and Mahalia walk into the bank together, Caren eight months pregnant and Mahalia almost six feet tall, Caren slips her arm through her grandmother's purse strap and they bump along together, holding onto each other as they walk through the crowd, talking animatedly the entire time. While they walk, Mahalia earnestly advises Caren about managing her money. After going to the bank, Caren goes to the cookie shop and buys a bag of cookies for herself and a brownie for her grandmother. Mahalia exclaims, "$1.89! She always wants to take care of me." Back at home, the two women walk toward the house, both still chattering, hanging onto each other, smiling, and laughing, delighted to be in each other's company.

Molly and Mahalia often give Caren advice. This ranges from Mahalia's gentle fussing when Caren arrives with the baby, "Where is his hat?" and "He needs more blankets," to Molly's, "As their mother, you'll be the one to teach them values, teach them what is important." All three women frequently echo one another's sentiments.

Molly's and Mahalia's observations are not restricted to child rearing. When Caren asks her mother to babysit so that she can "go out with the dudes," adding that she likes men better than women because women are "so catty, mean, and backbiting," Molly tells her wisely, "What they mainly want is your man." With many young African American men in prison, there is a serious shortage of men in their community that influences this view.

There are strong intergenerational bonds between Caren, Molly, and Mahalia. Mothers and grown daughters raise their children together, and between grandmother and granddaughter, there is a special connection. While the relationship between mother and daughter is sometimes strained with the stress of raising children and accommodating male partners, the grandmother-granddaughter relationship is consistently warm and nurturing. Mahalia, at age fifty-nine, is clear about her relationship with Caren. When Caren hints about babysitting, Mahalia is adamant that it will not work, saying proudly, "Caren don't just drop [the kids] like most teenage girls. 'You the mama and you have to keep 'em.' That's what I had to do. My mama helped me . . . she'd babysit when I'd work or had to go somewhere once in awhile . . . but other than that I had my own children."

Caren also depends on a network of young women. Her friends, in late adolescence, are not as reliable as her family but can be counted on at times. These friendships offer insights into the struggles that young black poor women face. Pregnant and with two babies, Caren is on the periphery of the street scene, but she often deals with the inevitable repercussions of her friends' problems.

Caren's eighteen-year-old friend Maxine, her son's godmother, often stays with Caren because she does not get along with her own mother, and in exchange, she helps Caren with the children. Currently Maxine is in jail for a traffic violation, and Caren worries about her, trying to take money to her, hoping that Maxine's boyfriend will bail her out, and calling Maxine's mother to urge her to go to the court date so that Maxine will not be alone.

Once Caren's friend Nairobi and her baby traveled on the bus at night with Caren to visit Caren's sister Shani at Children's Hospital. As I drove them home, the young women spoke with familiar horror about a recent violent episode involving one of their friends. When we drove down 23rd Street, the link between North Seattle and the Central District, Nairobi pointed out, "That's where Rhonda was killed . . . she was only fifteen, trying to buy school clothes." Rhonda had never been in trouble but then she sold "bad dope to a guy from Boeing." Nairobi had warned Rhonda not to get in the car with the man, but she did. Nairobi described graphically how the man murdered Rhonda by lifting her large breast to stab her. Although Rhonda's mother tried to prosecute, nothing happened to the man.

I left Caren and Nairobi and her baby at Molly's, where Caren's children were. The girls left the car in a whirlwind of adolescent energy and friendly chatter on their way to watch their three children together and eat the bucket of Kentucky Fried Chicken Molly had for them.

"He's in a Gang, but It's Not Like That"

Caren acknowledges that her boyfriend Derrick, age twenty, has been a member of a well-known gang from Los Angeles. Caren explains that "the gang" is simply a group of boys that Derrick knows from when he was growing up and that the name of the gang was taken from a street where Derrick once lived. Derrick has been on his own since he was fifteen and pretty much "raised himself up." His mother has eleven children and uses drugs, "smokes that stuff," so Derrick does the best he can. Derrick's mother lives in a motel with seven of Derrick's young brothers and sisters. Derrick and two of his almost-grown brothers (one of whom is in jail) try to help their mother as much as they can.

Caren notes that Derrick is more helpful to her than the fathers of most of her friends' babies. The couple has been together for five years, and Derrick buys the children's clothes or sometimes pays for cable TV or the phone bill. In general, Caren says she likes to take care of herself.

Molly and Mahalia like Derrick and feel he is a "nice kid" and "bright." They also mention his gang affiliation, adding, like Caren did, "It's not like that." When Molly first heard he was in a gang, she thought he would be "rude, obnoxious, somebody-I-was-gonna-haf-to-slap-up-side-the-head kid." But then she says, "My daughter, she wouldn't bring anybody home that was just gonna out and out disrespect her mother."

Molly believes that people generalize about "kids and gangs and kids on the street and unless you know a kid on the street . . . you can't just group them all in one stereotype." Derrick has a police record, but Caren says his arrests were "juvenile." However, he was in jail recently, once for a probation violation from an earlier firearm possession charge and once for a traffic violation. Derrick, like many poor people, cannot pay his traffic fines, and when they accumulate, he loses his license and/or does jail time, often because he is driving without a license. Caren does not like the police. She says, "They's mean. They's dirty. I want to stay as far away from them as I can!"

Derrick makes money sporadically by fixing up old cars and then selling them. His father is a mechanic in Los Angeles and taught Derrick the trade. Derrick wants to get his GED and more training; he would like an outdoor job where he can move around.

Derrick takes care of the children when Caren goes to her doctor's appointments. One day he arrives forty-five minutes late to a quietly fuming Caren. Good looking, tall, and dark skinned, with close-cropped hair, he climbs out of the car with a friend and a "Sorry, baby." He smiles at me and shakes my hand when we are introduced. Although the little boys cry as he takes them inside with him, Caren brushes this aside, saying that Derrick will "spoil" them all day, drive them around, take them to McDonald's. She says firmly that the boys need to be with their daddy and that he has to take responsibility for them.

Caren reports that she and Derrick get along well, that they argue, but "no fist fights or nothing." Molly claims Caren is very hard to live with when she is pregnant and laughs as she describes how Caren and Derrick still act like children:

> I guess, coming from single woman, single parent, have a different kind of outlook, a different strength. And it's like . . . he can't slap her unless he going get slapped back. So—it's just a fight and it's [male voice] "Mom, she hit me." I said, "Hit her back, Derrick." "No, Mom, I can't hit her, I can't hit her" . . . So she abuses him . . . 'cause when she's pregnant, she's totally obnoxious. . . . She looks at him and she can't stand the sight of him, then she starts fighting with him. He got dressed to go somewhere and I guess she wanted to go and I guess she couldn't go—"I can't go nowhere. I should throw this water on you. . . ." Before he left, she throw water at him so he had to change his clothes [*laughing*] . . . so they call me. I say, "I stay out of you guys' business. You're grown. So that's your house. As long as he don't abuse you or misuse the children I gonna stay out of you guys' arguments. . . . Long as you calls me and ask for my advice, I'll give it—grow up! . . . You guys need a couple more years to . . . get over all your hang-ups."

Molly and Mahalia often say that they are sure that Derrick will continue to be nice to Caren. The couple is engaged, and Molly wishes they would "formalize it. I don't like this shackin'."

Obviously in love with Caren, Derrick often tries to pacify her, to take care of her, and to protect her. She seems to accept his gestures but responds impassively. It is easy to be impressed with Derrick's likable sweetness, his enthusiasm, and his charm. Caren notes, "He gets better looking as he gets older. At first I didn't think so 'cause he was so black—different from the other guys."

After the birth of their third baby, Daniel, Caren and Derrick are happy to have me visit. They seem a little lonely, and Derrick is on the telephone—first with Mahalia, then with his mother. His mother has not been able to get the Section 8 house she planned on, and she has already spent the two hundred dollars Derrick gave her to use for the house. Derrick worries about her living in a motel with cockroaches and a leaking roof and calls the health department. He talks to his mother on his three-way phone as he simultaneously tries various phone numbers for her. He relates to me: "So much has been going on. . . . I just got to stick by my mama and hope she gets through this. . . . She brought it all on herself, I know that; but she my mama and maybe if I see her through this one. . . . I know how it feels for the kids 'cause I been there, but I got three babies of my own to take care of."

Derrick speaks loudly and laughs readily, moving constantly. He recently sold a car and he fingers a wad of bills while he talks to his mother. When he hangs up, he appeals to me, saying, "This is all I got left, but I got to help her. What can I do? I got to get me a job!" Caren silently watches him, keeping her feelings to herself.

Caren and Derrick are full of everyday conversation about their children, happy to share their parenting stories. Caren complains that she slept through her baby's two-week checkup appointment and forgot to make her Women, Infant and Children (WIC) appointment for the baby and Dameon. Three-year-old Derrick Junior no longer qualifies for WIC "'cause he's healthy and growing well."

Derrick answers a knock on the door and says he is going for a walk with a friend. He goes to change clothes, chastising Caren, "Woman, don't you put my clean jeans in the laundry!" He soon returns in jeans and a black-hooded sweatshirt.

Before Derrick leaves, Caren gives him a silent signal, and he makes a bottle for the baby. She complains as he pours the milk, "Don't waste it. I'll just have to throw it out." He heats the milk in a pan and makes jelly sandwiches for the boys, all while talking to and entertaining me. He asks for advice on cleaning the stove burners and shows how he is repairing a cabinet. Finally Derrick makes an obvious point of putting his money on the table and leaves. The apartment is much quieter with him gone.

The following week when I bring Caren and the baby home from the clinic, Derrick's mother is there, cooking for a birthday party for Derrick's twenty-three-year-old brother. The apartment is crowded with children and young adults. Derrick's brothers, unlike Derrick, look "down and out" and do not speak. Caren considers Derrick's family to be her family, but she rarely allows his mother to babysit. There is "too much going on there" with "too many children" and the question of drugs. Caren immediately says she has a slight headache and goes to lie down.

When I pick up Caren the next week for the baby's checkup, Derrick and five of his friends and brothers are working on a car parked in front of the apartment. As we leave, Derrick bounds away from the group and slips Caren some money, hiding the gesture from his friends. Earlier Caren was unable to find her purse because Derrick had hidden it because friends were coming over. They do not live in an entirely secure world.

"Bought Sense"

Caren and Derrick are setting up housekeeping with few resources. Caren's furniture consists of two nice sofas, a TV, and a children's table where the little boys eat their meals. Caren is purchasing the sofas on time at a store that specifically advertises to "low income." She worries that it is a "scam" when she receives a notice saying she has missed a payment. To prove that she has paid, Caren must obtain a mail-order check receipt showing that her money order has been cashed or she will lose her furniture. This conflict with the furniture store charging her extra periodically goes on for several months. She says she will never buy on time again as she ends up paying a total of $1,800 for a $900 set.

Caren is restless and wants to move. She is often trapped at home with three babies and no transportation. She does not live close enough to walk to any friends homes, stores, or activities. West Seattle is about half an hour away from her mother and grandmother in the CD, and Caren wants badly to get out of the projects. She decides to move with or without her Section 8 and starts to look at apartments and houses. Molly wants Caren to stay in the projects for a while to take advantage of the Head Start, day care, and GED programs. Her grandmother Mahalia tells Caren quietly, "Once you leave, it's hard to get back into any of them."

Within a short time, Caren decides to move the family to Los Angeles. They plan to leave at night and drive straight through in a car Derrick recently repaired. Molly sees, since being involved in the birth of his third baby, Derrick understands the seriousness of fatherhood, that it will be good for Derrick to be with his father and that he needs a strong male role model. It is hard for them to do well in Seattle, where Derrick feels responsible for his mother and siblings. Molly will miss her grandchildren, especially her favorite, Dameon, who always says, "I want to go to Granny's" when he is in trouble.

Molly wants Caren to pay an additional month's rent to keep her apartment until she sees how things go in California, but Caren disagrees. Caren's uncle puts her things in storage, but he is unable to move everything, and some of her belongings are left behind. Molly comments, "Maybe next time she'll listen to her mother." Caren and Derrick and the children plan to stay with Derrick's father and stepmother in Los Angeles. Molly says, "All Caren gets is one mistake and I'm coming to get those babies."

Shortly after the move, Molly relates that Caren is homesick and will probably be home soon—"I know my daughter." When she is "short [of funds]," Caren cannot go to Derrick's family for help because "we aren't that kind," and the neighbors in Los Angeles cannot be trusted. It is hard to find doctors for the children, and Caren has to wait thirty days "after approval" for welfare. Molly worries about Caren and says, "I just want to get Derrick Junior, Dameon, and Daniel back here," and, "It's hard when you're young." She believes that if Caren decides to move again, she will be more prepared—"You need money for a trip and money for whatever . . . and money to tide you over."

Molly says that when she returns, Caren will stay with both Molly and Mahalia—"I imagine Caren will flop down wherever she can." Molly comforts herself that Caren is gaining "bought sense." She sees that Caren is learning to take care of herself and her children and that she cannot depend on a man.

Caren surprises her mother by flying home with the children. For a few months, things settle into an uneasy pattern with Caren and the children staying at both Molly's and Mahalia's apartments. Gradually Molly begins to talk about how crowded it is with nine people (Molly with her husband, Will, and three children, and Caren with three children). With a one-year wait for the projects and a six- to eight-month wait for a Section 8, Molly decides to use her tax return to help Caren find an unsubsidized apartment. In the meantime, the house is messy and chaotic, and Caren is subdued and dressed in old clothes with her hair sticking out all over—not the usual Caren. Molly says Caren tries to clean up, but there are too many people. The children are sick and, with Dr. Margaret no longer at the clinic, Caren says that she cannot find good health care for them.

When Caren and the children stay part time with "Granny," Mahalia complains that the kids and music are noisy, and she spends time in her room with the door closed. She remembers that her own three children napped but also went to bed early, and she feels that Caren's children should be in bed by nine p.m.

Caren looks pregnant again, but Molly says, "No—I don't know—she could be." For some time Molly does not talk about this pregnancy, but she mentions that Caren still really wants a girl. Caren stops looking for her own place and decides she will stay with her mother "for a while." Derrick returns to Seattle and is in jail for several months for more traffic violations.

When I visit Molly, Caren does not come out to see me, and Molly admits, "Caren don't want you to know [about her pregnancy], but she can't help it if she can't take that birth control. God wants her to have all those babies." Molly reinforces, "Caren can make it," and that she just has to go to school. Eventually Caren comes out of hiding, at least to yell, "Hi, Mary!" when I visit.

Caren moves into her own apartment about two or three months before her fourth baby is born. In September, one year after Daniel's birth, a little girl, Ciara, is born after a two-hour labor with no problems. Church members say, "Maybe she'll stop now that she has a girl." Derrick has a temporary job at a gas station, and Caren is once again waiting for her Section 8. In early autumn the family moves back to California, this time to a smaller town where Derrick's father and stepmother have moved for a "better opportunity."

Molly feels Caren has matured and will be more flexible and under-standing of Derrick's stepmother and that this time the move will work. Unlike in the previous move, Caren can begin to receive welfare right away, as she was not receiving assistance in Washington State. Molly says "Plenty girls move away," but also notes, "I can't help her down there."

Molly is saving her money to go to California and says that "those kids, especially Dameon, better be well cared for or I'm going to go get him." She worries because Dameon is being spanked daily and is wetting the bed. Molly protests, "You have to give him time to adjust, too." But Caren complains that Derrick's parents spoil him.

By Christmas things have not yet settled down. Five-year-old Derrick Junior has not started kindergarten because the school requires that an immunization record be sent directly from Harborview Clinic, but Caren has not been able to arrange this. Mahalia and Molly say that Derrick's father has been "murdered" and no one knows who did it or why.

Caren is a very personable and bright young woman who is trying hard to find a good situation for herself and her children. But it is clear that her struggles are draining the resources, both emotional and financial, of her extended family system. However, she remains persistent and hopeful and takes good care of her growing family, and Molly and Mahalia take good care of her.

Six months later, Caren and her four children are back in Washington, spending the summer with Molly and Mahalia. Derrick is trying "to get himself together" after the death of his father. Caren, once again, is taking good care of herself. She says the housing situation in California is better than in Washington. She has let her apartment go for the summer, but she plans to return.

MAHALIA LAKE

"I Don't Ask the Lord to Move the Mountain; Just Give Me the Strength to Climb It"

Mahalia Lake asks me to meet her for the first time at the office of the Yesler Terrace Low Income Housing where she lives. The office is busy with staff members joking, residents coming and going, and the telephone ringing loudly. A large white woman with waist-length hair bargains on the phone with a caller, "No, I can't let you have that many diapers. I can give you a few, but not too many. You come on in and I'll see what I can do. . . ." A truck backs onto the cement sidewalk outside, and two men unload tired vegetables and moldy-looking bread into grocery carts. Project residents of all racial and ethnic groups and languages, some in their country's native dress, materialize out of nowhere to sort through the food. Staff workers compete with residents, bagging it up into smaller portions for needy residents. Soon all but the bluest bread disappears, and the crowd dissipates as quickly as it has formed. This ritual is a daily occurrence. When Mahalia arrives, a staff member tells her she saved some broccoli for her.

Mahalia Lake, fifty-nine, is an impressive woman at five feet eleven inches. She wears a flowered dress, a heart pendant necklace, knee-high stockings, a knit cap, and a full-length down parka that she shares with Molly. Mahalia likes to meet visitors at the office, in part because she feels people might be afraid to go into the residential areas of the projects, but also because she becomes depressed if she spends too much time in her apartment. She can stay home about two days, but by the third day she needs to get out. Sometimes she simply boards the bus and rides around the city looking at the scenery. When she feels better, she goes home again.

There are two sides to Mahalia Lake: the Sunday church, going-out-on-the-town Mahalia and the everyday Mahalia. The "Sunday Mahalia" is articulate, "blessed," congenial, intelligent, and carefully dressed at church. She sings and sways to the music with her daughter, Molly, eyes closed or lifted heavenward, her patterned skirt moving softly around her. On other days, Mahalia struggles with everyday life—the effort to survive on $450 per month, the pain of never having enough of anything, the fatigue of fighting her own "down days," and the grief of trying to raise her grandson. When she is down, she looks down, wearing old and stained clothing, too-short dresses with knee-high hose, her hair askew or covered by a knit cap. On these days Mahalia lacks affect, frets over her grandson, and is distracted and impatient with questions.

Protective of herself and her family, she never gossips and often refuses to answer questions with an abrupt "I don't know" and unmistakable body language. Wanting only a limited part of herself to be known, she keeps much of her life, including her innermost thoughts, within a private space. As Collins (2000) notes, "This private, hidden space of Black women's consciousness, the 'inside' ideas . . . allow Black women to cope with, and in many cases, transcend the confines of intersecting oppressions. . . ." (98).

Though Mahalia alludes to the fact that her life has been a terrible struggle, she steadfastly refuses to talk about the things that have made it so. While Molly shares how it feels to be poor and to live on the edge; Mahalia simply discusses the pragmatics, or the "how tos," of survival. Mahalia willingly talks about the things that help her: her faith, her knowledge of how to manage a limited budget, and her gospel music. (In recognition of the importance of music in her life, Mahalia chose her name for this research after the famous gospel singer, Mahalia Jackson.)

Growing Up in the South

Mahalia was born in 1932 at the height of the Great Depression in Georgia to a family consisting of her mother and an older brother and sister. Mahalia's mother had thirteen siblings, but Mahalia knew only one of her mother's sisters. When she was a child, her father died of diabetes after having both legs amputated, and Mahalia never knew her father's family. Mahalia's mother went to school through the sixth grade. There was no welfare system then, and her mother did domestic work for white people.

According to Mahalia, her mother never complained about working for white people—"I think people got used to a way of life and. . . . It's just the way that they know they had to do, because Negroes didn't have nothing. You couldn't work for them. . . ."

Mahalia loved school as a child and walked ten miles each way along the road to the school for black children. When she was "twelve, eleven, thirteen, something like that," Mahalia and her mother moved to Chicago to live with her grown brother and sister. She states, "I never liked Chicago. I come from a small town and being thrown into a big town like Chicago it was hard to get yourself together. . . ." Living conditions with her sister were crowded, but her mother no longer had to work because her sister and brother took care of them. Mahalia explains:

> [My mother] found that life could be better in Chicago. . . . Life wasn't that easy in Chicago back then either, with jobs so scarce. I don't know—jobs always seem to be scarce and they're still scarce. . . . I think she never wanted to go back because she never wanted to go back to the fields, the washing, the ironing, the cleaning she had to do to survive. Being uneducated, if she went back to the South, that's all she would've done.

At age fifteen, Mahalia quit school when she finished tenth grade, saying, "Somewhere along the way it got complicated. It was overcrowded. . . . We had to just, you know, feel your way." She compares Chicago schools to those she had attended in Georgia:

> Most of your teachers in the South at that time were just like your mother. You didn't do nothing because they would whip you just like your mother . . . so you had to mind. I think that's where a lot of our minding come from, the old Southern manners and things. They taught you how to take care of yourself and if you was raggedy, you didn't have to be dirty. Just 'cause you . . . couldn't afford clothes, you could wash what you had on and hang 'em out by the fire at night and let 'em dry. Next day you could be clean. So it was a lot of things the same way your mother would teach you at home. They give you the foundation and when they said you had to get your lesson . . . they didn't stand no playing around.

Mahalia was seventeen when she met and married Robert Lake. They were married for nine years, then separated but never legally divorced. Mahalia says, "We was just so young," adding that he was the "type" who always put a person down, telling her, "Who'd want you with three children?" and "You can't do that." But Mahalia was always confident, frequently saying, "I may not be able to do it as good as anyone else, but I can do it!"

In 1959, Mahalia was twenty-seven when she moved with her mother and children to Seattle, where her mother's sister lived—"Sometimes you don't want to move, but that's best to get away and get a fresh start. Sometimes you can't get a foothold in the land you were brought up. Jesus said, 'I came to my own but they received me not.'" Mahalia did not ask God about this move, but knew that God understood that she had to leave the marriage because He never wanted "His children to be unhappy." At this time, Mahalia says, she had not yet learned to pray for guidance in all life's decisions but learned this later, only after suffering greatly.

In Seattle Mahalia worked in a nursing home as a nurse's aide, but there were no housekeepers or orderlies, so the aides did all the lifting and cleaning in addition to patient care. Mahalia was "too tenderhearted" for the job, especially with her own family to worry about. She became ill and could no longer work. Around this time, Mahalia found Morning Sun Church and became involved with her faith on a deeper level. She has been "studying" her faith for the past twenty-five years.

Although she can no longer work, Mahalia keeps her spirits up through her church work and volunteer activities. She is a neighborhood representative on the board of the Yesler Terrace Housing Project Community Center and is in charge of the Christmas giving tree. She has been involved with Block Watch and was honored for helping decrease crime and drug traffic in her neighborhood. She volunteers at the housing office and at Head Start, answering the telephone. She is a practice client for the student nurses from the Catholic college two or three times a year, teaching them about her "culture." To her, "Volunteering is a little like nursing—you have to give a part of yourself and really care about what you're doing." Mahalia says that her life now is "about trying to do better the next year than the last year. That's what I'm living for."

"Keep Them in the Hollow of Your Hand, Keep Them from Hurt, Harm and Danger"

When I ask Mahalia to describe the main stressors in her life, Mahalia immediately says, "Children. Period." Mahalia loves children, but she says that if she were raising children today she would "get in trouble because I would turn them over my knee." Like the other churchwomen, she is afraid that the use of physical punishment might result in a visit from Child Protective Services. Mahalia has three children: Molly Lake Lander, forty-one; Harry, forty; and Robert, thirty-six. She has five grandchildren—Molly's four girls (Caren, Roberta, Shani, and Bebe) and Robert's son, Robert Junior. At the beginning of the study, her grand-daughter Caren has two children, and she has four by the study's completion.

Mahalia has raised her own children and her grandson, Robert Junior, and helps with all her grandchildren and great-grandchildren, but she says she does not take in additional children. Her life would have been boring and empty without the children, but she adds, "I have given so much, been stretched so far, between my kids, my mother, Robert Junior. You've got to have some time for yourself!" From time to time she is "sick of all of them," saying, "I been raising children [for] over forty years. I'm tired and I'm trying to get out of it as much as I can."

Mahalia rarely discusses her grandchildren or children, other than to say they are "fine." Her son Harry lives with her, and, when working, gives her money for rent and food. Her youngest son, Robert, is in the penitentiary for a parole violation, but he supports Mahalia when he can. Her daughter, Molly, and three of Molly's children live in the same apartment complex as Mahalia, and they are in and out of each other's apartments many times a day. Mahalia sees or talks to her granddaughter Caren every day, giving her advice on the children and sharing the daily goings-on.

Although Mahalia is often with all of her children, her relationship with her daughter, Molly, is the most important connection in Mahalia's life. There are times of tension between the two women, but more often there is love, affection, and laughter. Molly fixes Mahalia's hair every week for church; they sing and rock in unison—the only two choir members. When Molly falls asleep from exhaustion in church, Mahalia's heart goes out to her and one can see her longing to pull the grown woman into her soft embrace. Mahalia acknowledges that she and Molly "were brought up helping each other."

During dinner at Molly's house, there is a comfortable and intimate rapport between Molly, Mahalia, sixteen-year-old Roberta, and the two small girls, Shani and Bebe. The family eats, spread around the room at the table and on sofas, chatting and watching "Jeopardy" and "Wheel of Fortune." They flip through catalogues and discuss clothes. Caren calls several times, and Mahalia says, "Ask her how she can stand to not talk to me for four days?"

On holidays Mahalia, Molly, and Caren cook together, each separately buying a few ingredients over time. Caren might buy the fixings for the sweet potato pies and have Derrick deliver them to Mahalia, who will bake them at her place. Then Derrick picks up the pies for dinner at his family's house. If Caren has her holiday with Derrick's family, she makes Mahalia "a plate," so that Mahalia can try what Caren has cooked. For a holiday like Thanksgiving, things are relatively simple, without linen, china, and silver. There is no table in two of the three households—if the family goes to Molly's, there is a table but only three chairs. It is not a "Norman Rockwell Thanksgiving," but they do eat, and they are grateful to be together.

"Heavenly Father, Bless Robert as He Needs a Blessing"

Mahalia loves all of her offspring and depends on her grown children for support, but raising her grandson, Robert Junior, has been a demanding job. She has cared for Robert Junior since he was a baby. His mother was an alcoholic and a drug addict, and when Robert Junior was eighteen months old, Harborview Medical Center called Mahalia and asked her whether she would take the baby. Robert Junior had been brought to the hospital with a broken leg. His mother told the doctor that he fell down the stairs, but he also had an iron burn on his thigh that his mother blamed on her sister. Mahalia told the hospital "yes" immediately, "because he was my first grandson—I had other granddaughters." Robert Junior has many problems, which Mahalia calls "disabilities." At age six he spent six weeks at Children's Medical Center in the psychiatric ward as the doctors evaluated him and tried various medications. When the doctors started him on a combination of Ritalin and Dexedrine at home, he accelerated and would "just jump out the window and go." His "real problems" started in school, and "he just couldn't hack it." Robert is currently at his grade level but is in special education, and Mahalia does not know whether he is learning anything.

When Robert Junior was ten, his thirty-year-old mother died from a drug overdose. With this new crisis, his behavior worsened. Mahalia tried "to hold it together" by keeping Robert Junior with her until his father was released from prison, hoping that Robert could take over management of his son. But Robert Junior skipped school, ran away, and was disrespectful to his grandmother. She could no longer manage him and asked for help through the court system. At age thirteen, he was recently placed in a youth facility. Mahalia worries over and prays for him constantly.

Mahalia is grieving deeply over these changes in her life. It is hard not having Robert Junior with her after all the years of caring for him. She is ill and depressed and complains often about feeling frustrated and not being able to think straight. She is accustomed to looking after him, and now that he is gone she is always looking for something—something is missing. In addition, without Robert Junior she no longer qualifies for the two-bedroom apartment where she has lived for fourteen years, and she is given one week's notice to move to a one-bedroom unit.

As Mahalia watches Robert Junior move through the system and waits for his evaluations, she becomes more and more upset. There are midnight prank calls from other children in the youth facility telling her: "Mahalia Lake, your grandson passed," and then, "Mahalia Lake, you an airhead." Mahalia feels that if the facility cannot supervise him better, he might as well be at home. He is then placed in a foster home while they await his hearing. The foster mother makes Mahalia angry by saying, "I don't put up with that [running away]." Mahalia says, "Just as if I did!"

The doctors do not want to medicate Robert Junior until he is in a stable living situation, but this does not seem likely to happen unless he becomes more manageable. Mahalia and Molly feel that a reliable placement is Robert's only hope. They understand that, as an infant, he missed out on the development of "basic trust," and they wonder whether he has fetal alcohol syndrome even though the doctors do not feel his characteristics and behaviors "fit" the criteria. After many evaluations, Mahalia does not believe that the doctors know what they are doing. She says in frustration, "Who know that child? You do! You raised him! I had him since he was eighteen months and I know his problem, know how to handle him!"

Mahalia and Molly do not blame themselves for Robert Junior's problems, but they regret having to place him in foster care. Mahalia says:

> It's something that had to be done . . . he's still running away, so it doesn't make too much difference. At least all of it is not on me. I don't know . . . he may get better as he gets older . . . I couldn't handle it. . . . There's so much more to get into now than when I was raising my children and the law is more slacker. . . . If they would stop taking the law out of the home and enforce the law that's in the home, I think the children would do better.

When Robert Junior comes to visit he is a bundle of jiving energy and cannot sit still in church. He jumps around in his seat and runs up and down the basement stairs until Molly and Mahalia finally trap him on the inside of the pew. Even then he does not really stop moving. Although he is a handsome boy, well dressed with the latest haircut, there is something off about his features, and his face seems to twitch and move with the rest of his body. Mahalia touches Robert Junior and gently smiles at him as they sit together in church.

A year and a half after Robert Junior has been placed in foster care, he is "bringing up himself," and Mahalia notes that he could have done that at home. By the time Robert is fifteen, he is six feet two inches tall. He has been through several more evaluations, including one at Western State Hospital, with no definite diagnosis. In three years he will be eighteen, and then Molly and Mahalia fear that no one will be able to help him. The pastor's wife says, "They did the best they could with that boy, now they have to let it go." Mahalia and Molly have turned it over to God.

"The Church Is the Foundation of Everything I Do"

Although Mahalia has many interests, she prioritizes her church work at Morning Sun, saying, "The church is the foundation of everything I do." She is a leader and a strong participant in all of the church activities. As "Missionary Lake" she is responsible for introducing newcomers in church and for planning the Mission services to help the women live Christian lives. Missionary Lake often represents Morning Sun when invited for "fellowship" at neighboring churches, frequently spending her entire Sunday morning at Morning Sun followed by services later in the day at another church. Many things about fellowship appeal to Missionary Lake: she loves to pray and sing; she likes the social aspect of seeing old friends and making new friends; she has the opportunity to represent Morning Sun; food is always served; and she avoids hours in her apartment where she can become depressed.

In addition to being an active choir member (along with her daughter, Molly), Missionary Lake often leads the devotional prayer at the beginning of the service. In "devotion" there are certain phrases that are used week after week, but there is always spontaneous material as well. Missionary Lake's devotional prayer is chanted in a strong sing-song rhythmic voice, using repetitive words to passionately thank and praise the Lord as well as request His assistance:

> Heavenly Father, once again we come thanking Thee for the many blessings Thou have bestowed upon us. . . . We know that without You we can't do nothing. Bless the ones that don't have nobody, Heavenly Father. We know that they are Your children whether they know it or not. Have mercy on them. Bless the ones that have to take care of the little children. Ask for a special blessing on the ones that sick, Heavenly Father. . . . You a doctor and a sick room. You a lawyer and a courtroom.
>
> Heavenly Father, bless Robert as he needs a blessing. Asking You for a special blessing on all my little offspring, Lord. Keep them in the hollow of Your hand. Keep them from hurt, harm and danger, I pray Thee. Lord, lead them and guide them in the way that You would have them to go.
>
> Heavenly Father, when I've done all that I can do, when I can't do any more, when I go in my room and can't come out any more, give me somewhere where I can lay my head on Your breast and breathe my life out slowly. These and all blessings we ask in Jesus' name.

Mahalia practices her faith daily. If she finds a dollar on the sidewalk she immediately says, "Thank you, Jesus." She bows her head in grace before meals, no matter what the situation. She listens to gospel music and gospel hours on radio and TV to relax, to ward off the blues, and to block out the noises and the rap music of her grandchildren. She studies the Bible and prays frequently throughout the day. When Mahalia talks about her faith, her affect changes dramatically. If she is quiet or "down" she sits up straighter, and her tone becomes more confident as she speaks forcefully and fluently about her beliefs.

Mahalia believes that prayer "always works!" She often says, "We don't walk by sight, we walk by faith." She uses her faith to help her in situations of discrimination, believing like the other members of Morning Sun that she must love her fellow man and be kind to everyone. She feels, "There's a lot who do [discriminate] but some, once in a while, who will be good back to you. It all comes around somehow." Although she is "not one to protest" she acknowledges, "Some people got to do something, but prayer just beats it all."

"God Will Provide Not What You Want but What You Need"

Mahalia's faith informs all of her beliefs and her worldview. She trusts in God and in His Son Jesus to help her through life. However, Mahalia also has to contend with the day-to-day material concerns of food and shelter. She receives $450 per month disability income plus $67 per month in food stamps. She pays one-third of her income for rent and also pays for her phone, utilities, and life insurance. Whatever little she has left she spends on extras such as gifts for her children or needed clothing. It is never enough.

When the study begins, Mahalia lives in a two-bedroom apartment in Yesler Terrace Low Income Housing Projects. She moved there in discouragement after three houses were sold out from under her, one of them to create the Interstate 90 corridor. (She exclaims, "And then the housing levy can't pass!") She feels Yesler Terrace is one of the best of the projects. She likes how the apartments have small, separate kitchens, the bedrooms and bath upstairs, and a small fenced yard. Mahalia's apartment is badly in need of repair. The walls are stained and peeling. The linoleum is cracked and dirty. The baseboard heater is falling off the wall. Mahalia tries to cover the linoleum bit by bit, using carpet squares and scraps that she finds or buys one at a time from the downtown Woolworth's and carries home on the bus. The result is a raggedy, unfinished patchwork carpet.

The main floor consists of a living room and small kitchen. Stairs lead to a landing with a table filled with family photos and then on up to two bedrooms and a bath. In the living room there are two TV sets—one very old and one a newer model—a stereo, a worn sofa, a straight-backed chair, two easy chairs—torn and patched—and stacks of miscellaneous items on the floor—books, magazines, shoes, cassette tapes. The walls are covered with an assortment of inexpensive pictures, wire sculptures, and a large frame filled with snapshots of family and church members. There is a portrait of Mahalia with her two oldest granddaughters, Caren and Roberta, and another portrait of her son Harry in his Marine dress uniform with a picture of Caren softly superimposed in the background. One wall is devoted to pictures of Jesus, framed prayers, and religious sayings. The uneven curtains are pulled shut, and the rooms are dark.

The grass in Mahalia's yard is a foot tall, and there are old soda cans, broken toys, and decrepit lawn furniture scattered about. While a few project yards are well manicured with tulips popping up and little bushes carefully tended, and one yard has row upon row of cultivated rice, many are similar to Mahalia's. In order to mow her lawn, Mahalia has to walk two blocks to the project office to borrow a small electric lawn mower and then carry or push it back to her apartment. Mahalia cannot mow the lawn herself but waits for her children to do it.

When Mahalia does her spring or Christmas cleaning, it is an elaborate project. She first plans it out carefully—otherwise she gets "going in circles." She does the house in sections, pulling everything out of the cupboards a room at a time and then cleaning that room thoroughly. Since she has no place to store things while she cleans, the cupboard's contents stay on the floor while she works around them for several days. She generally starts her Christmas cleaning in late October so that she can have it finished by Thanksgiving. Cleaning involves not just wiping down and organizing the cupboards, but also moving and cleaning behind all of the furniture, thus making room for her Christmas tree and a few decorations. Mahalia's spring-cleaning is similar and generally goes on through March and April.

Mahalia tries to pick up frequently, but she has no vacuum, and her hypertension prevents her from bending over without dizziness. The constant in-and-out of grandchildren and the smallness and poor condition of the unit make keeping the house clean a futile task.

Besides maintaining her home, Mahalia's other main survival task involves shopping for supplies. After mandatory expenses, not including food, Mahalia lives on less than $250 per month. She is a veteran shopper who turns survival shopping into a necessary adventure and an art. Mahalia handles this chore with skill and pride. She is often thrilled with her bargains and rarely allows her discouragement to show when she cannot afford something (usually) or cannot find clothes that fit (often) in her price range (next to nothing). She considers it a successful day of shopping if she returns home with one item.

When Mahalia shops, she wears her "working clothes"—her print skirt and knee-high hose, her wool cap pulled over her hair, and a cardigan sweater buttoned up the front. She generously shares her expertise, preparing me for some unknown future when I, too, might be poor and in need of these same skills. I now know where to buy a Christmas tree for $4.69; I know that senior citizens can get bus passes and discounts to many fast-food restaurants. I know how to order the most filling food and the largest portions for the least amount of money. I now know where all of the stores that specialize in clothing for large women are located—they are scattered throughout King County, and Mahalia often visits several to find something in her size. She occasionally has good luck "when the Lord tells me where to go." Once she woke up thinking, "Lane Bryant, Lane Bryant," got on the bus to the mall, and found a seventy-dollar jacket for twelve dollars. I learn that sometimes one has to buy an item if it is cheap, even if it does not fit exactly right or has a stain. I know how to put items on layaway and how to watch for sales and use coupons. I know that buying fresh produce is not as practical as buying canned or frozen foods and that there are some stores where it does not look so good anyway. There is a chance that there might be produce in the daily free giveaway at the housing project office, and the staff will save you some if they know you. Eggs and milk are not considered staples in all families. It is too expensive to go to the corner grocery, and if you want to get the best prices you take a bus and carry groceries a distance. Chicken is the cheapest meat, and the best way to cook it is to fry it slowly. Pepsi and toilet paper are expensive "necessities," and it is important to buy large quantities on sale whenever possible, preferably at a discount store.

I also learn that it is smart to pay your bills in person with cash because it saves charges for a money order or a checking account (which poor people rarely have anyway). I now know that it is mandatory to share money and goods with your daughter and that it is inconvenient when you both forget your purses at the same time. Thrift shops and discount stores are good for children's clothes, but neither carry large women's sizes. It is best never to go into department stores at all.

If you do go shopping in a large department store, it is okay to gaze longingly at the toys, pretty scarves, and jewelry, but it is better to descend directly into the basement clearance outlet—a large, poorly lit, window-less room with a low ceiling that smells of stale cigarette smoke. Items are haphazardly stacked on tables, on racks, or on the floor. When Christmas shopping there, Mahalia buys two small items for her grandchildren and two special Christmas cards for her brother and sister, which she says are "too expensive."

The department store clearance sections are one option, but it is even better to start Christmas shopping in the after-Christmas sales the year before or in early September. By putting purchases in layaway at discount stores, you can pay a little every two weeks when you get your check and then be ready to bring the items home (where there is not much storage) right before Christmas. That way you have enough money left in December to buy the tree and your Christmas food. If your job allows you to take your check early for Christmas money, as Molly's once did, you will not have enough money to eat through January. It is best to buy cleaning supplies in late August or early September so that you do not have this additional expense when you are trying to buy Christmas presents. Besides, this allows you to start your cleaning and have it all finished by Thanksgiving.

I learn that even if you are very poor, you can still travel a little with Senior Citizens' Outreach. It helps if you are on the board of an organization and you get to go "hoboing," as Mahalia calls it. At one time, through her work on the board, Mahalia sells raffle tickets to "send an elderly low-income person to Vancouver, Canada." When I ask who is going, she laughs and says, "Me!"

Mahalia always knows precisely how much she can spend on any given shopping trip. She takes exactly the right amount with her, and when she has spent it she generally "runs out of steam" and goes home. Unless she has had particularly poor luck shopping, she rarely has money left over for lunch or a snack. After shopping, Mahalia recalculates the remainder of her expenses: "I paid my light bill, now I just have to pay my rent and my insurance." Once, when she is out of money, she says, "I can grab a piece of meat at Molly's and go on over to Caren's and grab a slice of bread." Mahalia describes how she makes ends meet:

> It's not hard with me. I don't have a lot of credit cards I have to pay off. If I don't have money this month maybe I'll save up and wait 'til next month or I'll put it in layaway. The bills come at the end of the month, you sorta have to dig out what you gonna pay and what you not gonna pay . . . always cut corners, look for sales. I don't have too much trouble. A lot of people run into problems, not to live within [their] means. Having to raise three children by myself I always live within my means and know how to cut corners. Like the light bill comes out, you can pay half on it one month and half on it the next. . . .

When Mahalia turns sixty, she has a new experience: "The Lord done see fit to bless me with a credit card." She and Molly charge the card to the limit. Mahalia always pays on her card before she spends more.

Mahalia accommodates her pace to her limited budget, time, and energy. She plans ahead carefully and prepares. She, like her daughter, Molly, has lived on the edge for a long time. She is private and accepting of her life, and so it is hard to know whether the family's daily existence is as difficult as it seems or whether, in fact, she minimizes her difficulties. Mahalia somehow is able to get by, and her music and prayer sustain her.

Black or White and Shades of Gray

There are many things to be learned from shopping with Mahalia besides the fine art of economizing. Most clerks and waiters avoid us. If I ask for help for us, even in small, uncrowded stores—Mahalia does not bother—clerks come grudgingly, help half-heartedly for a minute, and then drift away. Mahalia notes that at other times clerks "come up on you so fast! They act like they think you shoplifting." When I am with Mahalia, clerks are reluctant to tell me the location of the restroom or give me the key. Mahalia never asks.

Thus, when I am with Mahalia or Molly I learn about "association discrimination." Molly and Mahalia are deeply dark skinned and heavy, and they look poor. My presence and my assertiveness do not command better service for us: we are all ignored equally and treated rudely. I learn that I do not have to be black and poor to experience discrimination; I just have to walk with Molly and Mahalia for a while.

When Mahalia and Molly are together in predominantly white stores, they adapt their behavior, and their presence becomes a significant force. Their voices become louder as they shout at one another across the aisles. They are jovial, laughing loudly at jokes only they understand. Their nervous energy and rebelliousness make a statement.

On the other hand, being with Molly and Mahalia does not make me a part of their black world any more than being with me makes them a part of my white world. I often feel out of place and invisible when we meet black people who they know. There is one strong exception to this experience. One day Mahalia, her four-year-old granddaughter Bebe, and I take the bus downtown so that Mahalia can show me her routine. Mahalia is worried and distracted and leaves the care of the active child to me. Taking care of a black child in the company of the child's grandmother puts me into a new category. Black women on the bus or in the stores speak to me and smile as I hold Bebe by the hand. An old white man sharply reprimands Bebe on the bus, saying, "You're in my seat!" as she clamors into an empty chair. I quickly pull her away as the man scowls at her ferociously and looks like he may push her. A young black man jumps to his feet and offers me his chair. When I say I will take her to the back of the bus, he looks at me directly and says evenly and meaningfully, "You sure?" Caring for a black child shows an obvious commitment to their world that eases acceptance.

Christmas: "Bless the Ones That Trying to Make This Time of Year a Little Brighter"

On Christmas Eve day, Mahalia is at home alone. She is eager to open my gifts, a bright scarf and a religious plaque she admired. She proudly shows me a sweater her granddaughter chose for her from the housing project gift giveaway. As we sit together in the darkened apartment watching "In the Heat of the Night" on TV, Caren calls twice to make plans for Christmas Day. The little tree is pretty, if sparsely decorated with a few ornaments and no lights except for the tinsel shimmering in the flickering light of the TV. Wrapped gifts under the tree wait for the grandchildren, who are home guarding their tree and gifts—last year their presents were stolen. Robert Junior has not been allowed to come home for Christmas, and Mahalia doesn't understand "how that worked out." Mahalia's house is clean, and she has begun to cook for the next day. She "counts her blessings," saying that she wants to serve food to the homeless at Christmas, but has not been able to due to family commitments.

A few days later, on the Sunday after Christmas, Morning Sun is still decorated. A tiny tree sits on the piano, three small poinsettias are scattered about, and there is a small plastic crèche at the altar. Mahalia, her hair pulled back sleekly, is wearing her Christmas gift from her children—a softly patterned red and brown two-piece dress, one of her favorite brooches from her "pin collection" at the collar. As always in church, she is warm, gracious, and feminine in her gestures. Her Christmas devotional prayer reminds the congregation:

> Whatever your state, be content . . . we do know that "Jesus is the reason for the season" . . . Heavenly Father, bless the ones that trying to make this time of year a little brighter, a little happier for some. . . . Bless the ones that don't have nothing and nobody coming upon this year and this season. Heavenly Father, we know that if we have Jesus, we have everything.

After her prayer, she rejoins Molly, who looks rested and pretty in a bright red dress, red sling-back heels, and new gold hoop earrings. At a signal from the pastor's wife, Shani and Bebe, the only members of the children's choir, move to the front. Sister Kent plays the piano, and Shani sings her heart out while Bebe tentatively joins in. Mahalia shakes her head in frustration at Bebe for not wearing her shoes. As the children sing, Molly mouths the words with them and nods in encouragement from her place in the pew next to her mother. Mahalia and Molly look at each other and smile, and Mahalia lightly touches Molly's arm.

MABLE JACKSON

CHAPTER SEVEN
MABLE JACKSON
"All I Asked the Lord for Was a Man with a Cigarette and a Job"

Sister Mable Jackson lumbers slowly to the front of the church. As she walks, she winces and perspires in pain. She is dressed in a navy blue, short-sleeved dress with a white collar and cuffs and low navy blue heels. Her hair is pulled back with pretty clips, and she wears her large "Usher" pin prominently displayed on her ample bosom. She lowers herself slowly to her knees, holding firmly to the back of the folding chair that faces the congregation. She puts her face in her arms on the chair, her back to the members, and begins her morning devotion in a singsong voice.

Father, I stretch my hand to Thee, no other help I know. If Thou withdraw Thyself from me—where would I go? Thank You that my bed wasn't a cooling board and my cover wasn't none of my whining sheet. Thank You that the four walls of my home wasn't the walls of my grave. Thank You for having touched my feebled body this morning and having woke me up to let me know I was still among the living.

Father, look in all the churches that are opening in Your name. You know who's right and You know who's wrong. Bless all the sick and keep Your loving arms around them. Ease their strapping fever and ease their wracking pain. Bless the ones that want to be here and aren't here. Keep Your loving arms around my family in a far distant land. The world is done messed up. Please, Sir Father, can't nobody straighten it out but You. Father, look on the pastor and his wife. Keep Your loving arms around them. Father, send Your wind through here this morning like a wild rushing wind. All this I ask in Your name. Amen.

Sister Jackson agonizingly, slowly, stands up again as the sweat and tears flow freely together, and she walks unsteadily to the back pew of the church, holding tightly to each pew as she passes, pushing off from one to grab hold of the next. She sits down heavily, takes out her handkerchief, mops her face, and holds the bridge of her nose between her fingers, trying to stop crying. The congregation, seemingly oblivious, gives an inaudible sigh of relief to have her safely seated once again.

Sister Jackson is at the bottom of the church hierarchy. At seventy-one, she is deeply dark skinned, overweight, and the least educated member of the church. She was an alcoholic and a gambler for many years. She quit drinking and stopped "straddling the fence" a few years ago and now tries to "live the life."

Sister Jackson's house is around the corner from Morning Sun in Seattle's Central District. It looks tiny from the outside but is actually quite large inside. The front of the house is close to the street, and a shaky fence, secured by a rickety iron gate, surrounds the small front yard. The back lot is large, and its boundary backs several other houses until it reaches the border of the church's backyard. A locked outer iron screen door protects the entry to the house, and the windows are covered with iron bars. The yard is in need of attention. Mable is in too much pain to care for it herself, and she is too poor to pay to have it mowed and cleaned. The grass is long and littered with garbage and dog feces. Her old beige car is parked at the curb. She laughs about it, saying that people no longer pull in front of her: "They see my car and say, 'We better stay away from her, if she doesn't care for her car no more than that!'"

On the day of her interview with me, Mable waits behind several deadbolt locks with her little gray dog, Lady, who is almost blind. She is warm and welcoming and comfortable in her own home, dressed regally in a silky dressing gown that drifts to the floor. The bright peacock blue is beautiful against her dark-as-night skin.

The living room is cozy, picked up but crowded and cluttered with overstuffed furniture and tables littered with water glasses and medicine bottles. Photographs of family and friends are everywhere, including one of herself and one of the gospel singer, Mahalia Jackson, who looks a great deal like a younger Mable. Large portraits of Martin Luther King Jr. and John F. Kennedy, as well as religious sayings, prominently adorn the walls. The living room is painted a muddy brown, and there are sheets of cobwebs that Mable cannot reach hanging in the corners, crisscrossing the maze of electrical wires and extension cords strung across the ceiling that ultimately connect to the two television sets and two portable heaters glowing brightly against the gray February day. Her house is a firefighter's nightmare.

The kitchen is much larger than the living room, with a small table and chairs. Mable has not had time to clean the kitchen today, but on other days her kitchen is well attended to. The stove burners, like the electrical heaters in the front room, glow a bright orange in a futile attempt to keep the house warm.

Both TVs play without sound in the dimly lit living room, one with "The Gospel Hour" and the other with the soap opera "Days of Our Lives." Mable always watches both TVs at once but listens to only one set at a time. She knows her shows so well that she can tell what is happening without listening. As she talks, she chews tobacco and periodically spits into a tin can that she keeps under the coffee table.

Growing Up in the South

Like several of the other church members, Mrs. Jackson has chosen her name for this study by taking her mother's name, Mable. She starts her life history saying, "I didn't have it too good and I didn't have it too bad." Her mother told her she was born in 1921 but there was no birth certificate, and the social security office has informed her that she was born in 1920, "So that's what I go with. They're the ones giving me the money."

Mable Jackson and her brother were raised by their mother and father in rural Louisiana. Mable's father was a sharecropper but at one time owned his farm. Mable went to school and church picnics with her family and says she was a good child when she was in her mother's sight, but: "When I got out of her sight, I might have been the baddest girl in the world behind her back."

Mable attended school in a one-room combination church and school. She was "a high student," but quit school after she became "sickly." At the age of fifteen or sixteen she had "appendix" and "abscess" that ruptured and required emergency hospitalization in Shreveport. About this time, Mable also experienced heavy vaginal bleeding that lasted three months. The local midwife asked her if she had seen anything when she "sat on the stool." Mable had seen "a lump come out of me, blood behind." The midwife told her she had had a miscarriage and gave her some medication to stop the bleeding. Mable relates, "It stopped me and it put me on my right time." Mable had had sex with her first boyfriend by then but remained uncertain about the miscarriage, saying, "That's the only thing I can believe. By her saying it, but me knowing it—I don't know."

Mable was afraid the bleeding would start again at school, so her mother allowed her to quit school. She had "made it to the fourth grade" and "in the olden days, there wasn't no high school." Mable felt most of her learning took place "since I've been grown" and that she possesses a lot of "mother wit."

According to Mable, living on a farm "was pretty good 'cause I didn't have no other choice 'cause I was young, but when I got up to where I could have a choice, I left." Her mother told her, "Well, you can go where you want to, but when you come home you're under my jurisdiction." Mable states, "So that's the way I did. I was grown out but when I got home I was still a child."

Mable left home for the first time when she was nineteen years old. She met and married her first husband in 1939 in Mississippi:

> We were young and wasn't ready for it in the first place. But he seen me and I seen him and we just went on and got married. My auntie, she like to killed me. She whupped me. Mama told her send me home—"Stop whupping my child and send her home, and send the marriage license with her." And I went home and cried every day I left. . . . And Daddy told her, "Send her back over there a'fore that fool kill herself.". . . I thought I was in love.

Mable stayed with her husband for two years. But then, she states, "One day I was setting down and I got to thinking, 'What am I doing this for when I could be at home and happy,' and he went to work and when he come back, I was gone!"

As Mable walked the last mile and a half to her mother's house through the "little sawmill town" she grew up in, she wondered whether she would be able to live under her mother's rules again. But then she told herself, "Well, I'm going on home. I know I ain't be hungry at home." Mable's mother had heard she was in town and she ran out to meet her. Mable told her mother, "I was making up my mind whether you gonna receive me or not." Her mother told her, "Sure, you can come home any-time you're ready."

"Everybody Was Leaving"

Mable lived with her mother and father from 1941 until 1946. She then met a man named Joe who asked her whether she would come to California if he sent for her, and she said she would—"Everybody was leaving, going different places, and I left to go to San Diego." Mable found a job as soon as she moved because, "If you had a boyfriend and wasn't working . . . and he was taking care of you . . . they could throw you outta town. When my boyfriend brought me out there, I got me a job so they couldn't do anything with me."

Mable did not want to pay for a divorce from her first husband, so she never filed. He divorced her in 1949 without her knowledge. When he was killed in a gang war in Chicago in 1955, she felt free to marry again. But even though Mable stayed with Joe for fifteen years, they never married because Joe already had a wife.

Mable was still in California in 1951 when a telegram came that said, "Your father passed. We gon' bury him Monday." Mable said, "I'm going home if I have to walk." She made her way back to Louisiana by bus in time for the services. Her father had had a heart attack out in the fields. He had "been to see some people [about his sharecropping tract] and they made him mad and the doctor said his heart failed on him." Mable's uncle found him in a field with the horse grazing by him and the dog lying next to him. Mable still thinks often about her father—she remembers that he never "whupped" her but chastised her gently and sat down to talk to her.

"Ask the Lord to Send You Somebody . . ."

Mable had grown "tired of the life" she was living in California. She worried to her mother about her future and asked, "Mama, how come you been married five times and I haven't been married but once?" Her mother answered, "Well, only thing I can tell you, baby, pray. And ask the Lord to send you somebody and when He send 'em, don't turn him away." Mable returned to California and started to pray, "and it wasn't long before I met John."

> I was off work that day and sitting on the porch and here this man and another man come up the street and I called my landlady, "Look, here come two men, do you know them?" She said, "No." And he come up to me and he says, "My name John Jackson. . . . Do you want to go with me to pick up my check?" "Sure do!" And I had on shorts and I went and put on a skirt and I didn't lose him from that day 'til I married him. . . . All I asked the Lord for was a man with a cigarette and a job and I got it!

Mable was not in love with John and told him, "You don't be setting no time for me." But John said, "When I first saw you I told the boys I was gonna marry you." He insisted, "Mable, you gonna marry me and someday you gonna love me." Mable replied, "Well, if that's the way you want it, that's the way we'll do it."

Mable and John traveled to Yuma, Arizona, and were secretly married. But back in San Diego, Mable's landlady put their picture in the paper to let people know—especially the wife of Mable's former boyfriend. When her ex-boyfriend, Joe, saw the picture, he became enraged. When Mable saw him at a party, "He cut me."

> I passed him and I heard a girl say, "Joe, don't do that!" And I looked up and he was coming down in my back and I throw'd up my hand and then it happened. And John . . . went to say something to him and I say, "No, John, don't bother, come take me to the doctor." Because by me drinking my blood was hot, it was spilling out, bleeding. And we went and found the policeman and the police took me to the hospital.

Joe told people that if he could not have Mable, "ain't nobody else gonna have her." The doctor told her, "If you hadn't a throw'd up your hand and he'd a hit you in the back, he'd a killed you." She still experiences deep pain in her hand across a line on her palm where "this hand been split half in two."

Mable told the police to put Joe in jail; but John told Mable, "the district attorney have a field day with you . . ." and "Joe'll lose more, honey, don't, don't 'peal against him." So Mable did not press charges, and John bailed Joe out of jail. John was not angry over the stabbing because "he turned it over to ignorant."

Mable and John were married twenty-one years, from 1958 "until '79 when the good Lord took him." They lived "happily . . . [and] didn't have no trouble." In their time together, John "never done nothing but raise his voice at me. He never called me nothin' but 'Honey' and 'Mama.'" When people gossiped about them, "like people talk," Mable and John "didn't pay no 'tention and we got along."

John was a construction worker, and in 1962 they left San Diego for a job in Las Vegas. There they partied day and night. When John came home from work on a Friday evening, "I'd be setting there waiting on the money." Mable believed, "That's what pulled me to him, I guess, made me care more for him 'cause he done what I liked to do . . . he loved to dance . . . that would pull us together."

When work was slow in Las Vegas, Mable and John moved to Pasco, Washington, and then to Seattle. Mable "kept house" for John and didn't work "'cause I had a husband then." They continued their lifestyle of dancing and drinking in the Central District, where there was a lively jazz and nightclub scene centered on Jackson Street. Mable loved to listen to "those dirty blues," and if John did not go drinking with her, Mable would "be with someone else." She felt that, "Me 'n' him, you'd see us, you'd thought we were sister and brother 'stead of husband and wife." Mable and John understood each other well from the beginning. When Mable agreed to marry him, she told him, "John, you know I drink. You know I love to dance." She made it clear that even if people saw her with someone else, "he's not my man." John told her, "It don't make me no difference. If I don't catch you in bed with none of them, it's okay with me."

Mable and John accepted and helped each other. John always gave Mable his check, and she says, "Lotta people hated me for that because I took care of everything and we didn't hide nothing from one another." Some people said John was "a father figure." She acknowledges, "Anything I said I wanted, I got." John occasionally saw a funny look on her face and asked, "Honey, what's wrong?" When she replied, "Oh, nothing, I just ain't got no money," he would "walk out the door and when he come back, he had it. Where he get it from, I don't know and wouldn't care."

"I Can Get Another Husband, but I Can't Get No Other Mama"

When Mable was forty-six years old she went home to care for her sixty-seven-year-old mother, who had suffered a heart attack. But her mother told her to go home to Seattle and "see 'bout your husband." Mable told her, "I can get another husband, Mama, but I can't get no other mama. That's the onliest way I'd be leaving is if you can get up doing something for yourself." When Mable woke up the next day, "[Mama] had breakfast and everything fixed, the table . . . set pretty. She said, 'Now you can go on home,'" and Mable ate breakfast and left the same day. When Mable was gone, her mother "got in the bed and didn't get out"; and she died the following day. Mable feels "she didn't want me there. She knew I was scared of dead people and she didn't know how I was going to act."

"Settling Down"

Mable never wanted to have children, and she was not worried when she did not get pregnant. Neither she nor the doctors related her infertility to the abdominal and pelvic infections that she had suffered as a teenager. Mable relates, "What was I gonna do with kids? I didn't have time to take care of myself. . . . When you here and yonder, you don't want no kids." A doctor told her that her uterus was "twisted" and she needed surgery to have children. Her husband "never minded," so she never bothered.

Growing up, Mable did not know of any birth-control methods, but she saw even then that "a lot of people don't have a whole lot of kids." Her mother was married five times but had only two children. She notes, "If you caught a woman with a gang of kids, she didn't take care of herself. She didn't care how she went, cleaning up and everything like that. . . . If a girl have two or three babies, she wasn't taking care of herself." There was no such thing as abortion. "If they was pregnant, they had the baby. If it died, it died." Mable is opposed to abortion, calling it "killing babies," but birth control "is up to them. Each to his own. . . ."

Although Mable was married, she had not "settled down too much." She finally began to live a little quieter lifestyle when she brought her nephew's son, Timmy, home to raise. Timmy's father lived in Las Vegas and was Mable's brother's child from an "outside woman" (not the woman her brother married). When Mable visited him in Las Vegas, she saw that his wife had nine children, was working and looking for day care for Timmy, the youngest, who "was the spit of my brother." Mable said, "Let me carry him back home with me. You won't have to pay no babysitter."

Timmy's mother agreed that thirteen-month-old Timmy could live with Mable and John.

Later Mable and John also took in a newborn baby girl from the same family who stayed until she was nine years old. Although Mable had warned John, "Don't let her get under your skin too far," when she returned to her Las Vegas family, "it broke my husband's heart."

John died when Timmy was ten, and Mable asked Reverend and Sister Kent to help her with the boy, and they "raised him right behind me." Church members and neighbors also watched Timmy, "so if he got too far outta line they would call me. And he'd tell them, 'Don't call Mama. Don't call her.'"

Timmy lived with Mable until he was twenty-two years old. She and John wanted to adopt him, but his mother would not allow it. After John's death, Mable struggled to help Timmy in school and asked the school principal and teachers to assist her because "the stuff Timmy taking in school, I never come in contact with." She told Timmy she'd stick by him through the twelfth grade and then "he could do anything he wanted to." When Mable felt that one of Timmy's teachers discriminated against him, she told the principal, "I don't want him to hurt my child." The principal put Timmy with a different teacher, "a Filipino, [who] took him under his wing. Filipinos are smart."

Mable was strict and "whipped" Timmy many times. Once, after he lost a job, she roused the fifteen-year-old out of bed to go look for another job. She reached for him, and he grabbed her. She said, "Lord, give me strength," and "when I said that, I downed him and sat on him. I told him 'up!' And I never had no more trouble out of him."

Timmy finished high school and his "Filipino teacher" helped him get a college scholarship, but Timmy went for only two of the four years in electrical engineering. Things began to fall apart around that time. He had been an usher at church and in training to be a deacon, but he became discouraged when another member was chosen to be church secretary. Simultaneously, the "outside world" tempted him, and he started smoking marijuana. Mable told a policeman that if they got a call for her address "about some child doing something he didn't have no bizness doing, don't come 'cepting to bring the dead wagon 'cause that's what he's going to be. . . ."

Timmy then moved to Las Vegas. Although Mable was sad, she was also relieved because she worried about him coming in at all hours. She was afraid she might kill him by accident, thinking he was an intruder. She loved him, but she knew he would leave someday, and she tried to protect herself by keeping him "a distance from me."

When Timmy left, Mable told him, "If he ever got in trouble, I didn't care how old he got, don't call me." At the time of the interview, she had not heard from him in ten months. When he had last called, she had reprimanded him and now wishes that she had said gently, "Hi, baby, what you want?" She heard from her brother that Timmy was in jail: "He was using 'the stuff' when I had him, and I know he done got into it with his brothers."

Now Mable worries about Timmy but says, "I ain't gonna lose my life over it." A policeman once told her, "Don't worry about it, Mrs. Jackson. You raised him, he'll fall back. He wasn't raised up in the world. He want to try the world." Reverend and Sister Kent feel that Timmy has "the foundation" because he was in church every Sunday until he was twenty years old. Mable notes that he is like her in this respect, saying, "I drift off from it, I went back to it. So that's the way he has to do it, too."

When Mable once again hears from Timmy, he is out of jail and has a job. He promises her that he will come and see her when he has vacation. Mable plans to leave him her house when she dies. She has purchased a cemetery plot for him from the Purple Cross door-to-door salesman along with the plots for herself and John, but she doubts that he will ever use it.

Womanhood: "Take Care of Yourself"

Mable has always been a down-to-earth and lusty woman. Now in her seventies, she has a strong sense of herself as an attractive and sexual person. Mable felt like "a woman" for the first time when she had sex at about age fifteen. However, she was not "an adult," because she was "'shamed" and could not take care of herself. She did not know what to do.

Mable makes a subtle distinction in her behavior growing up—she was "wild" but not "fast," meaning she "never stayed in one place long" but she "wasn't fast with boys." Her mother thought she might be gay because Mable mainly went out with older men or other women. She did not "care too much for boys," telling her mother, "The old man can take care of me; the boy can't . . . give me nothing." Mable advises young women:

Take care of yourself and don't be around on the streets because it's not healthy. . . . If you been a girl, you know what's out there. . . . That's all I can tell 'em, "Get tame." They don't got to settle down and go to church and nothing like that. Take care of yourself and don't move too fast. . . . All men gonna talk about it, white and black.

I got proposed to by two marines when I was in San Diego. . . . But I asked them, "Can my brother see your sister like you seeing me?" And he didn't give me no answer, so forget it. . . . The dog is like that. Every hour of the night you can have the dog and any hour of the night you can have a man.

Mable was sixty when she had a hysterectomy. Her "floating tumors grew together" and "I couldn't get out of the bed [during my period] . . . . Looked like it paralyze my legs." After her hysterectomy, she says, "My home affairs was okay. . . . I could satisfy my husband or anybody I went with."

Mable currently has a male friend who calls. After John died, he proposed, and she considered remarrying. However, when she checked on her social security, she found that marriage was not a good economic decision. The woman at the social security office told her, "If you marry, you marry a rich man." Mable said, "'Well, that's out.' Go back home and be satisfied ever since."

"How Many Quarts of Water Does It Take to Mop the Floor?"

Mable sees that racism is pervasive. Keenly attuned to its nuances, she notices how waiters bypass her without filling her water or checking on her during a meal. She tells stories of racism, and she meets discrimination with resistance. An early lesson in racism happened as Mable watched her mother in the sharecropping fields and a white overseer called her "Auntie." Her mother challenged him, saying, "Was your auntie black as me?" The head boss told the man, "From now on, call her Mrs. Jenkins. If you think you can't do it, find you another job."

Similarly, Mable learned to demand respect. She once applied for a "civil servant job" in San Diego to do cleaning work in a government building. During the interview, the woman asked her, "How many quarts of water does it take to mop the floor?" Mable walked out after telling the woman, "Lady, you can take this thing [her application] and put it anywhere you want." She stated, "As long as I have been in this world working this thing, I ain't never had to measure no water to mop no floor. I know how to mop!"

When Mable later did domestic work, her employer told Mable that her former maid had "mopped [the floor] on her knees." Mable responded, "Lady, I don't get on my knees to say my prayers. If you don't have no mop and broom, I'm going home." The woman found her the mop and broom, and "from then on I never had no more trouble." When Mable's knees hurt from her arthritis, she laughingly wonders whether "maybe the Lord was punishing me because I told her that."

Mable moved to Washington State in 1967. However, she says she preferred Las Vegas or California because "I could go more and have more fun and it wasn't 'Jim Crow'. . . . [Washington] has always been prejudiced." When she first came to Seattle, "It was better because most of the people from back down there [South] had come up here, so that put a little bit of hope from the prejudice. . . . It's still Jim Crow now! . . . It's still prejudiced, but when you don't come in contact with it, you don't worry about it. Even down to your own color, some of them is prejudiced." In spite of this discrimination, Mable was not afraid to go out and about in Seattle when she first moved, saying, "When I was drinking, I didn't care." However, she says that things have changed: "I been free, a colored woman, free all my life, but you have to put a limit on it. I ain't never been raped. I ain't never been held up or nothing like that, but still I have a limit to myself. . . . I generally stays at home, go to church and back home, store and back home."

Mable sees that both black people and white people can be good and can be racist. Deeply dark skinned, she experiences discrimination from both races. She notes that black employees in the stores "don't know how to treat people. . . . They act like they don't want to wait on you. . . . When they get a nickel above breakfast, they think they rich!" Sometimes the white clerks are more courteous to her than the blacks, and she feels that one's color does not always matter.

Mable is very aware of institutional as well as individual racism. She notes that having a black mayor did not change the racial situation in Seattle. She contacted the mayor's office about her senior citizen status and "didn't get no service." She went there twice, but "I still ain't met him. . . . So I don't worry about the mayor 'cause when I called down there you can't talk to him no ways, so I don't bother about it."

She sees that institutions have always been racist, telling how at one time a white man could keep a black man out of the military service—when John's boss did not want him to go to World War II, he did not go. She recalls, "Some white men would say, if you stay out of the ground, they could keep you out of jail. Didn't care what you did." When Mable encounters racism, her blood pressure goes up:

> Some people, you can look at 'em and take sick. You can tell the way they talk . . . 'cause they don't have nothing to say to you. . . . You know they're prejudiced! . . . It upsets you but you just have to live with it. . . . Even down to the colored. I never could mix too well with people. . . . I didn't think myself no better than them, but if they didn't have anything to do with me, I wouldn't have too much to do with them. . . . I treat you like I want to be treated and that's all there is to it. . . . I never tried to run over nobody, but I can get 'em off me when they get on me.

"I Did It to Myself"

Mable is not a healthy woman. The years of alcoholism, old injuries, and past surgeries have all taken a toll. She is in continual pain from her arthritis, which became worse after John's death. She has medication for this and for high blood pressure, but, unable to afford it, she takes it only when she "needs it" instead of as prescribed.

She experiences pain in all of her joints and at the sites of her past injuries and surgeries: her hand and her arm hurt where her boyfriend "cut" her; her leg hurts where she once broke her ankle in a drunken fall; her stomach hurts from past surgeries. She believes her arthritis moves to these locations, transported by her "high blood." She does not "worry about" these pains because she knows their source, saying, "I know the Lord is putting it on me 'cause I did it to myself. Don't worry about things you do to yourself. Just sit there and do with it!"

But Mable has trouble understanding the continual and sometimes sharp pains in her back—"My back isn't my fault!" She blames the spinal anesthesia during her tumor surgery since her back has "been worrying" her ever since. She struggles to move and often wears a brace. Once in a while her back does not hurt, and she says, "The Lord blessed me today. I feel pretty good."

Mable has tried physical therapy but cannot afford Medicare's 20 percent matching charges. The therapy helps her but also sends pain through her shoulder, down her arm, and into her thumb. She now wears a copper bracelet on her arm and winds a piece of elastic tightly around her wrist, pinned with a safety pin. She complains that her thumb is on fire and her whole hand is swollen and bluish colored. I point out that she is cutting off her circulation, and she willingly takes the elastic off her wrist.

Mable is devastated when the doctor tells her she weighs close to three hundred pounds and is at risk for "sugar," but she wonders how she can exercise when she can barely walk. At one point she was "going to the spa," but one doctor told her to quit "because when you stop, you gonna gain weight faster 'n you lose it." Another time she went to a special weight doctor who tried shots and pills, but "they come to find out he wasn't no doctor and arrested him." She says that at three hundred pounds, she might "just as well go on and eat!"

Mable dips snuff and chews tobacco regularly, but she knows she should stop because "it gets on my nerves," and sometimes "it hurts me . . . makes me sick." However, when she had "pyrrhea of the gum" her doctor told her that snuff might have prevented worse problems. She believes that by spitting snuff, she also spat out the illness, "so it didn't go down in my system." Her teeth became loose at age forty and she went to Tijuana, Mexico, to have them pulled because "it was cheaper over there." She has worn false teeth since then.

Many of Mable's problems are related to her former lifestyle of drinking, smoking, and gambling. As Reverend Kent says, she "owns" these problems. Mable started drinking in 1941 and did not stop until 1985: "I was drinking like a fish! Every day! But I'd have [John's] food ready before I started drinking. He'd come from work sometime and I'd be in the bed, drunk. He didn't say nothing, but go in and get in his room and go on about his business. I lived pretty good. That's the reason I say I don't worry 'bout it."

When Mable gambled, she played bingo and the numbers. At one time she risked losing everything:

> Lord says, "You stop" . . . and if I hadn't stopped, I couldn't been here—drinking and all. I'da walked off and left this place. . . . Because when the music gets to playing I get to rambling. . . . You get to hearing them old dirty blues . . . and gone! I got a record player and I don't even want to play it . . . gets your mind all stirred up. . . . I know it's bad for me. Where you gonna wind up?

Mable quit drinking when Timmy "shamed" her. During a hangover, he told her, "You mean it making you that sick? Mama, I wouldn't do this if it made me that sick." So she decided to "just let it alone"; and people were surprised that she could quit because she had been a heavy drinker, buying a gallon at a time. Mable says, "I done found out who my company was since I stopped drinking and you the longest company I had in a long time." Mable quit drinking, gambling, and smoking all at the same time because she was tempted by any one of the three to do the others. Mable tries to "just go on" with her daily life, asking "the Lord to give me strength."

"Everybody Got a Little Portion of Jesus . . ."

Four belief systems influence health and healing for Mable: traditional Western medicine, folk remedies, voodoo, and the power of the Spirit. These days Mable likes her woman medical doctor, but she has not always felt welcomed by her. She once confronted her, saying, "'You act like you don't want to wait on me. If you don't want to wait on me, let me know and I'll get another doctor. . . .' She been treating me pretty good ever since." When Mable is treated badly, she does not want to go to the doctor. But she says softly, "I go ahead on. Forget it, y'know. It makes you feel bad. You don't know how to do, when you ain't never been reared up against it you know. Really feel bad." Mable does not believe her experience would necessarily be better with a black doctor as "some of the colored's the same way."

Mable says that Western health care is too expensive, "but 'the man' got to have it." When doctors order medication not covered by Medicare, she tells them, "I am paying for it myself. Welfare not paying it. . . . I pay every month, money out of my pocket and I want the medicine to do me some good!"

Mable is afraid of hospitals and knows that people of all races receive better care if their families visit frequently—"The more you visit them, the better they treat 'em. . . . If you put 'em there and never go back to see 'em, you can forget it." When Mabel is hospitalized, she likes to go to Providence Hospital, a Catholic hospital, because she thinks care is better at religious hospitals. The nurses put her by their station so that she can see them at night, but she still does not feel safe and cannot sleep: "People coming in like they do in the stories . . . taking you out and killing you . . . taking dope and stuff. . . . People can walk in the hospital and they be paying no attention and walk out."

Mable frequently uses home remedies and over-the-counter medicines when she is "hurtin' so bad" and she can't afford her prescriptions. She tries Epsom salts and table salt in the bath. She rubs herself with Watkins liniment. Home remedies like castor oil and hog foot tea and black broth work for constipation. She takes aspirin for pain and Contac for her "asthma." Some of her home remedies do "better than the doctors now."

In addition to home remedies, Mable believes that voodoo can cause illness. She tells of two men who were fighting when one of them borrowed the other's hat. When the borrower returned the hat, the man who owned it went blind.

Mable finds healing in the power of the Spirit and is moved to sing out loudly in church. She is more verbal than the other church members and uses a lot of "call and response" as the minister speaks and the music moves her. She often shouts out, "Thank you, Jesus!" Once she "got to the place I couldn't catch a breath" and wondered whether demons possessed her. But usually she sees that, "When you hear me moaning and going on like that, I be feeling pretty good. 'Cause I'm used to that. I was raised up on it. Sometimes I hear my mother moaning and groaning, praying all the time."

Mable tells of a woman who became so full of the Spirit that she tore up her own house. Mable's mother explained to her, "The Spirit would be on her and wouldn't be off her." Sometimes Mable feels the way the woman did: "I gets to hollering and crying. I see why she tear up her things when she come home. You get that feeling on you. You got to touch something. . . . It ain't pitiful. It's just a good feeling."

However, Mable feels "some people can kill the Spirit." She sometimes wonders whether Sister Kent wants her loud participation. Occasionally when she starts to sing along with the choir, she feels that Sister Kent looks at her to hush. She wonders whether Sister Kent sometimes hits the wrong notes on the piano to "throw her off." But Reverend Kent encourages her, saying, "That's right, Sister Jackson. That sure is right!"

Mable experiences both release and physical pain (which begins when she feels criticized) at church. She says, "I be hopped up when I get there and if don't nothing cut it down and I can't get it back, I feel release when I leave. I enjoys it. . . . But I have come from there, I hurt so bad I couldn't see. I ask the Lord to help me, 'cause I got to understand them like they understand me."

Mable believes that "Jesus [is] the doctor, the onliest doctor." When she is "hurting," she goes to Jesus. To her, Jesus guides the hand of the doctor during surgery and "speaks to him and gives him a vision." Thus a person can be a good doctor even if he or she does not believe in Jesus because "everybody got a little portion of Jesus but they don't know it."

"Having Half of What I Want"

When Mable and John were raising the children, she wanted a home for them on a safe street. She rented a house, but the bank was threatening foreclosure, so the landlord offered to sell the house to Mable and John for $90 a month. They made their first payment on July 1, but John "took sick on July 26." He needed surgery for an acute bleeding ulcer. After his surgery "he wasn't gonna live 'cause he had laid up there and thought he was [worth] more to us dead."

Mable went to the welfare office in tears. An elderly welfare worker asked her what was wrong, and she said, "My husband's in the hospital, cut half in two, 'n' I got two kids and I don't know how I'm gonna make it." The woman helped her fill out the necessary papers; when Mable said, "Lord, please, I got no money," the woman told her, "Don't leave. Don't leave." She issued her a check for $255 and asked Mable, "Will this help you?" Mable said, "Oh, yes, ma'am." Mable went directly to the hospital and laid the check on John's chest. Relieved, John said, "Oh, you and the kids can live now, huh?" Mable told him, "You ain't got to die," and he came home two weeks later. Mable adds, "So I can't look to nobody but Him to help us. . . . I know the Lord has brought us a long way."

Mable and John kept their house and worked on it. John was never able to work in construction again, but he raised a big garden and did small jobs around the home. Mable has had little help since John's death, and the house is run down. When she considers moving, she realizes, "Something of your own is better than something of somebody else's." She wants to just "go on and work with it."

Living alone frightens Mable. The doors and windows are secured with iron bars. At night, she takes an iron bar with her in the car if she goes out and keeps it next to her at home when she watches TV or sleeps. Mable also keeps a gun handy in her bedroom. She hopes her neighbors still believe that John or Timmy lives there, because she does not want them to know that she lives alone. The violence on television contributes to her fears, but without it she would be "so lonely." She adds, "At the quiet of night you can hear everything. I sets up 'til twelve, one o'clock, two o'clock in the morning and then I gets my biggest sleep from then on 'til day. And so sometimes I hear things. You look out there, you don't see nothin'. . . ."

Mable lives on her husband's social security check of $600.06 per month. She pays about $117 per month for her house payment. The taxes, the insurance, and the fire insurance are all included in the note. She always pays her mortgage—"The first thing that come out of my check is the house note. All the rest of the people don't get paid, they have to wait."

Mable pays her bills in person as much as possible. She does not like to use money orders because of the check charges. She often makes trade-offs, paying her bill from the water department and then wondering, "Oh Lord, now how am I going to eat?" Something always seems to come along. For example, once the water department found it owed her money! She attributes these lucky coincidences to the Lord. Ever since July 1969, when John first became ill, "The Lord has helped me. I ain't had no man to come in and help me."

Mable admits she sometimes worries, saying, "Lord, I want this and I want that . . . [but] . . . it come to me, the Lord will help your needs, not what you want." Having accepted this, she is okay with "having half of what I want." She relates, "I feel pretty good all the time. . . . When I got the money to pay my bills, I feel better. When I wanna eat, I have money to get some food with, so what else do you want?" When Mable has unexpected expenses, she often gets behind on her bills but has decided not to worry about it. She tries to follow the advice she always gives—"Just be happy!"

Mable does not ever want to go to a nursing home and plans to keep her house. Owning her home gives her a certain amount of power, security, and freedom—"If I don't want people in the house, I don't let 'em in, cause that's my authority. . . . That's the reason that fence across there." Her home is her refuge. She says, "If I played around out there in the streets and I got tired, I went home. People said, 'Mable thinks she's something because she can go home' . . . That's why I keep this place. If the Lord can help me to keep it. . . . If I walk around here buck naked, this here's my place." Others are jealous and urge her to sell, but she says "For what?" Rent would never be less than what she pays on her own home.

Mable wants to fix up her house if she ever has the money. A year after her interview, she manages to do this. The inside of the house is freshly painted white, she has an expensive electric radiator to keep her warm, and the webs of wires (and cobwebs) across the walls and ceilings are gone. The rug has been cleaned, and she has a new upholstered chair. The yard is well maintained. The back steps on her little porch have been rebuilt by a contractor who often works on the houses of the elderly poor in the Central District and charges too much (he now carries a lien on her house).

All of the repairs and new comforts took place when a friend helped her fill out an application for a credit card, telling her she was "sitting on plenty." The friend then took Mable to the bank and showed her how to get a cash advance of five hundred dollars. Mable charged her account to the limit, asked for another thousand dollars, and was allowed it. She is soon using four credit cards regularly. Reverend and Sister Kent try to talk to her about the dangers of credit, but she feels she has struggled for long enough. She does not have that much longer to live, and she wants to be comfortable. But soon bill collectors begin to call night and day, and she is eventually forced to declare bankruptcy to save her home. However, for a short time she is happy and comfortable, and the house is warm, and she has been able to buy all her medicine.

"Follow Me and Maybe We Can Make It In"

Mable's security revolves around her home, a good friend with whom she has a check-in system, her car, and her life at Morning Sun Church.

She has gone to church practically all of her life, but she became more involved when she was forty-six years old and moved to Seattle—"There wasn't too much to do up here but go to church and home, 'cause clubs wasn't like they was anywhere else." The Central District nightclub scene changed dramatically in 1969, when the police, who had been "paid under the table for winking at illegal practices such as gambling, drinking and prostitution," cracked down (de Barros 1993, ix). Jazz subsequently went into "a decade of near hibernation" (ix). Mable joined a large church at this time on New Year's Eve in 1970. Timmy and her husband, John, were already members of Morning Sun Church around the corner from their house. When John died, Reverend and Sister Kent helped Mable with the services at Morning Sun. Sister Kent "went all the way with me and showed me what to do and act . . . and I . . . didn't [have] nobody to help me but them and I love 'em to my grave for that." After John's death, Mable joined Morning Sun.

During the 1970s and 1980s, Morning Sun was a lively church with many young people involved. The church was full every Sunday, and "people used to say soon as they hit the sidewalk, they could feel the Spirit." Mable remembers a time when she and the other women wore evening gowns to Morning Sun, when there was "cooking and eating going on all the time." The same members are still at the church, but their children are grown and have moved on. Although the church still overflows on special occasions, church activities have declined with the loss of youthful members, and there is little to attract young people.

In a church where every member matters, Sister Jackson has the important role of church usher. But she is old and slow and makes mistakes. Reverend Kent corrects her, and this "grieves" her and then her back hurts her so much that she has to sit down. Usually a very kind man, the pastor, when he has small lapses in patience, directs them at Sister Jackson, complaining that he needs male ushers. Sister Jackson believes that he should be more appreciative of his congregation—"Ain't nothing over there but women. Some of them is able and some of them is not." But she has known Reverend Kent for a long time, and sometimes she does not "even hear what he is saying." Occasionally she goes to sleep during his sermons.

Sister Jackson is a proud woman in church, but she is also lonely. She holds herself aloof from some of the activities, often leaving immediately after services. People rarely seek her out to talk, "as if I ain't good enough to talk to." She does not stay to eat because she cannot get down the steps to the basement church hall, and some members think she does not want to socialize.

Sister Jackson is an active participant in Sunday school, but her attendance drops off when Missionary Mahalia Lake takes over from Sister Kent as teacher. The sessions become more formal, and Sister Jackson is embarrassed that she has difficulty reading aloud and Sister Kent has to help her. She gradually comes in later and less often, explaining, "I haven't got the learning that [Missionary Lake] got. I don't know the Bible to teach it like she want it to. . . . I don't understand too much in it. . . ." With Sister Kent, she was comfortable, but with Missionary Lake, "I don't say nothin' because if I explain it one way, it may not be the right way."

Sister Jackson may not have specific knowledge of the Bible, but she has no doubt she believes in God. She always prays before she arises in the morning, saying that when she "wake[s] up hurting, if I start praying, I ease it out." She notes, "When I get ready to go somewhere I say something to the Lord before I leave so He go along with me and bring me back home." When she goes to the altar to pray, she leaves her worries there: "Don't take it back with you."

Mable is determined not to "straddle the fence any longer." She tries to stay on the "right side," praying, "Lord, I need help." She states, "I'm trying to live the life and that's all I can do." She tells another struggling church member, "Follow me and maybe we can make it in." Mable sums up how she sees herself "living the life":

> I don't say I got everything. I don't know everything and I haven't been everywhere, but in a way I'm living straighter than any of them. I'm not in the streets. I go to the store and come on back home. I ain't got Dick and Harry running through the door, and I ain't lying. I'm here at home setting next to my TV. And I talked more to you than I talked to many. . . . You have to live it. You don't talk it, you live it. You don't know who watching you. You just walk your straight line. That's all you got to do. I can't tell you how to serve the Lord. You have to learn that for yourself. I treat you like I want you to treat me. That's all there is to it. . . . You don't be more than what you are; you don't be more than what you not. This is me.

It is easy to see Jesus in Mable.

"They with You All the Time Like the Lord Is"

John's passing was a critical passage for Mable that marked the beginning of her life alone. When John first "took sick," Mable remembers she "just had come off a big train [drunk]." She relates, "He say, 'Honey,' but I didn't move, but when he said, 'Mable,' my foot hit the ground. . . . I know somethin' was wrong 'cause he hardly never did call me that. . . . [His ulcer] busted and [the bleeding] come through his mouth. . . ."

John had his surgery in 1975 and lived until 1979, but during those years he was a partial invalid. Eventually he had a stroke and "he got to the place where he couldn't do nothing." Mable bathed and dressed him. One day when John was seventy-two, Timmy came out from John's bedroom saying that something was wrong with him. Mable found him "laying there looking one way." The aide car came, but John had "passed." A neighbor comforted her, "Mrs. Jackson, dry them tears." "What you mean 'dry them tears' when my husband laying back there dead?" "Dry 'em 'cause ain't nobody in this town did for their husband what you did."

The neighbor urged Mable and Timmy to come and stay with him that night for fear that John's spirit would reenter the house where he had lived and died. But Mable could not sleep and "that was the longest night in my life." The next day she told Timmy, "We going home tonight! 'Cause Papa didn't hate us, he loved us. He ain't gonna bother us."

However, the dead often do visit Mable, and she accepts these visits as a part of life. After her mother died, she appeared frequently to Mable until she "had to let her go." Mable often sees and hears from John:

> I was setting here and I was used to cooking every day . . . and I said, "I'm tired of cooking," and after a while pots and pans went to falling in the kitchen and I went in there and they was laying out there and I just said, "John, I ain't cooking today." And I come on back here and sit down and it started again and I went in there and put on some food. I wasn't bothered no more. . . . Now I don't wait 'til I get hungry to cook, I just go ahead on and cook. . . . So I don't worry about it when things get to dropping and going on in there, if I got on some clothes I go 'head on and get in the car.

A suitor came to call after John's death, but Mable could smell the scent of embalming fluid, and then she knew that John was watching and that he did not want her to be with the man. So she told him, "You get on out the house. John don't want you here." Another time Mable was driving and it was clear to her that John wanted to drive the car. She released the wheel and let him drive for a while.

When Mable and John moved to Seattle, they came with several friends who have since died: "I'm the onliest one living. . . . All of them gone and . . . it kinda gets you when all pass around you, you know." Sometimes at night she feels her friends around her. Once she caught a vision of a former neighbor drinking coffee in her house just as he always had; sometimes an old friend knocks on the door and she sees her out the window; another time a neighbor boy came by to visit and she found out that he had died just before he came to her house. When Mable is in pain, John often comes and sits silently on the bed with her. At one time she was able to give all of her pain to him, but his presence no longer seems to take her pain away. When she goes to the cemetery she says wistfully, "I wish I could leave all this pain here with him."

Mable describes her visions by saying, "There's a vision . . . but they be's with you, they with you all the time like the Lord is. They with you. All the time. So I don't bother . . . 'bout it cause I know they're gone." She sometimes wonders "why I have to have so many!"

"I Don't Want to Linger on My Dying Bed"

Mable is getting ready to move on. At times she is in a liminal space, at a threshold of perception, and she maintains relationships with people on both sides of the line on a daily basis. After a few minutes of visiting at John's grave, she says, "Let's go. I can talk to him at home." She is in constant pain and poor health. When she thinks about her death, her belief in another world sustains her. She is "gonna try" to see John in the afterlife: "I believe he was a Christian . . . but he didn't [officially] join church. . . . He wasn't no bad man . . . he wasn't no rowdy man and I do believe . . . his soul went to heaven and I'm gonna try to see him again." Mable reflects on her life, saying:

> I done had a pretty good life all the time. Any way it go, it's okay with me. If it ain't right, I just won't do it and if it's right, I'll help. I ain't hard to please. . . . I ain't had no kinda trouble or nothing. Sometime now

I feel sorry for myself but I soon gets over that. Sometime I sitting up here and I laugh about the old days. They was pretty good to me. But I never did forget the Lord because I was raised up on Him. . . . I haven't regretted none of my time. None of it. . . . I never try to hurt nobody, steal, be unkind. . . . I never was no big talker. . . . I never tried to run over nobody. . . .

As Mable struggles with her physical body, reviews her life, and has daily interchanges with people who have "gone on," she thinks often about her mother's words, "I don't want to linger on my dying bed. . . . If I'm going, take me now!"

THE JONES FAMILY

BETTY JONES
"I Like to Go!"

The Jones family is a large extended family that spans five living generations. The following chapters tell the stories of four of the women from three generations. The Jones family, like the Lake family, has struggled, but they have also managed to build up assets, and, as a family, they have a small safety net. Family members attribute their success to the determination that they have learned from Martin Jones, husband, father, and grandfather to the women who share their stories. This determination is the central theme and foundation of their lives.

Mrs. Betty Jones is eighty years old at the time of her interview. She grew up in a small town outside Shreveport, Louisiana. Her parents were married for sixty-seven years and had seven children. Her mother lived to be ninety-nine, and her father lived to be ninety-three—she is a woman with a lot of life left in her.

As Mrs. Jones talks, she sits quietly on the sofa in her daughter Joann's house. She is ageless in the way of certain old black women. She eats her breakfast cereal and smiles through missing teeth as she visits with me. Her hair is coal black, and glasses cover the bright, dark eyes that see everything and sparkle with smiles. Mrs. Jones is eager to be interviewed but says frequently that she is a shy person and it is difficult for her to talk. Her memory is sharp as she discusses her large extended family and speaks proudly of her children and grandchildren.

The Growing-Up Years

As Betty Jones remembers her childhood she softens, dreamily describing the house on a seven-acre parcel where she and her brothers and sisters grew up. Her grandfather worked "all his days" for a white man, who left the property, which had three houses, to him. The family held onto the property through the generations, and family members still own two of the houses.

Even though Betty was raised during the Depression, she does not remember it, saying, "If I was home, Daddy was taking care of me!" Her father worked "on the railroad track and my mama was working for a doctor . . . clean up the house and cook . . . and babysitting." She describes a rural lifestyle:

> Papa raised everything and we, oooo, Mama have eggs and everywhere you look in the bottom of the refrigerator, just full of eggs. And go to the garden and cut all the greens you want and pull up all the turnips, okra, corn; go to the cornfield and get all the corn just by [the] sacks. Dig potatoes, big sweet potatoes, great big things like that, they raised plenty.

Betty, like other members of Morning Sun Church, was "raised in church." She sang in the choir, was in the Baptist organization for young people, and taught Sunday school. She was well behaved as a girl, walking with the older people to church and Sunday school.

When Betty was thirteen years old, her father followed a job to another small town in Louisiana where Betty finished high school. Although she wanted to go to college to be a teacher, her father was financially unable to send her. An uncle, the president of the college in Baton Rouge, offered to help her go to school there, but Betty's mother was afraid for her to move so far away. Her mother said, "Noooo, she go off there and go away from us and stay [there] and come back with a houseful of children. Uhnnn." Betty said, "I sure did want to go to be a schoolteacher so bad, but after I couldn't go to school and do it, I just stayed and did something else." Betty told her father, "That's all right, I get me a job and go to work . . . and that's what I did." At age eighteen, she began her lifelong work as a domestic servant by keeping house for the superintendent of the high school and helping raise his grandchildren so that their mother could teach school.

As it turned out, Betty later moved away to the Pacific Northwest and had "a houseful of children." Before Betty's mother died, she said, "Oh, I wish I hadda let Betty went on to school." Later one of Betty's six children became a teacher, giving Betty a great deal of satisfaction.

Betty met Martin Jones at a school party. He was raised much like her in the same small town, and had finished school through the eighth grade. Both families belonged to the same church, and their parents were good friends. Betty knew Martin Jones "for years" when she married him in her early twenties, and they have now been married fifty-six years.

It was during these growing-up years in the 1920s that Betty and Martin first met Joseph Kent and Bessie Freeman (the Morning Sun pastor and his wife). Martin and Joseph were "some kind of kin." When they met, Bessie was a schoolteacher, teaching Betty's younger sisters and brother and boarding with Betty's aunt. Betty's sisters adored Miss Bessie and would bring her big bags full of okra and corn. Both families predicted that Joseph Kent would become a preacher, and Martin stated, "If he be a preacher, he gonna be a good one." It was by chance that Joseph and Martin both came to Seattle in the early 1940s and later sent for their families.

The friendship between the Jones and Kent families spans from Louisiana to the Northwest and has lasted for more than seventy years. When Betty's father died, Joseph Kent's parents comforted Betty's family in Louisiana. When Betty and Martin celebrated their fiftieth wedding anniversary in Seattle, Reverend Kent preached and Mrs. Kent played the piano. The Joneses' children and grandchildren now attend Reverend Kent's church, and Reverend Kent has married, baptized, and buried many Jones family members.

When Betty and Martin were first married in Louisiana, Martin did road construction for logging companies, and the couple lived with Martin's mother. Betty had her first baby in her early twenties, and the ensuing years were filled with the births of her next five children. All of Betty's children were "born and come in the world" without problems. Betty, her aunt, and her mother all worked for doctors, and they learned from them about good care during pregnancy. The first four babies were born at home with the help of a doctor or a midwife. When the doctor was out of town, he would recommend the midwife, Mother Abbie, saying, "She's just as good as I am." (Mother Abbie died at age 107 and, "you couldn't get in that church!") The last two babies were born in Seattle hospitals.

When Betty had her babies at home, she had help from her mother-in-law and her family, and she could rest for several weeks. However, when she had Joann in Seattle at St. Francis Cabrini Hospital, they sent her home after three days. She was forty-two by then, with a "houseful of children" and no extended family. Although the older children helped, Betty remembers, "I be tired, I sure would—washing, ironing, cooking and cleaning house and running the store. Oh, boy, I tell you!"

Health and Healing

Betty's children were healthy except for minor illnesses like colds and sore throats. Betty used both Western medicine and folk healing strategies to keep her children healthy. She still protects her grandbabies and great grandbabies from catching illnesses by putting a little string bag filled with "asifibity" (asafetida—a gum resin that smells like garlic) around their necks. At her grandchild's recent checkup, the doctor said about Betty, "[She] know what she doing. . . . She put that on the baby, you can carry her in a crowd where they got a cold . . . and your baby won't catch it." Betty also treats colic with asafetida: "You mash a little, you take your little pinky of it, put it in a teaspoon and mash it up and put a little breast milk, warm breast milk in that and give it to the baby. Oooo, that'd sure stop that colic!"

Betty Jones has other remedies as well. Her grandchildren receive a dose of cod-liver oil three times a week to help prevent colds. She remembers what her mother and her grandmother taught her:

> Get this piece of flannel, like you have a hurting in your side, anywhere like that, and they put a little Vicks salve on that. And then they put that tallow on that. They keep that thing real hot . . . they lay it to that side. My brother had pneumonia once. Mama has greased him down so with tallow and Vicks salve and give him hog hoof tea. . . . She wondered, said, "I think I'll call the doctor and let him check him and see," 'cause he kept crying, fretting so with it. The doctor come. . . . When he checked the baby out Mama was in there washing dishes. He say, "Aunt Rosella, you come here." Mama came and he said, "The baby had the pneumonia but you done killed it on him."
>
> *Recipe for Hog Hoof Tea*: You get that hog hoofs, people save 'em from down there when they kill the hogs, put 'em up and dry 'em. They get

hard. You cut 'em up, chip 'em up with a hammer or somethin', then you . . . let 'em boil. Pour some hot water over it, steep it. Like a tea. And let it sit and it turns it red, that water be red! Just like another kind of tea. Then you pour it in a teacup and with a little sugar, and drink it hot as you can bear. . . . It tastes like any other tea . . . kinda got a funny little taste but it's good. You have to drink it hot.

When Betty's girls have menstrual cramps she advises: "Your period be coming and it don't look like it comin' free or nothing, you steep some . . . like peppermint tea. Smells good, too . . . that's really good to stop them cramps."

Betty follows certain other traditions to stay safe and well. Like other elderly church members, she turns off all electric appliances and covers mirrors and other reflective surfaces with sheets during thunder and lightning storms. She believes that lightning can hit against the reflection and strike a person down. Betty warns her children and grandchildren about "the witch riding you at night." Her granddaughter Linda describes this belief:

> You'll be like pinned down in your sleep and you'll be trying to move . . . you can't get up and move anywhere. My grandmother says that's called "the witches are riding you" . . . maybe you've been doing some dirt that your grandmother or your mother doesn't know about. So when you go tell her a story about that, she says you been real bad about something and the witch is riding you. . . . What you do to prevent that is to put a bowl of water underneath your bed and that drowns them.

Although Mrs. Jones relies on her home remedies for treating everyday illnesses and supernatural problems, both she and Mr. Jones see the doctor for regular checkups and always follow his advice. Mr. and Mrs. Jones have been treated with medicine for "high blood" in the past, but neither has hypertension now. When Betty found out their food was too highly seasoned, she "just cut on eating." She describes her diet:

> We eat lots of vegetables, salads, fish, baked chicken. And greens, peas and beans, boiled corn, fried corn sometimes. . . . I like mine boiled right off the cob. Martin can eat up—I don't know how much salad, tomatoes and lettuce and cucumbers. I do too, I love that. Fish, baked fish. Baked chicken. I like all that kind of stuff.

Although Mrs. Jones trusts doctors, her belief in them is tempered by a healthy degree of skepticism and an overriding belief in God's power. When Mr. Jones had back surgery after a severe injury at Boeing (he lifted a heavy object with a woman who dropped her end), the doctors predicted he would never walk again. Although Mr. Jones was disabled by the accident, he is still able to get around slowly. Mrs. Jones relates, "The doctors don't know it all . . . they know some but they don't know it all. God knows it all."

Mrs. Jones is clear about her belief system. If she or one of her children is sick, she chooses both the doctor and the Lord, but she depends on the Lord. Mrs. Jones is happy and healthy because "I just pray and move to the Lord. I think that's what makes me happy. I found I could trust in Him."

Everyday Life

During Mrs. Jones's young adult years, when she was busy raising children, she and Mr. Jones were temporarily separated due to his job demands. Martin, like many black men, sought available opportunities while his wife and children stayed in the South with extended family. In the early 1940s Martin became determined to get his family out of the South. His daughter Marie says, "He was getting out from down there and he said he wasn't going to stop until he did." Joann adds that the South "was not a place he wanted to be with his family—especially raising boys." He first found a job as a sandblaster in the shipyards in Vancouver, Washington, then went to work in manufacturing for Boeing Aircraft in Seattle. In 1945, he rented a house in Seattle and sent for Betty and the children. The two oldest children, John and Anne, stayed with their grandmother in Louisiana while Marie, at that time a baby, and her younger brother, Martin Junior, came ahead with Betty. Within a short time Betty and the children returned to Louisiana for her fifth child to be born at home. They stayed for one and a half years, and Marie remembers that this was a difficult time. She tells how as a baby she was pulled behind Betty on a cotton sack as Betty worked in the field: "I wasn't old enough to, but she was out there picking cotton . . . so she'd just sit me there . . . at the end of it, and I thought 'Oh, my God.' I was so glad when my father came and got us and we . . . came back."

Mr. Jones worked "day and night" and bought land with a grocery store, a house, an apartment house, and ten garages on the property in the Central District. Martin had been working for the people who owned the property in addition to his Boeing job. When the owner decided to move to California, he offered to sell the place to Mr. Jones, who was able to get a loan. The Joneses bought the property and raised their children there until 1960, when it became too much work with the job at Boeing and Betty's outside domestic work. They moved to another house on Yesler and 12th Avenue and managed a café that was part of the property.

The Central District at that time was a very safe place to raise children. The children slept on the porch on hot summer nights. The family left the front door open, and the breeze would cool the house. Mrs. Jones says, "You do it now you won't have nothing in there when you wake up. And you liable to not be there."

Mrs. Jones feels that other things have also changed since she raised her children. Then children knew how to behave and if they did not, they would get "paid for it" with the strap. Like many of the church members, she feels that discipline has fallen apart because parents fear that Child Protective Services will take their children if they discipline them in the same way that they were disciplined. This fear has left a gap in parental power. She looks sorrowfully at the problems in the black community and feels, as Reverend Kent frequently says, "We got to return to the old ways."

Although Mrs. Jones firmly advocates strong discipline, she quickly intervenes with her grown daughter when she is too harsh with her toddler, saying, "Don't hit him, Joann. Now don't! That's why he is like he is." Mrs. Jones often takes the little boy away from his exasperated mother and holds him and rocks him in church until he falls asleep in her arms.

Mrs. Jones sees that grandparents have a very strong role in raising their grandchildren. Her parents and her grandparents raised her, and her own parents and Martin's mother helped her raise her children—"[The grandparents] didn't have to whip the children either, they'd talk to 'em and they listened. . . . These children now, you have to get a baseball bat. . . . Then you can't get them to listen."

She does not know what goes wrong when children are "bad," because as a girl she "always let that bad crowd go. I try to follow that good crowd." She says that peer groups have influenced two of her grandchildren who have been in trouble with the law: "[They] do things and they say, 'I ain't gonna do that no more' . . . and then turn around and they did worse. . . . Like Martin says, 'They know right from wrong.' They do. And still they do things wrong. . . . If they won't listen, that's they hard head."

Mrs. Jones raised six children and influenced twenty grandchildren, great-grandchildren, and a great-great-grandson. They have, for the most part, done well, and she speaks proudly of them. All of the Jones children have finished high school and have gone to college or participated in training programs. Betty's daughter Marie feels that there were more opportunities in the sixties for black people and that she and her siblings took advantage of these. Betty's oldest son, John, has a college degree, is married to a schoolteacher, and works as a general manager for a major clothing store in California. Her oldest daughter, Anne, is a Boeing mechanic and has raised six children and is raising two grandchildren. Marie has her teaching certificate and is a day-care teacher. Martin Junior works "for the city lawyers" in Portland. Both Jeremy and Joann are Metro bus drivers.

Betty turns to her daughters for day-to-day conversation, help, and comfort. Grandmother, mothers, daughters, granddaughters, sisters, nieces—the women in the family—are in contact several times a day, calling back and forth on the phone, sharing the day's happenings, eating together, "going to the mall," working on church business, and attending church services. Betty, her three daughters, Anne, Marie, and Joann, their children, and their grandchildren are all "regulars" at Morning Sun Church, although only Marie is an official church member.

Betty, Anne, Marie, and Joann are each other's best friends and helpers. This closeness of all the women in the Jones family provides a good example of "othermothering." The sisters' children all see their aunts as "mothers" (unless they are close in age, and then the aunt is more like a sister).

Although a good portion of Betty Jones's life has been spent raising children, she has had other interests. For many years she played the horses, she and the children worked in the family-owned grocery store, and she did cleaning work for individuals as well as for Seattle companies such as the Bon Marché and Frederick & Nelson department stores. Mrs. Jones still does "chores" for one family and babysits her eighteen-month-old grandson three days a week. Mrs. Jones admits, "I can't stay at home.

Not me. I like to go! I'm like my mama. That's in me. . . . I just love to get out and mix amongst people. Like on a Sunday when they fix up and going to church. I say, 'I'm going!'"

Mrs. Jones is a practical person with strong values of hard work and education. She is eighty, and Mr. Jones is eighty-two. They live on his disability income and on what she earns from her work. Her children will help her if necessary, but so far she and Mr. Jones have been able to handle things independently.

Betty Jones also has a deeply spiritual side and is comfortable with ideas of death and the spirit world. Her beliefs are based on her religious orientation and on her personal experiences. In death as in life, she puts her trust in God, and this allows her to see the possibility of continuing relationships with people who have "passed." Betty tells of dreams or visions in which her parents visit her:

> I saw him [my father] sitting out in the back in a chair and I looked around and look like I viewed him and I went running over that way where he was. And when I got to where he was I say, "Daddy," and he looked up at me and said, "Betty, how you doing?" I said, 'I'm doing fine. How you doing?" And he just disappeared.

The fluidity of life and death is comforting to Betty. She believes, as do other church members, "If you been good and did good in life, everything will kind of go smoothly for you [in death]." When people are grieving, Mrs. Jones tells them "to pray and look to the Lord." It is best to "just go on with the program until it kinda gets better or worse."

Throughout her long life Mrs. Jones has had her ups and downs. She depends on her closely knit family and on God. She sees her daughters daily and often holds a sleeping baby in her arms. She says with serenity, "The Lord has helped me a lot. He returns all my prayers."

JOANN JONES NEWTON
"When God Comes,
He's Getting Some of Every Race"

Joann Newton is a thirty-seven-year-old athletic woman, about five feet five inches tall. As a city bus driver she still fends off passes from her riders and co-workers, saying that she is married and means it! She likes to stay at home, cooking and cleaning and doing things for her family. Although she describes herself as shy, she has firm ideas and speaks her mind.

Joann's husband, Jimmy, is an imposing man. At six feet three inches tall with thick, curly hair and a full mustache, he is burly from working for twenty-three years at City Disposal. He is at Joann's side at church, dressed handsomely in a dark suit, talking quietly with the few men or holding their sleeping baby boy. Jimmy Junior is a bright, active toddler at eighteen months, described by his mother as "bad." He is often "ssh'd," threatened, and disciplined in church as he wiggles his way through the services.

Christine, Joann and Jimmy's fifteen-year-old daughter, is a tall, lean, long-legged girl just coming into womanhood, with long straight hair like her mother's and a coltlike grace to her movements. As Joann watches her grow up, she experiences both fear and pride. Sister Kent pulls Christine aside and earnestly talks to her about having boys respect her and making them watch their language in her presence. Christine, still a child, listens carefully and agrees vigorously with Sister Kent.

Life in the Central District

As the youngest child in the Jones family, Joann has a different perspective on her childhood than do her siblings. She nostalgically remembers it as an idyllic time when she was taken care of by both her mother and father, her father disabled and retired from Boeing. Her father walked her to school every day, coming back to bring her a hot lunch or a hamburger. Although the family was living on disability income and on Betty's salary from domestic work, Joann remembers that things were stable financially. She regrets that her children's experience, with both parents working, is different from hers, even though she and Jimmy work in shifts so that one parent can be at home at all times.

Joann has always lived in the Seattle Central District. She attended Garfield and Franklin public high schools and participated in special programs that involved temporary voluntary transfers to suburban schools for "a week, a month, a quarter." As an adolescent, Joann lived for a time with her sister Marie, then a single working parent with three girls, to help her by managing the after-school household, cooking dinner, and babysitting.

Joann participated in Upward Bound programs and in Summer Youth Corps, where she learned office skills. She attended Western Washington University as part of the Upward Bound program but decided against finishing college because, "My spelling is terrible. I was walking around with too many dictionaries. And then, I don't speak clearly with my words, you know, my big words. So . . . after I got a job I just stayed on my job."

Joann was sixteen years old when she met her future husband, Jimmy, through her sister Anne. He was twenty-one at the time. They waited for five years until Joann was twenty-one before they married. Her early married years were the happiest time in her life—"When we first got married we didn't have no children, we could just eat and go to sleep. That's fun. That's why I tell my daughter, 'You better enjoy your life.'"

Joann and Jimmy lived with her parents, Betty and Martin Jones, for the first seven or eight years of their marriage in order to save money to buy a house. Joann did not like office work and so she "cleaned toilets at the phone company." When Jimmy was laid off from City Disposal for a year and a half, she went to work for Metro as a bus driver to make more money. She continues to work there.

When Jimmy was called back to work, they bought a fairly new split-level home on a well-kept road off Yesler Street in the Central District near Morning Sun Church. The house is well cared for—their dining room chairs and off-white carpeting are covered with sheets of plastic in concession to "baby Jimmy," who travels with his juice cup. The furniture is new, moderately priced, and comfortable. The walls and tables are decorated with family photos and portraits, children's bronzed baby shoes, and various awards from Christine's drill team.

Joann's daily life is quiet. She does not put up with any "in and out" during the week. Occasionally a friend of Christine's comes over to play, or Joann's brother stops by, or Joann goes to the mall with her sisters. She talks to her mother, Betty, on the phone or sees her daily. Joann's main activities revolve around work and church, and she feels exhausted most of the time from working full time and getting up at night with her baby. She loves the Central District. She is close to work and hospitals, and she likes being around people. Her children have opportunities to "go to things," and she knows the families of her children's playmates.

Raising Children: "There Are Things I Allow and Things I Don't Allow!"

Even though Joann and her husband are financially stable, with a combined annual income of around fifty thousand dollars, they are not untouched by the problems of the African American community. Joann worries about how to raise her children safely, how to protect them. Patillo-McCoy (2007) notes that young black middle-class children are prepared for success through working adult role models but are also tempted by "youthful experimentation, the consequences of which can be especially serious for black youth. . . . The in-between position of a black middle class sets up certain crossroads for its youth . . . connected to the black poor through friendships and kinship ties, as well as geographically. . . . The right and wrong paths are in easy reach . . ." (139).

Joann and Jimmy's daughter, Christine, attended a private Catholic elementary school, but the Newtons cannot afford to send her to Catholic high school. Joann and Jimmy, with a great deal of hesitation, have enrolled her in Franklin, the local public high school. Joann believes that in order to get a good education from the public schools "you have to go really far north or south or east." Christine is not used to the "commotion" of a public school, and Joann worries about this. Sister Kent, in her role as "othermother" and advisor to the young women in her flock, always recommends the individual attention found in a private, religious school.

This frequently leads to lively discussions as few in the church can afford such an option, nor do all believe that it is best for their children.

Joann has held Christine back a year prior to her freshman year, even though her grades are good and she has a solid group of friends. But her friends have all started their periods and seem more advanced than Christine, more interested in boys. They have been pushing Christine to do things she is not ready for. Joann's decision is an example of the protectiveness in black mother-daughter relationships (Collins 2000).

Although her daughter's emerging sexuality is of concern, Joann plans to handle this issue much as she herself did. When she and Jimmy became involved when she was seventeen, she went to Planned Parenthood and "watched the movie" and started taking birth-control pills. She has asked Christine whether she wants to go and see the movie, but Christine says, "No." Joann makes this offer with qualifications:

> "Just because you have protection don't mean you lay down with every Tom, Dick and Harry." I hope, what I'm really wishing for is she listen to me and have the sense I have, and I know that's not going to be possible. Everybody is not like me. . . . I'm too old-fashioned. I'm like my mother [who] had the same man for sixty-eight years. I probably have the same man for whenever. . . .

Joann wants Christine to be able to "enjoy her life!" She wants her to finish school and sees that going to college "would be nice . . . if she wants to go." Joann notes that Christine likes taking care of her baby brother but tires of it quickly, and she hopes this will discourage Christine from any early sexual involvement.

Joann fears that innocent girls risk becoming involved in gang retaliation. She sees that many parents deny their children's entanglements, thinking that their child can do no wrong—and then ordinary actions can create major problems:

> [If a boy] calls your daughter . . . and if your daughter don't like them or somethin', they just go off . . . there is a retaliation. . . . These boys feel if you quit them or don't like them, that they can kill you or beat you and they'll come talk smart with your parents. . . . This type of life that these kids are going through is sad . . . when they get mad at each other, they want to kill 'em. . . . They are seriously physical, it just don't matter

to them no more. . . . You know they are all packing guns like machine guns and stuff. . . . I don't like it and the system can do something about it, they could stop it but they don't want to. . . . I feel if these boys want to be shooting up people, innocent people, just to join a gang, put them in the army . . . these gangs . . . they just killing each other.

Joann worries about the world that is out of her control. She tries to drive Christine everywhere to make sure she gets there and back home. When Christine is out with friends, Joann watches the news on TV and worries. When Christine comes home, she tells Joann, "Mama, they were shooting. I'm sick of it. Everywhere we go, we can't do this, can't do that, . . ."

In spite of its worries, life with a teenage daughter has many positives. Joann proudly shows pictures of Christine's African American drill team, the girls dressed sharply in bright blue uniforms. She points to a photograph of Christine dressed in a formal at the Tolot dance at Franklin High, her date the son of longtime family friends from Morning Sun Church.

Raising a toddler has its own set of challenges. Joann worries about her eighteen-month-old son's future as a young black male. She sees that he needs firm discipline and that she "has to" spank him. Disciplining Jimmy Junior is not always easy: sometimes when he sees the belt, he grabs a book, sits down, and loudly says, "I'm reading!" It is difficult for his parents to stay serious. The safety of her children is Joann's biggest challenge:

My mom and them keep saying "You gonna be old before your time." I got a bald spot up there from worrying. But when I was young I could go anywhere and do anything. But you can't now. And it's scary. It look like you sittin' trying to mind your own business, raise your children the right way and bam! Something happens. . . . All I do is pray and hope for the best. That's what my grandparents did and they made it and they lived to be ninety-nine and they believed in it. They did a lot of [praying]. It's like, it gives me a good feeling and looks like you could feel things, if this is gonna happen or if it's not. . . . That's how I do. I can't say for everybody. But to me . . . that's the way I was raised. My parents did it and they made it and they didn't give up hope. . . .

Prayer is part of daily life for the Newtons: the whole family prays at night before bed, they play church music on Sundays before church, and Joann sometimes reads Scripture after work.

On Men: "It's Treacherous Out There"

Joann has been married to Jimmy for sixteen years and has strong opinions on men. She is protective of her marriage and worries about other women: "I haven't had a problem with him so far. . . . It's treacherous out there." She states:

> These men today are boys. They're not men. They are nothing like what my mom knew . . . and they are still trying to do the same old thing. Wanna mess with this one, that one, this one. They makin' babies over here; they makin' babies over there . . . everybody want to have a piece of your man. . . . It's getting worse, 'cause the single women out there, they don't want the single man, they want the married man because they have somethin'. They want to have a part of what they have. They want to entice them . . . and then the next week they got a baby, just wrecking your home. . . . I can't say for the white race, but . . . there's a lot black women I know that's going through that. . . .

Joann does not worry about Jimmy as long as he pays the bills and brings home his paycheck—if he stops, she will know there is a problem.

Joann is not alone in her comments about protecting her man, home, and family from other women. The women of Morning Sun often discuss the shortage of good black working men due to incarcerations, homicides, unemployment, and partnerships with white women. They recognize that they need to hold onto their good men in the best way they know how.

Working: "It Takes Two to Be Ignorant"

Joann's job as a bus driver is "a good job." She receives many written commendations from her mostly white riders. She watches for her regular customers and waits for them, asking, "What happened to you?" if they miss the bus. She states, "I treat them just like I want to be treated—like human beings." Still, some people get on the bus who "cuss [her] off. . . . Sometimes you don't get close to the curb; well, you can't because of the way the cars park. . . . They'll start 'You could get closer.' Or you could be two minutes late or a minute, 'You late.' Any old thing."

When people treat Joann this way, she tells herself, "It take two to be ignorant. So why should I start cussin' and actin' a fool, too?" She says philosophically: "I don't let it get under my skin, 'cause if you do, they gonn' work you. But if you say 'you're right' or 'thank you, have a good day' when they get off, they'll think about it."

Joann is sometimes afraid on her bus route. She always uses a pseudonym to protect herself from people who bother her; and, although it is not allowed, she carries Mace in case she needs to "back 'em off." When she is frightened, she turns to prayer, and it helps her "feel good about things":

> Crazy folks would get on there and I would want them off . . . you could tell that somethin's up. I was "Please get out of here," you know, whisper somethin' in my mind and it look like that person would just calm down or I would feel better about myself, or I wouldn't fall to pieces 'cause. . . . Some people get on there—just me and that person, and they scare you to death. . . . There's a lot of strange people. They're homeless. They're mad. . . .

In general, Joann feels she has not been mistreated because of the color of her skin:

> I'm not into that black and white thing. 'Cause I can handle myself. It's the way you talk to people—you can let 'em know in an intelligent way and everything. You don't have to get crazy and loud and act ignorant. . . . I could speak up for myself. . . . I'm just one of them that go to work, do what I'm supposed to do; they don't bother me, I don't bother them. I don't give them no trouble, they don't give me no trouble, but there is a lot of it going around and it's happening to some people. But sometime I feel people bring that stuff on theirself. . . . Then I feel some just bring it out more than others. I don't know . . . I get confused on it sometimes.

The following story illustrates her confusion. For six months, she regularly parked her bus on her break to run into the same grocery store in the University District for a snack. Then the following happened:

> I walks into the store, I has on my uniform and my sweater. In my sweater pocket I have my coin purse, I always have it in there so if they steal my purse they won't have my license or my money 'cause, you know, you have to redo that and your ID. Then you can't work until you get it. . . . So that morning when I hit the door, I pulled [the coin

purse] out . . . and I kept walkin' as I was doin' it and when I got to the lady's counter where she was checking, I put it in my pocket . . . and ran back there and got my milk and came and put my money down and said, "Is it okay?"

Well, she turned around from checkin' and says, "Give me those cigarettes." And when she said that she shocked me 'cause I thought—I thought she's tellin' me a joke. So I stood there and I looked at her and she said, "You heard me, I said, 'Give me those cigarettes.'" So I said, "What cigarettes? You talkin' to me?" She says, "Yeah, out of your pocket." I looked at that lady, I say, "What?" She say, "I say, 'give me those cigarettes out of your pocket.'" By then she all up in my face.

To be honest with you, Mary, she shocked me, she made me speechless. I couldn't believe it—she's been seeing me since September come in there. . . . So I pulled out my coin purse and I said, "This?" And I leaned so she could see and she looked and there were no cigarettes in there. I said, "Lady, I don't even smoke." Then I put my purse up there . . . and I says, "Here, go through, I want you to go through my purse to see if I have cigarettes." I mean, I couldn't believe it. I was in shock. When I got on the bus I couldn't hardly drive because I just couldn't believe this lady had seen me come through this store for at least three or four months with her all the time, every day and then she wants. . . . So she didn't really say she was sorry for accusing me. So I says, "I'm sorry if I made you feel that I was stealin' or anything."

When Joann got off work, she returned to the store to speak to the manager and let him know she was considering hiring a lawyer. The manager apologized and, after investigating the incident, sent her a two-hundred-dollar gift certificate. Joann feels that she made her point and that any legal action would have been difficult and too expensive to pursue.

As Joann describes this event, she acknowledges that this probably would not have happened to her if she were white. She qualifies this, noting, "It's certain people," and "Some bring it out and some don't." She remembers that other white checkers in the store have been nice to her. She rationalizes the woman's behavior, saying, "Maybe she thought I was being too cheap buying milk and juice." She thinks about what she would have done if she were the checker: "If I would have accused her of stealing, I would have said, 'Ma'am, I'm very sorry.' I probably would have been on my knees." Joann says it was important for her to go back and "make sure I go through her line. I don't have no reason to run or hide or nothing." She finishes her story: "But then there's some black people that the same way. Like I say it's hard, it's a toss up. But the only thing people gotta realize, there's blacks that steal, there's good blacks; there's white that steal, there's good white; there's good Jews, there's bad Jew; you know of every race."

Joann speaks painfully as she tells this story, relating her innocent surprise and the subsequent feeling of betrayal that she experienced when she was faced with the overt racism that she could not deny.

Race and Health: "They Kept on Insisting . . ."

When Joann had her second baby in Seattle, she chose a wealthy private hospital because her doctor had recently moved there from a hospital that served low-income people and people of color. Joann had undergone natural childbirth with Christine, and her husband was there to support her, but she was not allowed to have a natural birth the second time. She tells the story:

> They kept on insisting to go in my back . . . for them to put that needle in my back [an epidural]. And they were stressing me out. They had made my blood pressure go sky-high because I didn't want them messin' with my back . . . after you have something poked in your back, your spine, you have back trouble. So they just kep on and kep on and kep on. So then she told me, "Well, you're gonna have to get somethin'." I said, "You don't have to go in my back." I know better than that. They just sit down like they were psychiatrist with me, 'cause my mind was made up when I went in there, and then I really started freaking and gettin my blood pressure up because I said I shoulda went to [another] hospital. I was really upset. 'Cause I didn't want to be there no more. . . . And then after my blood pressure went up so high and they put a monitor on me, they kind of convinced me, maybe I do need it . . . but I've had natural birth and I can stand pain. . . .

Although Joann was angry about her treatment, she does not see it as discriminatory. Rather, she says, "I think they want to give everybody epidurals and I think [that] hospital is overcrowded. . . . I'm not really into that black and white thing. . . ."

Joann also feels her postpartum care was unacceptable. When the postpartum nurses did not help her to the shower or change her linen, Joann again rationalizes: "It could have been my particular nurse 'cause the lady across from me had a different nurse and got her bed changed and she was up—the nurse was helping her walk."

But Joann has no clear explanation for why the doctors refused to do a tubal ligation when she requested one, instead prescribing birth-control pills:

> I wanted my tubes tied and they wouldn't. They put me on the pills. . . .
> They said I was still young [for a tubal at thirty-five years old], and I
> had signed the papers and he [Jimmy] had signed and everything. . . . I
> think what it was, my doctor wanted to make more money. You know,
> 'cause I right there having a baby—I'm already open—"Do 'em, tie 'em
> up." "Well, no, let's let you heal and come back. . . ."

Joann blames her inability to lose weight on the birth-control pills and now suffers from edema and hypertension. She believes her back problems are related both to the extra weight and possibly to the epidural. Although she used a diaphragm successfully for thirteen or fourteen years and wants to do so again, the doctors have discouraged her. After her hospital experience, she is afraid to return to have her tubes tied.

Many times the churchwomen describe a lack of clarity in their experiences that creates a sense of unease and uncertainty about their own perceptions. This uncertainty comes up time and again related to discrimination. Joann's senses tell her one thing, while society and her desire to "get along" tell her differently.

In the end, Joann looks at issues of outright discrimination, such as what happened at the market, and those of questionable motivation, such as her hospital experience, and she relies on her philosophy, "When God come, He's not just getting white people. He's getting some of every race. That's how I feel." This belief helps her stay "grounded" in times of discrimination and in times when she is uncertain about why something occurred—those times when her instincts do not coincide with the explanations she receives.

The Jones women believe that "it's how you handle yourself" and "some people bring it on themselves." It is shocking for Joann to discover that how she acts does not always matter. The Jones women have been raised to believe that if they work hard and play by the rules, discrimination will not hurt them. This approach allows them to manage fairly well in a white world. However, when discrimination occurs, in spite of all their efforts, they feel betrayed and deeply hurt. Joann, her sister Marie, and Marie's daughter Linda all make the same statements about racism—that it rarely affects them—and then each describes an intensely moving story about how much an experience of racism has hurt.

Joann uses tools to help her cope in the face of these worries: prayer, a strong belief in God, knowledge that she is "grounded," and a solid family support system. Her beliefs are reinforced over and over each week at Morning Sun Church services.

CHAPTER TEN
MARIE JONES SMITH
"Getting That Made-Up Mind"

Marie Jones Smith is Betty and Martin's third child. At forty-eight years old, Marie is lean and rangy with fair skin and straight, reddish hair; she dresses beautifully and her clothes drape stylishly on her slight frame. Marie is an energetic person and an outspoken and reliable church member who is vice-president on the board of directors of Morning Sun. Hardworking, intelligent, and clear thinking, Marie typically "says it like it is." Reverend Kent frequently refers to her responses in church, chuckling, "Sister Smith, I don't know what I'm going to do with you!" She begins her interview by flatly stating, "Black women's lives have mostly been struggles."

Like Joann, Marie has strong opinions on child rearing, health, discrimination, men, work, and God. These opinions have evolved from her experiences and those of other family members. For African American women, the importance of experience in "assessing knowledge claims" is "a criterion for credibility" (Collins 2000, 257). With three grown daughters and two sisters, Marie has many women's experiences to draw on as she articulates her beliefs, values, goals, and knowledge.

Womanhood: "Getting That Made-Up Mind"

Marie chooses to start her life story with her marriage to Carl Smith. She was in high school when she met him, an older boy already in the air force. She was a tall girl, weighing only ninety pounds and working as a model at

137

a department store. She planned to be a stewardess, "but after high school I got pregnant and that was the end of that then, because they didn't allow you to have children." Traveling with Carl's air force career, Marie and their baby Linda "got a chance to go to Taiwan," and lived for a while in Oklahoma City. In the summers Marie and Linda went to Louisiana to be with Linda's great-grandmother.

Marie and Carl soon had two baby girls, Linda and Caroline, and, out of the air force, they returned to Seattle to put themselves through school. They managed with help from his family, who were "brainy people"—teachers, police officers, a professor. By the time they graduated from college they had a third little girl named Patricia. Marie started teaching in the Seattle school district, and Carl was awarded a grant to attend medical school at University of California, Davis. The couple commuted; but the marriage was not working well, and Marie "could see him changing." Carl became a doctor, but the marriage ended and Marie was on her own with three little girls.

It was during the time just prior to her divorce at age twenty-eight that Marie began to feel like a grown woman. She says, "I knew that I was going to have to step up there and take over and get things going . . . be the breadwinner. . . ." Marie terms this attitude "getting that made-up mind." She demonstrated this quality during her divorce:

> He told me—I won't dare tell you what he told me. I had filed for child support in my divorce. . . ."Well," I said, "are you going to pay for the divorce?" He said, "I don't want no divorce; you want it, you pay for it." So I did. Then when I told him about the child support, he called me up and he said, "What on God's earth do you think you was doing, having them white folks write me some papers telling about what I have to pay for child support?" He says, "You would have did better asking me yourself."
>
> And I just forgot about it. I just dropped it and went ahead and did my thing and then he would come across when he got ready. . . . Like I told him, "Honey, you haven't seen anything yet. . . . The older you get and the older [the girls] get—they going to really make up for lost time."
>
> I was determined after he said . . . that I shouldn't have had the white man to tell him what he had to give, do for his children . . . he was very strong on that—I didn't have . . . the white man to tell him nothin'. I went ahead and did what I had to do for my children and raised them.

. . . I felt he would eat those words one day. . . . Out of all of them [his
wives from later marriages], I think I've been the one that wouldn't ask
him for a dime and I'm the one that they say he respects the most. . . .
I was very determined I was going to do it. And the thought of being
able to have him fly in each year as his girls graduated from high school
[kept me going].

Carl remarried several times and has two sons. Today Carl and Marie function as an extended family, with Carl's sons coming to stay with Marie, and
Marie's girls going to California to stay with their father's family.

Raising Children: "Marie and Her Three Little Girls"

Marie's girls are now grown, with Linda age thirty, Caroline, twenty-
nine, and Patricia, twenty-eight. Marie is glad she has her girls and is
proud that she raised them alone, but she acknowledges that she paid a
heavy price:

I worked two jobs. I worked for the [school] district and then in the evenings I would work out at Western Electric where they repaired phones
. . . close to Kent. I did that for about four years . . . so that my kids
would have things like other kids . . . without having to go out and want
this and that. And then during the summer . . . when they got of age,
they would get summer youth jobs and make their money . . . that would
buy their school clothes and then I always had them to pay me rent. And
then the rest of the money was theirs to do whatever they wanted to do
with it. So we kind of helped each other.

As a young woman, she was able to maintain this pace, but "If I had to
start it now I couldn't." Her sister Joann helped her, as did "Grandma," a
neighbor who prepared dinner and got the children ready for bed.

While working two jobs, Marie obtained her foster care license so
that she could take in her daughter's friend, an eleven-year-old girl whose
foster mother had died. The child was raised "just like one of mine . . . it
was no different" until she was twenty-three years old. Marie eventually
gave up her second job and took in more foster children.

In the first six years after her divorce, Marie and the children lived
in Yesler Terrace Low Income Housing Projects (where the Lake family

currently lives). Marie's daughter Linda says about the projects, "They're worse now but they were really nice back then. The only thing I didn't like was they had no carpeting on the floors." Linda relates how her mother budgeted and worked two jobs to move the family:

> It was like we was there but we didn't belong there. . . . My mom always kept a nice house and nice things. She's always been that way. And she always wanted to move out of Yesler Terrace and she finally got . . . somebody to rent to her . . . because a lot of people when you say where you lived previously, you say that type of housing program, they look down on that.

Marie adds:

> You can get comfortable with that! You work every day and still you settle for nothing—just what you have. There's nothing to pull you to say, "I want to do better," or "I'm going to do better." Your goal is to just get the money to pay that rent . . . you can't see beyond that! . . . You have to have a desire to want to do better. . . . I believe in when you set a goal and accomplish that, it's time to set another one. It gives you something to strive for. . . . When you start to settle for nothing . . . to me, it's almost like no hope.

When she had saved the money, Marie rented a four-bedroom house in the Central District. The family and several foster children lived in this house for fifteen years. When the house was for sale, Marie tried to buy it, but a real estate agent bought it out from under her.

Raising Women: "People Have to Go through Things"

Because Marie's children are grown, her focus is now different from Joann's with her blooming fifteen-year-old daughter and toddler son. However, she understands Joann's concerns because she was devastated when her oldest daughter, Linda, became pregnant during her junior year of high school:

> I thought I was gonna have a heart attack because my hopes was up in the air. I felt she wasn't going to be able to finish school. . . . She was

always an honor roll student; trophies she'd bring home like that. . . . I never had to tell her much. I never had to spank her. All I had to do was talk to her.

Joann says:

> [Marie] went off the rocker, she almost cracked, because Linda had so much going for herself. She was a very smart girl. She graduated on time even with that baby with a 3.9. She's got a good job. She's got a good head on her. She could have been an airline stewardess. Marie just hated to see her wreck her life.

Linda acknowledges:

> It was hard for me to tell my mom because of the fact—I guess she kind of depended on me a little bit more because I was the oldest. And when she did find out she had a real hard time with it. She really broke down. We thought she was going to have a nervous breakdown because all she could think of is—I was in the eleventh grade, I wasn't going to finish school, and what was I going to do with my life, having a baby! I wasn't married. I ended up having to move out of the house and live with my grandmother.

Marie's dreams and hopes for her daughters have changed with time. Linda eventually married the baby's father, but Marie now wishes that Linda had not married because of what she subsequently experienced (see Linda's story). Marie now believes, "I can do bad by myself. I don't need another person to help me do bad—if you see it's not going to work, get out of it." Marie's second daughter, Caroline, is unmarried and has a child. Marie says, "Like I tell my girls now, 'It's no biggie.' My thing with them is, 'Be happy. And whatever you get or have through life, take care of it, because you're going to need that someday.' So it has worked so far." Marie's third daughter, Patricia, is pregnant for the first time at age twenty-eight, and Marie comments, "She don't want to get married right now. She says, 'Wait a while . . . financial reasons . . . get more stabilized.'" Marie states philosophically, "I believe strongly that people have to go through things in order to really benefit."

Although her opinion about marriage has changed, her values about grandchildren have never varied. Marie consistently repeats to her girls,

"If you bring [children] in here, baby, they're going to be taken care of. I don't care if you work day and night, you're going to take care of them." Marie "laid it on her girls," telling them that if any child were ever neglected, she would take the child and rarely allow her daughter to visit.

Marie understands that young girls want to have husbands, but she, like Joann, sees a shortage of good men. Marie and Joann call on their experience and observations to support this claim. When Joann supervises her daughter's drill team at Monroe State Penitentiary, she is appalled, saying, "You should see all the good-looking men just locked up. It's terrible. There are all these women out here. . . ." When Marie goes to Western State Hospital with a friend, she finds the same thing, "all black . . . and good looking. . . . My girlfriend's brother was in there and you talk about a kid that has talent . . . he blows the horn . . . and here he is, just flipped out."

Homicide, incarceration, and unemployment of young black men have diminished the women's hopes for responsible partners for their daughters. Marie notes, "When you look around—and I can speak from the black. . . . What on earth is out there for our children? Mine might have . . . escaped some of it but just look at what the grandkids—what's left for them?" Joann and Marie say there are very few men who take care of their families, even shopping for groceries and paying all the bills, like their father and Reverend Kent have done.

There are many dimensions to "raising women." The dialectic of simultaneously protecting and moving young women toward independence is apparent (Collins 2000) as Marie stresses independence from men and welfare, yet offers safe haven in times of financial need, helps with grandchildren, and protects her daughters in times of trouble. They all talk to one another several times a day, and "If we don't, we wonder what's wrong."

Everyday Life

Marie gave up teaching in the public schools when she became ill a few years earlier and the work became too stressful. She now works as a child-care teacher with ten to twelve children, running a small center owned by a woman with three centers. She is thinking about "setting another goal" of working for herself. She dreams of having her own licensed day-care center, reasoning, "If I'm licensed just to keep my grandkids, that'll pay off. Then I have my sister's kids and my nieces' kids. If I just took care of my family, the ones that are starting to have babies, I would have a load." Her daughter Linda does not believe that Marie will fulfill this goal, saying that Marie protects her savings in order to help her children out but rarely spends money on herself. In this close-knit extended family, one person's success or failure affects everybody. This "spider web" effect—where all make it together or all fall together—is a constant influence on the decisions that Marie makes.

Marie has a partner, fifty-seven-year-old Sam Peters, and he is as important to her as is her extended family of women. Sam and Marie met through friends at church and began sharing a life six years ago. They first dated off and on when Sam visited from Minnesota, where he lived. Sam began to send Marie money to put away for their life together, demonstrating that he cared deeply for Marie and was dependable as well. Today Sam is "settled" after an adventurous life that included riding freight trains, and he works as a cashier in an underground parking lot. Sam and Marie are active church members and make a handsome couple at church. Sam helps Marie with the grandchildren and has recently taken over the care of his eighty-year-old father. He helps Marie with "hers" and she will help him with his father—"It's give and take." The most important thing in Marie's life is to "have that peace of mind" that she finds with Sam.

Experiencing Racism

Marie relates two pivotal experiences of racism when she tells her life story. In the first experience, Marie was hospitalized with a severe IUD infection. She had been sick for quite a while, had lost a lot of weight, and was extremely weak. When she was admitted to the hospital, she told the nurses that her ex-husband, a doctor, would be calling to check on her. When her sister Anne visited, the nurses told her that Marie had been hallucinating, saying that she was married to a doctor. After her ex-husband called, Marie's care improved dramatically.

In a second story, Marie faced racism when trying to buy her own home. She had helped an elderly woman friend for many years and inherited her house. With this house for collateral and ten thousand dollars in the bank, Marie applied for a ten-thousand-dollar loan from a major

Seattle bank to buy a townhome. However, "They denied me . . . and I confronted the management there . . . and I sat down with her and I said, 'What is going on here? . . . Do they have a freeze on letting black people . . . ?' And, do you know, she told me 'Yes.'"

Marie was astonished that they refused her a loan when she had the same amount in the bank, plus a house for collateral. She questions, "What could they lose?" With characteristic resolve, she decided, "Goddamn, I'm gonna fix them!" Another bank sent her an unasked-for preapproved loan of seven thousand dollars, and she sold the inherited house. When she returned to the original bank, the manager asked whether she could be of any further assistance. Marie answered, "You can't do anything for me but cash this check . . . when it clears I'm taking my money to [another] bank. . . . I asked you for ten thousand dollars. . . . You're so stupid. I had that much money in my account, but I didn't want to use my money, I wanted to use yours."

Marie believes that this happened because "the white man wants the Central District back." She says, "They used to have it at one time. This is going to be one of the most livable places . . . and those blacks that have property, if they can hold onto it, won't regret it." Whenever there is a house for sale in Marie's neighborhood in the Central District, it is bought by white people.

In addition to the difficulties blacks have had in obtaining mortgages, Marie believes that increased police activity in the Central District is putting pressure on blacks to leave, with the idea of "cleaning up" the area to make it more marketable for whites. Although fueled by the economics of desirable property, Marie sees that a secondary effect of these market pressures is that they are destroying the strong black community and social system of the Central District.

With the money from the house and her savings, Marie and Sam are buying their two-bedroom condominium, a first-floor walk-in, one of only four units. Marie pays about three hundred dollars per month for her home, and she plans to hold onto it. The house is cozy and warm, with stylish furniture and carefully chosen photographs of her family.

"My Peace and My Clearance"

Marie tries to pray every day, and in a crisis she turns first to God. She is a member of Morning Sun because, "I wanted to find something that was small, cozy; where there was less problems because you [don't] go to church for problems." Marie feels Reverend Kent is "one of the most sincere people I have met in a long time."

When something is worrying Marie, she tries to make it a practice "to pray about things, and then step out." She says, "It's just for me. It seems like things work better when I put Him first." She then receives an answer and feels a sense of peace—"that feeling comes or something that lets me know." When she was deathly ill and almost died from the IUD infection, she agreed to go to the hospital only after she had prayed and "received my peace and my clearance." She adds, "I really believe we're on a journey. And I don't think we're going anyplace until the Good Lord's ready for us. And when He's ready, there's no way around it."

Marie's basic personality has an influence on and is influenced by her life as a Christian woman. She is a very determined person. She speaks often at church about being "resolute," and frequently mentions that she is a fighter, stating, "You push me—you push me against that wall and I'm coming out!"

Marie feels that her family's success comes from everyone "pushing and striving together." She sums up this belief by saying:

I look at it like this: If I live I'm going to get old and as you get older a lot of things that you could do, you can't do them anymore. And I'm going to need to rely on my children. And if they can see to where I took out this time and give for my parents, maybe they will think, "Well, we need to do this for our mom." Then maybe they won't, but at least I would have said to myself, "I tried to do what I could while [my parents] were alive."

LINDA WILSON, MARIE'S DAUGHTER
"All These Years I Have Become Stronger"

At church with her four little children, Linda is a beautiful young mother, wearing bright colors and big hoop earrings and short skirts. Her three little girls are dressed pristinely in pretty ruffled dresses and dress-up coats, and her little boy Simon wears nice slacks, a white shirt, and a vest. The children sit quietly with their cousins, writing on little bits of paper during the service.

At home in Federal Way, a suburb of Seattle, Linda wears a comfortable sweat suit to be interviewed at her kitchen table. The youngest children, ages two and four, run in and out, and Linda tries futilely to quiet them until she relaxes into the conversation amidst the everyday background of play, meals, squabbles, and Popsicles.

School Days

Linda begins her life history with her junior year in high school when she became pregnant. She had always done well in school, attending Lincoln High in predominantly white north Seattle. She won fourth place in the "Miss Black Teenage Pageant," danced with her school African drum ensemble, and marched with her drill team, performing for audiences at basketball and football games. She says, "My school days were real calm."

Linda was a junior when she met Nicholas, when they were both participating in a talent show. When Linda became pregnant she was determined to finish school at her high school and not be forced to go to an alternative school, which was the policy for pregnant girls at the time. Linda hid herself well, staying in the back of the class and doing her work. She had her baby in August at Virginia Mason Hospital, returned in September for her senior year, and graduated in January with a 3.9 GPA. Linda says that the pregnancy was a blow to Marie:

> [My grandmother Betty] had to remind her what goes around, comes around. . . . She [told Marie], "Well, you were like Linda, you were eighteen years old. Don't you forget what I had to go through." So she was kind of letting her know, "I know you're hurt, but it's not nothing we can't live through together." But you got to think about that, too—"What goes around comes around. You did it to me, now you're getting it back."

When Linda became pregnant, she "decided to leave [Nicholas] alone." They had talked about getting married, but when she saw "the type of group he was hanging with . . . and it didn't lead to nothing but trouble," she quit seeing him. Not long afterward he got into trouble with the law. He was with friends when they robbed a convenience store, and, although he was innocent, he was apprehended and sentenced to the penitentiary for five years. Linda and Nicholas reconciled during this time, and he urged her to move in with his family after baby Natalie was born so that the family could help Linda with the baby.

Nicholas's family was "church oriented," and his father was a pastor of a Pentecostal church. His father drove Linda and the baby to the penitentiary, two hours away, to visit Nicholas every other Saturday for two years. This time of Linda's life "was real harsh. . . . You think about . . . some of the dumb things you did, but that's what I did at that time." Linda describes how Nicholas's mother helped, "When I'd come home and had homework. . . . I had to go to the library—she was always there to help take [Natalie] to her doctor appointments and all that kind of stuff because I was in school." After graduation, Linda's father urged her to come to college in California where he lived, but she felt, "I can't really afford to go to college—I have to make a living for me and my child. . . ."

Nicholas's parents' house was crowded with ten children and additional grandchildren, and as soon as she graduated, Linda applied to the Seattle Housing Authority and qualified for low-income housing. She moved into a two-bedroom duplex with her baby, found a roommate to help with the costs, and got a job at an insurance company as a file clerk. She soon changed jobs, began working at "Check Company" (a pseudonym), and stayed for eleven years, growing with the company. At first she worked the evening shift, finishing at 11 p.m., boarding the bus to go to Nicholas's mother's house to pick up the baby, and getting home at about 12:30 a.m. Her mother, Marie, and grandfather Martin frequently picked her up on rainy or snowy days. At the time of the interview, Linda had recently left the company after it had been bought out—she had been supervising twenty-five people and making $3,000 a month.

Motherhood: "I Was Real Protective of Her"

Linda, like her mother, Marie, is determined. She has needed this determination in motherhood. When she was four or five months pregnant with Natalie, the doctors did a routine ultrasound:

> They were doing a lot of talking but they wouldn't really say to me what was going on. . . . They really couldn't tell, but something looked like it wasn't normal. I was really far into the pregnancy by then. . . . After about seven months, they said she might be a little mentally retarded because her head size is not formed with the rest of her body. . . . And they did a lot of treatment on me as far as blood tests to see if I had been on drugs or anything like that, which I had never tried that stuff—I was never raised around it . . . my friends wasn't on it. . . .
>
> When she was born, they had a lot of specialists come in because her head size was smaller than normal; and what they told me was that she might not live to the age of one year because of her head size. Well, I don't really think they had that much information on the different type of problem that she had, so we ended up having to take her to Children's Orthopedic Hospital and they did a lot of research. . . . We were at the Birth Defects Clinic . . . and they worked real well with me. They were a lot of support, my family was a lot of support. . . . [Then with] the first shot . . . her regular immunization, she started getting seizures.
>
> I was real protective of her . . . and they wanted to go inside of her head at Children's Orthopedic, take a look inside, and I just couldn't do

it. She never was on any medication. When she turned one [the seizures] disappeared, she never had them anymore.

Nicholas was released from the penitentiary after three years, and Reverend Kent married the couple in a big wedding at Nicholas's uncle's much larger church. For two years things went well—Nicholas was a counselor at a home for developmentally disabled children, and Linda advanced at her job. They decided to have another baby. The Birth Defects Clinic had not warned them of any danger, so they believed Natalie's problem was rare. But Linda exclaims that the second baby, Charmian, "came out the same way!" When Charmian was about three years old, she, too, began having seizures. Her seizures have continued, and she has been on medication for the past five years.

Today twelve-year-old Natalie has a normal appearance—her head size has grown with her body. She is in special education classes at school and functioning at a seven- or eight-year-old level. Charmian at age eight is a tiny child with a small, slightly misshapen head. She has tremors when she is excited or not feeling well and has distinct small-child mannerisms, such as hiding her head inside her coat when she feels shy. She is functioning at a four-year-old level and is in special education in public school.

Early in the evaluation process, the doctors told Linda that her children's small head sizes were caused by placental problems—"The placenta was detached from part of their body and it didn't preserve their whole growth they were supposed to have." However, family members believe that Nicholas's drug problem may have contributed to the children's problems, but Linda says he did not use drugs before the children were born.

Linda's marriage ended a few years after Charmian's birth, and much later, Linda fell in love and became pregnant again. She went to the doctor immediately, "worried sick" about having another baby with problems. She considered having an abortion—

> because of the fact I just knew automatically [it] was going to happen again to me. But something said, "You need to check it out a little further. You have time." Because I didn't want to bring another child into the world like that. . . . It's hard enough dealing with Natalie and Charmian. . . . I was just afraid, is this going to happen again? Because I'm thinking it might have been my fault. You always have that in your

mind—what could have happened? . . . What could I have done to change anything? . . . When I was pregnant with Natalie I had to vomit so much they had me on them pills to help me keep my food down, which I heard in later years they're not too good for pregnant women. So I don't know what happened. . . .

Genetic studies were done with the children, Linda, and her new partner, Scott. The genetics team also gathered as much information as they could about Nicholas, who refused to go for testing. Linda had a normal amniocentesis and ultrasound during her pregnancy. She interprets the explanations she was given:

> The geneticist said, "What we came up with is that the father of Natalie and Charmian and your blood—it just was not compatible. . . ." A lot of people don't think about the background and the seed of another individual. You just go into these relationships thinking things are okay. . . . And what it came out to be is that our bloods—we just didn't match at all. And [the geneticist] says that if we [Linda and Nicholas] ever was to . . . continue having babies, they would all be like that. . . . They tested Scott and they says, "Your blood . . . it's fine together." But she says "it's all a mixture of blood, which a lot of people don't understand. Some people are not meant to make children."
>
> They kind of touch base with it at church. Sometimes when Reverend Kent talks about "You don't know about their seed or their background. . . ." [My grandfather] has always said to us . . . "It might not be the right blood." And that's what the conclusion was. It wasn't the right blood with us. . . . There are people out there that their bloods do not mix and they can come up with retarded children. It turned out that Angela and Simon [her children with Scott] came out perfectly normal. It was just bad blood between me and Nicholas.

"It's Time for Me to Go!"

The early years of Linda's marriage to Nicholas went well, but then "all of a sudden he started 'getting involved.'" She becomes upset as she relates the story:

> He wouldn't come home at night or come home in the morning. At first I thought it was a woman, but it turned out he was on drugs. . . .

He had got into a lot of cocaine and he had deep-time problems with that. We went to a lot of counseling. He lost his job behind it. Well, they tried to help him, they sent him to [counseling]. . . . The last straw is when he walked off and left those kids by theirselves [at his job with developmentally disabled children].

He would get paid, he would either say somebody stole the car, somebody beat him up. He had cut up his own self, all up in the face, just to come home and say somebody had stole the money. . . . These are things he was doing to himself. He called me late one night and said somebody had him under a gun and if he didn't pay them all of their money. . . .

It was absolutely draining, me trying to go to work each day, having to worry if he's coming home or not. I left him a few times and thinking—praying for him and hoping to God that he'd do better. And he'd plead you and say, "I'm going to do better," this and that and the other, and end up not doing anything for [himself]—do well for two weeks, three weeks, and he's back on a binge again. And it was getting scary for me.

When he didn't come home, I couldn't sleep through the whole night. I just was worried to death. I would call a babysitter over at two in the morning, one of my sisters or somebody, get in a cab to go see if I could find him and get him off the streets, trying to bring him in, but he would run from me if he seen me. He would run from me! And I would call his parents and cry about it . . . they tried to put him in different programs. It just didn't work. He just wasn't ready to really give it up.

And he came in the house about three o'clock in the morning—and what scared me, he went in the kitchen and he picked up a knife, and I ran in the room real quick and bundled up my kids and I put them around me. And the first thing they teach you to do is don't make them any angrier than they are if they're angry about something—you try to get on their side and stuff—because I went to [counseling] with him for . . . sixteen weeks. . . . He said, "Somebody has just took my money and I give them money to go get me something and they took my money. I'm going to kill them." And he had this long knife in his hand and he came in the bedroom and it just absolutely freaked me out—"My Lord, what is going on?" . . . [He] walked back out with the knife in his hand. I packed up my clothes and stuff and called my mama and told her we were coming because I was scared to stay there.

I didn't even know this—he had called the landlord and said we didn't have any food or we didn't have any money, begging for money from the landlord. And she says, "I never did give him any money but I directed him to food banks and things like that," which that wasn't even the case. . . . He had went to the pastors of churches and said we didn't have this or we didn't have that so he could get money to do the things he needed to do.

And I says, "It is time for me to go!" So I came in one day, me and my girlfriends, it was about three of them—they were going to help me pack my stuff and make sure I was okay to get out. And I opened the door and there was something against the door. And I'm like, "What's this against the door?" and I heard a bunch of people in there and they said, "Somebody's at the door. . . ." He had this stereo up against the door and there was about two other dudes in there looked like they had been up all night. . . .

What they used to make this stuff in a pipe is this alcohol where they had waste alcohol all over the coffee table and just brought up the wood, bubbled up the wood on it. And he had clothes and stuff all over the place—"What is going on?" So I went next door and I called the police. I said, "Look, I live here, I know he's my husband, but he's a drug addict. He has people at my house I don't even know," which the police knew some of those dudes because they were on the streets. Well, they made them leave and told them if they ever catch them back there again they were going to jail. And they really got on Nicholas real hard: "You have a wife who is trying to work and raise kids, and you're sitting here on drugs and she has to come home to this every day. I advise her to leave because you're no good." They kept saying, "What's your name," and he wouldn't tell them. "You'd better tell us your name or we're going to take you to jail." He was . . . not being very cooperative, and that was really making them mad after that.

And they gave me a sheet of paper of places I could go talk it over with people and help I could get to get away from the situation. . . . [The policeman] was trying to say to me that he sees this every day: "He's not going to change, no matter how much he pleads and begs, unless he's ready to change. You can only just worry yourself with him by now, debt, debt, debt," because I'm used to two paychecks coming in because he was very responsible the first two years, very. There was nothing that we wanted for.

And for him to get on those drugs, he had a problem. And [the police] made him leave and then they stayed there until I got all my stuff out. . . . And I got my own place again. A small little place for me and . . . Natalie and Charmian. And he had—his father has his own landscaping business so he usually works with him and he can make about

$150 a day working with his father—and he was doing that for a while and kinda straight . . . for about a month and a half or two, and I was still married to him then. He was going to counseling, AA counseling, day after day after day, sometimes two times a week, and he would call me.

And we being married and me being in church, I'm saying I want my marriage to work, but it's a two-way thing. I only could do so much for it. So he had saved up enough money . . . and we had bought brand-new living room and dining room furniture, a new coffee table. . . . He just redid the whole apartment and the kids' room. . . . I went to work one day. In eight hours I come home and everything was gone. . . . And I just fell—I just said, "Oh, no!"

I had become very sick. I went to the doctor. I had two ulcers. That doctor looked at me and said, "Mrs. Wilson" . . . because I kinda talked with him about my situation because I was going back and forth to him, talking with him to see what he could give me to keep my stress level down and keep my body going and what classes or something I could take to keep my health up—And he says, "To be frank with you, you have to leave him alone or else you're going to kill yourself. You're not going to be any good for your own kids. You're running behind him"— and I had lost about sixty or seventy pounds in about a month and a half. I wasn't eating. I was just really stressed with the whole situation.

And when he sold everything in the house . . . the police couldn't do anything because it's a community property state, and it's his as much as mine. Well, he went and sold it to the dope man to get what he needed to get. That next day he went to jail because a cab driver said him and a young man tried to rob him. His probation ended in the year of '93, so any trouble he got into he had to go back. So they put him on a probation hold for ninety days when he went back in there. But by that time I had moved in with Mom again with Natalie and Charmian, and I stayed there with her until I could get my health back. I had to take three months off of work to get my body back in shape because I was really ran down.

And Sister Kent would come over sometime and talk with me and she said, "Linda, you have to let him go. I know this seem funny coming from me saying that, but God understands you've done all you can do for him, you can't do anything else for him. He is killing you. You don't have to stand for that." And a lot of my friends would tell me that. And it took a lot—I mean, I had taken him back so many times, thinking he was okay. . . . By the time he got out of jail, I had moved across the street from my mom. She had gotten me an apartment. . . . She says, "We'll do what we can do . . . until you can get better." And of course I went back to work and started getting income again. She went out and paid the first and last month's rent for me in another place and got me more furniture. And she says, "Linda, I'll do this and I'm tired of seeing you go through this. You need to go down and start your paperwork."

I was very afraid, because . . . he seen that I was going to put a restraining order on him while he was in jail. The probation officer was there to tell him when he got out, "You are not to go anywhere near her, her job, the kids' school, you are to stay away. . . ." I was scared because one day I was walking down the street and a guy came up to me and said, "Are you Nicholas Wilson's wife?" and I automatically said, "No," because I know he was out there. You don't know when he would come and he might have killed me. And I had my kids with me. I didn't know what he was doing. . . .

I kind of stayed away from his parents a while. I just didn't want to have anything to do with their family. I wanted to . . . start my life over again. My mom would be there to watch the kids after work and while I'd go to work she'd help me put them in a day care and paid half of the day care 'til I could get subsidized child care.

And I finally . . . started my papers for my divorce. . . . He had to come to Family Court. I was surprised he did come. . . . I was telling the judge, "I feel if he's going to do any better he needs to do it on his own. I can't go any further. I can't do anything for him any more. . . ." And I'm thinking, "Well, if I really leave him maybe this will straighten him up." [But] he even went a lot further with me leaving him; he just went deeper. . . .

He might have gone deeper anyway, but he would come and throw rocks at my window, harass me a lot. . . . I'd be scared sometimes to come in from work, thinking he might be hiding somewhere, because I've seen him in bushes; I've seen him sitting up in trees; and I will call the police and by the time they get there—because if they ever catch him he's going to do time. . . . I was so scared. I didn't know what he would do because he would threaten me all the time, calling my job and threaten me. . . .

Linda was twenty-one years old, working full time with two babies who required a lot of attention when her marriage ended. She did not want to go out, but her girlfriends urged her to do things with them. For several months she "just didn't want to be bothered . . . it wasn't the time for me right then. I had to find myself first."

Gradually Linda started seeing friends, and she met Scott. "He would come by every so often and. . . . He really liked me, but I gave him a hard time because I wasn't ready for a relationship. I just wanted to be friends with somebody. . . . And he would come by and give me grocery money or 'You need help on your light bill?' He was really being helpful."

One day when Linda and Scott were coming out of her apartment, she saw Nicholas and ran back inside. Scott approached Nicholas, saying, "Look, don't you have a restraining order not to be over here?" Nicholas replied, "You're over at my wife's. I've seen you over there lots of times." Scott replied, "Well, you might see me over here a lot more. You've lost your chance. You have her and children in there that you don't do anything for. You don't even know how to care for your own self. You need to get your own self together. You've lost what you had. If I catch you back here again, the police is not going to need to do anything for you—I'm going to do it."

Linda feels that Nicholas's family contributed to his problems by denying that he was addicted to drugs: "You know when they started living up to he had a problem?—When he started robbing them! Coming in the house, they go on vacation, taking their TVs, taking their cars, selling them, then they seen what I was going through. Before then, they just couldn't see it. . . ."

The courts eventually allowed the children to visit their father as long as he lived with his parents. Linda says, "All these years I have become . . . stronger. I have the upper hand over him. He cannot look me in the eye. If I come over there to get those kids from his mom's house, he's running somewhere to the back. He won't just come forward and just look me in my eyes. He can't do it."

"Welfare Has Nothing to Offer but Discouragement to Me"

Linda's attitude and determination have helped her face her problems, raise four children, succeed at her career, and buy her home. She talks about this, saying:

A lot of [my] girlfriends had babies then—I mean, just sit back and wait for a welfare check. I just can't—oh, I can't do that. That's no money.

You can go to McDonald's and do something and make double that. Welfare has nothing to offer but discouragement to me. You can get out there and do filing entry level positions and hardly know nothing and make more than what welfare is going to give you. I think it's for lazy people . . . if you're going to sit there from month to month and settle for that. I couldn't do it.

Linda admires her mother for getting them out of the projects and into a house, and she wants even "more than that." She says that girls she grew up with think, "We're black, we can't move here or we can't move there or we can't afford this or we can't afford that, we can't do this and we can't. . . ." Linda believes:

Even at work, I started off as a CRT operator and through the years made it up to a manager, but that was my goal. [My friends] said, "You'll never be that because you're black. . . ." I tell them all the time, "It has nothing to do with the color of my skin. I know what I want and who's stopping me?" . . . I'm just not into this black and white thing. I don't use that to say I have to stay centrally located because I'm black and I can't afford anything better than that. . . . I don't think . . . I'm too good—I love my mom and she loves the Central area because it's close to everything . . . but I want to raise my kids to where they can go outside, ride their bikes in the street; these cars are not coming through here like crazy. I mean, [the kids] are free. . . . They're able to get out here and you don't have to—you look out on them, but you don't have to worry too much: "Is somebody going to come by and shoot their head off?"

When I was living in the Central area, it's just so much commotion for me. When it's dark here, that's all you hear is birds. . . . I was looking for an area that I could raise my kids in just an absolutely beautiful atmosphere. I've had a picture of things, to be able to let my kids really have a good life . . . and it's beautiful out here. I just absolutely love it.

Linda and Scott are buying their current small suburban home using a lease option plan with owner financing and only $7,000 down, which Linda's father loaned them. They are selling this home and have recently purchased a five-bedroom home in south Seattle with financial help from Marie. Linda knows that there is discrimination and she has learned to handle it in a certain way:

I'm going to speak my opinion. . . . I go into a grocery store with one of my girlfriends, and . . . we might be standing in line and . . . a white lady up at the cash register [will] go to the next person, which . . . well, we were in line first. To me, there's two ways to it—maybe she didn't even recognize we were there first; or maybe she could have been trying to be funny about the whole situation.

I guess I put it on their ignorance. I don't let it bother me: "When you get to me, you will, sooner or later. I'm standing here with your merchandise." I don't make a big scene about it—some black people will. . . . They're getting just as ignorant as [the whites] are. . . . It's not going to kill me to wait. . . . That stuff, that black and white, it doesn't bother me. I don't let that get next to me. . . .

I do what I have to do and I believe in God and if I'm supposed to get it, I will. If not, well, so be it. I don't make it "because . . . I was black." I don't even think that way because if that's the way you're thinking, you're going to have some hard problems in life because every situation come up, you're going to use that as a crutch. . . . And maybe that's not the issue. Maybe you weren't qualified or maybe you weren't first in line.

When Linda's company was bought out she received a good severance package and she is eagerly looking for another job, taking advantage of outplacement counseling and career fairs. She is a trained CRT (computer) operator, but the entire family still worries over the loss of her job. Linda is anxious to find another job, in part because work is her "therapy." It keeps her "out of the house and away from worrying about my four children." Shortly after this interview, Linda was hired to help welfare recipients and the unemployed find work. She started with part-time work but quickly progressed to full time and was soon supervising other workers.

Family: His, Mine, and Ours

Linda has a safety net of family support, demonstrated by the hands-on, immediate help she received from Marie when she left Nicholas. But she has a much broader web of support that extends as her family grows. Linda and her mother both discuss the importance of extended family in Linda's upcoming marriage to Scott. Marie says, "Oh, he come from a lovely family. His grandfather's a minister. [Linda] has support. His grandmother helped to babysit. . . . She would keep the kids, go to their house every morning, be there. And his mother—she do for one, she do for all of them. So she's in a good family as far as having the support and helping her." Linda adds:

> I see us getting married and having a really nice life together. He's a lot different [from Nicholas] and his family support is a little different. . . . His parents—they don't take no time jumping on him if he's wrong on anything. I mean, they're not afraid to say "you're wrong" to him; where Nicholas's family tend to cover up for him a lot. . . . Scott comes from a smaller family—it's just him and his brother, so I tend to think they got more attention just with the two of them. . . .
>
> He helps a lot with the kids and he's been there when they were a lot younger. And that was another thing I was scared about—I have two special-needs kids . . . how would that man accept those problems? I had a real hard time and that kind of kept me from dating. . . . But he come along, he's very supportive. He goes to the doctor's appointments with me; tells them when they're wrong and they're right. . . . His family is very supportive of Natalie and Charmian, also. I mean, birthdays, Christmas, they get just as much as Angela and Simon. . . . So it helps a lot to make things run . . . smoother.

Scott's ability to father the four children and the support of his extended family are seen as positive predictors of a happy marriage by both Linda and her family. Scott is not seen in isolation from his family, but rather Linda sees that she is marrying into a small community. Stack (1974) points out that mothers often actively incorporate their children's father's kin, thus "consciously expanding the number of people who are intimately obligated to care for one another" (29). Linda's mother, Nicholas's mother, Nicholas's new wife, and Scott's mother and grandmother all act as "othermothers" to Linda's children. These five women, along with Linda, Scott, Nicholas, aunts, uncles, grandparents, and cousins, provide a rich environment for the children.

In addition to having a strong family background, Scott is a "working man." With a degree in electronics, he is employed at an import warehouse as a lead machinery operator. He attends school at night and wants to start his own import design store.

Although Linda has a good relationship with Scott, she does not necessarily see him as the "head" of the family:

The Bible does say men should be in charge, but [times] are not like that. I mean, there's a slim—I know if you did a count on how many men are really in charge, it would be very few, because women is what's really making and keeping things going. I even say with my own situation. . . . Scott does his responsibilities and he knows what he has to do, but I'm still the stronger one. I really feel that.

And there's not too many people I know that the man is really running the house. I don't think I could sit home every day and think Scott is going to be able to take care of me and my kids. There's no way he could do that. . . . Economy is so weird . . . there's no way one man can get out there with what they're paying and take care of a family. They can't do it. So it seems kind of confusing to me at times with what they talk in church and . . . what you're really facing day to day.

In addition to a solid family network, Linda, like her aunts, grandmother, and mother, frequently turns to the Lord, to prayer, and to the church family for help. She is confident that the Lord hears her prayers and has conversations with Him in her everyday life. When she has serious problems, she talks to her family, but she also asks Reverend Kent to pray for her and accepts guidance and counseling from Sister Kent.

Like Linda, Scott was raised in church, his grandfather being a pastor at a Baptist church. Linda and Scott are not yet regular church members, but Linda says, "I know what's right from wrong. I can read my own Bible and learn what I need to learn about the Lord. I still love . . . and know . . . the Lord. . . . Just because I'm not in church every Sunday, the Lord is still a part of my life. I go to bed praying, I pray all through the day, I wake up in the morning, thank God. . . . I live a Christian life. . . ."

"I Will Always Be There for My Kids Anytime"

Raising four children, especially two with special needs, has been a constant challenge for Linda that began when she was eighteen years old. She loves her children passionately and tries hard to protect them and make their lives better. Linda works closely with the public schools so that Natalie and Charmian can have the best education possible, saying:

Natalie and Charmian is mild, they're functional children. I had a fight with the school board about this when they wanted to put them in severe classes. I will not allow that to happen to my kids. That, to me, is holding them back. They're not learning anything but to mimic those other children that's sitting there doing things—they're not functional. . . . That's my only thing with special education in the Seattle School District because they're starting to want to do that. Every year you have to go and fight about that because they're low in funding and so they figure they'll just put all the special ed children in together when that's not going to help them.

Natalie and Charmian are in Special Olympics, and Natalie does well in track. Natalie is in middle school and taking two regular classes along with her special education classes. Charmian is in a special school and has a speech therapist. Both girls go to after-school day care with a teacher who has been trained to work with special-needs children. She helps Natalie with her homework and gives her "helping type of things to do—helping with the kids, teaching her how to clean, letting her wash the dishes." About Charmian, Linda says:

Charmian's the best one I have that will clean her room, clean house so well. Charmian's the one, when something has to be done, it has to be completely done right or she gets very frustrated with herself.

Basically all they [at the Birth Defects Clinic] could tell me now is just work with them, do the best you can, hopefully they can do the best they can do in life. They might not ever be the smartest kids, but they should be able to live on their own, depending on what type of environment they're around. . . .

Natalie, she seems like she's catching up a little bit more quicker than Charmian is. Because Natalie, she's just like any normal twelve-year-old child to me in a lot of ways. In her learning abilities she's slower, but for every day-to-day living-wise, she's just like a normal twelve-year-old child. That's what confuses me a lot. . . . I mean, I can see it coming now—she started on her menstruation already and she knows what to do with that. . . . She's not really interested in boys right now, so I don't have to worry about it yet. She's still into Barbie dolls and that kind of stuff. . . . She's pretty developed for her age. And I worry about that. I can't protect her always but I can tell her the facts so she'll know. But she has health in school . . . and they talk about it a lot there also . . . and my mom, she counsels her. . . .

And it's just really weird to me, with going through all the evaluations. I didn't think she could ever reach that point. They said she won't be able to do this, she won't be able to do that, and she's doing them. It makes me feel real good . . . it just goes to show you, you just don't know. I pray real hard about them and I know their grandparents does, too. And as far as me, I think that's what helped me to be a lot more stronger, also. I want to have the best for them. I mean, I want to have the best for all of my kids, but with them two being labeled as special-needs children, I want to really have the best for them. . . . I worr[ied] about when they were younger—setting a path to where it would just be a clean shot for them; but I'm not going to be able to do that. . . .

At the beginning of the school year they had called me because two girls had tried to take [Natalie's] lunch money, and . . . she wasn't going to let them have it. I mean, she was fighting both of them . . . they weren't going to get her money. And when I got there she was really upset and shaking and she says, "They tried to take my money. . . . I'm not giving them my money." The teachers [were] real proud of her, too.

But these are the type of things I worry about. . . . I'm wondering how can I protect her? But a lot of her counselors says, "You don't need to worry about Natalie, she's going to be able to protect herself." She doesn't let anybody run over her. If she knows it's not right to do, she's not going to let them do it. Anything that happened to them two, I'm really jumping on it quick because of the fact they're special-needs kids.

Linda's two youngest children, Angela and Simon, are healthy children, but both of Linda's pregnancies were "high risk" with difficult births. Linda was severely toxemic with Angela and experienced bleeding problems with Simon due to a placenta previa. She had to be hospitalized five times before Simon was born by cesarean section.

Today Angela is a precocious four-year-old and Simon is an active toddler. Linda works continually with them during her interview, listening, settling arguments, correcting them softly, chastising them sharply when she perceives danger, making them snacks and lunch. Once in a while she threatens to send Angela to her room to "think about it." When she asks them to do something, she always speaks gently and finishes with "thank you." As Linda talks, she works on Angela's hair, saying, "Oh, your hair looks bad! You look like you're crazy. . . . Angela, bring me a comb and brush and I'll just put a ponytail. You can't go out there looking like that!" As Angela sits patiently on Linda's lap at the kitchen table, Linda begins

CHAPTER ELEVEN

the steady tug, tug, pull, dressing Angela's hair with Pro-line Hair Food, and putting the little girl's hair into small plaits fastened with multicolored clips.

At this time in her life, Linda concentrates on how to best help her children lead strong, happy lives:

> I need to educate them, be there for them . . . live by example a lot—your kids, when they're growing up, [they] look at their parents and how they live and that kind of sets them on a track on how they're gonna live—I see my mom is a strong person and that's the way I felt—real strong, and saying, "I want to be like that." Letting them know . . ."this is the real world" and what's in it and what you have to do to deal with it. I will always be there for my kids, anytime. That's why I really want a big, big house, in case they ever have to come back home.

In the future Linda wants the same relationship with her children that she has with her mother. She sees that Angela will have a special role in the family — the continuation of the caretaker role that Linda and her mother have had.

> They want to put her [Angela] in a gifted school next year because . . . she's a very bright, observant child. I mean, she's really smart and she might need to be there for her sisters. I say, "Maybe the Lord sent me something like that to help me with the responsibility—to help out with her sisters." So maybe it just worked out that way. Because my mom didn't really want me to have other kids. . . . She was very worried what was going to happen then, too. But I wanted to take that chance, too, because I might need her and Simon to help out with their sisters. You just don't know. . . . I don't want them alone. . . .

Part Three
THE RESEARCH PROCESS

CHAPTER TWELVE
THE RESEARCH, THE WOMEN, AND ME

Beginnings

The first day of my research project was a gray Sunday morning in February. Driving to Morning Sun Church, I passed south of the Montlake Cut on 23rd Avenue. As I went deeper into the Central District I gradually began to see more black than white people on the street. At a busy intersection, an old black man was selling newspapers to motorists and pedestrians. There were several men standing with him, casually dressed, visiting on a Sunday morning, and I locked my car doors. I recognized this as a racist reaction, and I was not proud of myself. But I was worried about driving through the Central District—my perception was that it was not a safe part of town.

As I drove, I was nervous about being accepted in a black church. How would I fit in? I knew that the women dressed up for Sunday, but I did not want to overdo and look too well off. I finally chose a nice dress and high heels, but covered the dress with a casual sweater instead of my red wool coat. I selected earrings that my older daughter had made for me and took off my mother's diamond wedding ring. I tried to be early, but not too early, and parked around the corner for ten minutes before entering so as not to appear too eager.

Learning to Follow

This section is about my growth and development in the process of doing this research study. I originally wanted to understand more about African American women, health, and health care. In health-care research, black women, particularly poor and working-class women, are routinely represented as having poor health statistics. As a nurse, I was appalled at the statistics, particularly the pregnancy complication and infant mortality rates, but accepted them as factual. However, I was puzzled by the usual reasons given to explain the data—high-risk behaviors such as smoking, drinking, drugs, adolescent motherhood, poor nutrition, poor prenatal care, and so on. The focus was always on how black women contributed to their own and their children's health problems.

I recognized this "blaming the victim" attitude, and I questioned it as I started my research. I believed that the women from Morning Sun Church had probably come to some questions and conclusions of their own, and I wanted to hear what they had to say. Nevertheless, it was hard for me to get around my educational socialization, and I quickly discovered that my "routine" questions created brick walls over and over again as I asked them about health issues. My basic and most inaccurate assumption was that the women saw themselves as I had been trained to see them and as they were presented in the dominant discourse—as an at-risk and vulnerable group. Through trial and error and much painful experience, it gradually became apparent to me that this assumption was puzzling and insulting to the women, as well as subtly, blatantly, and pervasively racist. The women clearly and adamantly rejected the scientific and cultural stereotyping and the racial and gender objectification of African American women seen in the majority of research studies. Framing their lives within "poor health status" was not relevant to their worldview or to how they defined themselves (Abrums 2000b).

I do not claim to have completely or even partially overcome the problems that are inherent in research done by a member of the dominant social group who studies with poor people of color. All I can say is that the women led me in a particular direction, and I had to follow them to learn what they wanted me to learn. I tried to leave my assumptions behind and step away from the dominant ideology, and I started to pay close attention to the women's experiences and stories, as well as to the meticulous details of the everyday. It was only then that I began to move into the space that they wanted me to occupy in order to better hear and portray their life histories. It was only then that I began to look beyond the stereotypes and statistics and see how the women understood and influenced the world around them.

In our conversations, the women were willing to discuss their personal health, but more often, they wanted to talk about other interests: gospel music, spirituality, men, work, discrimination, teaching, family, cooking dinner, motherhood, loving Jesus, and surviving. It took me a while to learn that this *meant* something.

Later, when I asked the women to review their stories, they told me that what I had written was "just fine," "funny," "all right," and that they did not want to change anything. To me, these comments meant that I had presented, at least in part, the stories that they wanted to be told.

A Question of Entry

As in Stack's (1974) landmark study of poor black women, I believed that the question of how to enter the research setting was an important one. I wanted to join a small group in an environment where the women were comfortably at home and traditionally "held the cards" and I did not—I wanted to be where the women held the power. I also wanted a setting where I had some level of familiarity and where I felt safe. I recognized that this issue of safety was based on stereotypes I held, but I could not entirely get around the fact that the Central District had a high crime rate. When the opportunity arose to visit a small storefront church where another nurse anthropologist had studied, I seized the chance.

In retrospect, my reasoning was sound from a "power" perspective. I consistently felt that the church members had the power in our relationship. They could choose to reject or accept me as they wished, and they did so. The women were not dependent on me for social services or good health care or kindness to their children in a school setting. They did not have to invite me into their homes, nor did they have to agree to be interviewed (and several refused). All they had to do was tolerate my presence in church and be courteous to me between services. While I gradually developed relationships with some of the women, they were not under any pressure or obligation to forge these friendships.

There were drawbacks to this setting as well. As women meeting in church, we had certain roles to fulfill. No matter how they truly felt about me or I about them, we generally were on our best behavior with one another. Charity, tolerance, kindness, and courtesy were the order of the day. This role of "Christian women" might have precluded some measure of our truly knowing one another. For instance, one woman hesitated to tell me that she loved to play the horses. If the women partied, I never knew about it (and maybe they didn't). But being in a setting that essentially demanded thoughtfulness was good for all of us as we tried to get to know one another, especially because fears, stereotypes, and prior negative experiences all played a part in our interactions.

Fears and Stereotypes

Unlearning racism or becoming anti-racist was a process of "two steps forward, one step back" for me during the entire research experience. I found that I grappled with the racism within myself as much as I did with the societal racism that affected the lives of the women of Morning Sun (Abrums 2000c). This struggle and resulting growth will undoubtedly continue all my life. There has been progress: I now recognize many of the hidden dimensions of racism and I "own" what Sister Kent taught me—that we are all "unique" and yet are "all of one blood." I will never be able to see, feel, or hear the world as the women of Morning Sun do, but I have come a little bit closer to their angle of vision.

This process of learning a new way to see the world required constant and vigilant monitoring of my words, thoughts, and questions. For example, I felt reassured and safe when I saw a police car in my neighborhood. But the women of Morning Sun were nervous around police officers: if there was an incident on the street, they sympathized with the person in trouble; if they saw a problem at night outside their homes, they did not call the police because they feared someone might get hurt. Reverend Kent often said that police had a hard job and that "there are some good ones," but the underlying and occasionally spoken feeling in the church was that police were "mean." When I drove into the Central District on a Friday or Saturday night to pick up a church member, I was shocked at the differences between the CD and my north-end white middle-class neighborhood. Police cars were on every other block, and black adolescent girls and boys were spread-eagled against police cars by ten p.m. I began to understand that the CD was more dangerous than my neighborhood, especially for teenagers. But the danger came from both criminal activity and the ever-watchful surveillance of the police.

I worried that racist thinking motivated me to lock my car doors as I drove into the Central District, but the women of Morning Sun consistently locked their own car doors and locked me in when I dropped them off at home. Safety was an issue for all of us; and they had a realistic assessment of the dangers of in living in a poor neighborhood.

I also found that the churchwomen saw danger where I did not. I felt uneasy when I saw groups of young black men, and they were anxious when they saw groups of young white men, whether they were "skinheads" or athletes playing basketball. As we drove through white business districts near the university or on Broadway, they carefully checked their car doors and stared straight ahead. We often made different decisions about who and what situations were safe or unsafe; and these judgments related to our personal stereotypes, experiences, and histories.

Stereotypical and racist thinking clouded my view in other ways. One time when I was driving downtown with several of the women, I spotted a row of six white men and women in their twenties, sitting on the sidewalk, obviously homeless or traveling, looking grubby but healthy with sleeping bags and backpacks. An old black man walked by and reached into his pocket to give each young person some money. His passing kindness startled me. The whole picture was out of focus; and I was ashamed that I had trouble accepting this image.

I found that I was often distinctly uncomfortable as the only white woman in a black church, especially when the church overflowed and yet no one joined me in my empty pew. I became exhausted from going week after week into a community where I was unsure of my place and my welcome—even though the churchwomen were friendly and tried to include me. I had to take breaks from the strain of facing a black world and from constantly watching my thoughts, words, and actions. From these stressful, albeit illuminating, experiences, I learned how the many small discriminatory actions that black people face daily at work and school create the constant stress that causes serious health problems.

Gathering Data

The research study began in the early 1990s and took eighteen months to complete. I have remained in close contact with some of the women; however, the data in *Moving the Rock* represents only the experiences and conversations that occurred during the official research period. I began my research initially by meeting with Missionary Mahalia Lake, the church member responsible for outreach activities. She and I agreed on three approaches: I would explain my study to and obtain permission from the pastor of the church, meet with Missionary Lake every week to discuss church-related questions, and attend Morning Sun Church "to watch and see."

When I told Missionary Lake that I would like to interview church members, she said, "We'll see about that. We're a small church." So I patiently pursued traditional ethnographic methods, hoping that once the women knew me better, they would agree to do life history interviews. Meanwhile, I found that using participant-observation methods at church generated rich data as Reverend Kent interpreted life experiences and gave his congregation "rules to live by" from the Bible. The music and songs offered concrete lessons about how to make it in this world and eventually enter heaven.

Each week before church services I attended Sunday school with several of the older women and learned how they applied the church lessons in their daily lives. In between the morning and the afternoon Sunday services I joined the women for lunch and informal conversations. I often participated in additional services with neighboring congregations on Friday evenings or Sunday afternoons when Morning Sun members were invited to "fellowship." Outside of church I visited with Missionary Lake on a weekly basis at the housing project office, in her home, or out on errands. Gradually I became more involved with additional members of the Lake family. We did errands and ate out and went to doctor's appointments. I provided the transportation and sometimes lunch; and in exchange they tolerated my barrage of questions, sometimes willingly, sometimes impatiently.

The Interviews

In addition to using participant-observations methods, I interviewed eight of the women to learn their life histories. I spent fifteen months in the church prior to being granted the majority of the interviews that took place in the final three months of the study. In structuring the life history interviews I hoped to use a collaborative approach, so I asked Sister Kent and Missionary Lake to help me formulate the questions. But they said that it was my project, not theirs, and that I was the one who wanted "to know," so I should just ask what I wanted to know.

At last Sister Kent endorsed my credibility and "good heart" and encouraged some of the women to participate in the interviews. I finalized my questions and scheduled lunch and an interview at my home with Mahalia Lake. Mahalia dressed up and brought her photo album. She seemed to enjoy lunch, but the interview process was tense and uncomfortable. I learned quickly from this interview that I needed to let go of any ideas I had about controlling the interaction. I left my questions and all ideas about chronological order behind, and I let the women choose the meeting place—this was always in the women's homes with the exception of Betty Jones, who asked to meet at her daughter Joann's house.

At the beginning of each interview, I simply told the woman that I was trying to understand more about black women and that I wanted to hear her life story as if she were writing it herself. I told her that she could start anywhere that she wanted. I assured her of anonymity and told her that she could change or delete any part of the story. Each woman chose her own name for her life history. Using Minister's (1991) method, I referred to a single sheet of paper that highlighted topics of interest (see the interview tool in figure 1). All the interviews were taped and professionally transcribed. They lasted anywhere from two to six hours over the course of two days. During each interview, I acted as a "witness" to the woman's testimony through honest response, expressions of empathy, and laughter, and by sharing my own experiences, beliefs, and values. I never left behind the idea of "making meeting," and I always took a gift of food, sometimes lunch, but more often snacks of cookies and fruit for the children (Banks-Wallace and Saran 1992).

With these approaches to the interviews, the process was successful and enjoyable for all of us. The stories were told through conversations

Tell the story as if you were writing the story of your life

History of family   Development as a woman

                        Life as a child, young-middle-older adult

            Spirituality

Birth
Illness   Health
        Feeling bad   Feeling good
                        Hard times
        Racism   Death

Experiences with
medical care   Who helps you?
                How do you manage?
                                        Prayer

Basics: age, education, job history, number of siblings, children

Adapted from: Minister, Kristina. 1991. A feminist frame for the oral history interview. In *Women's words: The feminist practice of oral history*, ed. Sherna Berger and Daphne Patai, 27–41. New York: Routledge.

Figure 1. Interview Guide

about context, historical forces, opinions, beliefs, and spiritual searches. In short, they were dialogues of meaning.

Forging Relationships

During the interview process, I found that my own stereotypes sometimes got in the way of accuracy. For example, I misheard Marie Jones Smith when she told me that she was nineteen when she had her first baby, and I noted that she was seventeen. When I listened to the interview tape I realized my error. I became wary of the subjective influence of my preconceived ideas on the research data. If this error occurred in my interview with Marie, a clear-speaking, well-educated woman, how many more errors did I make when class and education, as well as race, were barriers? I learned to strongly value tape recorders and meticulous transcription.

Sometimes the women seemed evasive or guarded about their information, and at first this frustrated me. Things were left unsaid, and the women focused on the positive parts of their lives and on how they overcame challenges. I finally realized that each woman deserved the right to share her history, her memories, in the way that she saw fit. In trying to ferret out information that was not readily offered, I was often looking for content that fit my preconceptions. I learned to critique my questions and examine how I had led the interview. I learned that privacy was a valued space that I needed to respect.

Forging relationships, both during the interviews and in everyday life, took time and persistence. I had always depended on my ability to read people, accommodating my style accordingly to help smooth the rough edges of an encounter, but I found that I could not judge my interactions with the women accurately—I was at a loss as I tried to understand them and how to fit into their world.

I had originally wanted to model my research relationships on Stack's (1974) work, but I found I could not do this. I learned that I had to be myself. Unlike Stack, I was not willing to give up the convenience of my car and found it was more of an asset than a liability in that I traded transportation for the women's time and stories about themselves.

Marie Jones Smith, Joann Jones Newton, and I were similar ages and closer in terms of social class and educational level than were the other participants. These were important variables that helped overcome some racial barriers. I was comfortable visiting their homes, and they were comfortable having me. Mutual concerns about our children's health, safety, and education were commonalities that allowed us to communicate on many levels. Mable Jackson loved entertaining me in her home. In spite of the poverty of her surroundings, she always made each visit an occasion by dressing up and graciously welcoming me into her life.

In contrast, my most successful encounters with the Lakes were on "neutral territory." We went to their usual stores and fast-food restaurants, to church, and to health clinics; and we took field trips to places that Mahalia selected. In these settings I did not have to struggle with the poverty of their homes, and they (and I) did not have to be reminded of the privilege in my world.

My relationship with the Lake family was a complicated one. Over the months Molly and I became friends, but it was an unequal friendship because of the differences in our resources. Although Molly and I were close and her children sat with me at church, we did not trade child-care arrangements as did Stack (1974) and the women in her study. My children were older than Stack's were at the time of the study; they recognized and felt uncomfortable with the abject poverty of the project apartments, and I did not leave them there for any extended period of time.

I was frustrated with my inability to develop more trusting relationships with the Lakes, especially with Mahalia, but it was hard to gain the intimacy I hoped for. The Lakes knew and I knew that I could escape from their world into my nice house, safe neighborhood, healthy children, and employed husband; and they had no such escape. As much as I wanted to be a part of their lives, their intimacy was based on shared problems and mutual need as well as on love, affection, and trust. I was not, nor could I ever be, part of that context. I felt compassion for them and admiration for their pride and ability to sustain. I learned that it takes courage to face the lives they lead every single day. Courage just to keep going is an important virtue, and it is one that Molly and Mahalia have and that Caren is rapidly learning. I admire them for this, but I do not want to go through what they have had to go through in order to have it. I am not trying to idealize them—the women are simply doing what they need to do. In the eyes of the church community, Mahalia and Molly are neither better nor worse off than any other members. They are poorer, but they are required and expected to do their best.

I struggled and still struggle with the idea that when someone enters your field of vision, you have an obligation. However, each time I left Molly and Mahalia's homes, I "counted my blessings." And when I finished my fieldwork, I felt a sense of relief that I no longer had to face their pain and my own ambivalence about how involved I wanted to be with that pain on a daily basis. It was only later that I was able to try again.

On Social Context

My relationship with each woman taught me something important about the meaning of being black and/or a black woman in our society. From the Lake family members, the poorest women in the congregation, I learned the most about the confluence of class, gender, and race. Unlike the Jones family with inherited property and Mable Jackson with a working husband, the Lakes never had a break in any way. The Jones family could trace property and family through several generations, but the Lakes' knowledge of previous generations was sketchy, a legacy from slavery in some black families. In addition, for the past three generations, the Lakes were female-headed households. Although husbands, partners, and brothers/sons lived with and supported the women and children emotionally and even financially when they could, the lack of steadily employed men was a serious problem for the Lakes. With barely enough for day-to-day survival, family members were unable to accumulate any money for savings or a safety net.

In spite of these challenges, with each generation, Lake family members obtained a little more education—Mahalia's mother finished sixth grade, Mahalia finished tenth, Molly and her brothers earned their GEDs, and Roberta was the first in all the generations to graduate from high school. The Lake women were intelligent and articulate, but their educational history was variable: Mahalia, raised in the South and in Chicago, read and wrote fluently; but Molly, educated in Seattle public schools, struggled with these skills and could barely do math. Her daughter Roberta labored over English and language courses when she began to attend community college.

Because of their poverty the Lakes faced ongoing health problems related to stress, poor nutrition, and possibly environmental exposure. Molly had two miscarriages, a stillborn baby, and another baby born with leukemia, and her daughter Shani had a kidney problem. Mahalia cared for her grandson, who had behavior problems probably related to prenatal drug and alcohol exposure. Molly had asthma and hypertension, and Mahalia was prediabetic and also had hypertension. Caren suffered placenta previa with one of her births. These health problems took a continual toll on the entire family unit, depleting emotional resources and physical energy that might have been used to improve life for the family as a whole.

Giving Gifts

There were difficulties in maintaining equality in relationships given the vast discrepancies in resources between the women and myself, and I grappled with the idea of gift giving or of paying the women for their help with my research project. I often questioned my own intentions—did I give them gifts or food in the hope of manipulating further revelations, or were these gifts freely given? When they confided in me, was this a "payback" on their part for perceived favors from me, or was this information generously shared? Probably all were true to some extent. In anthropological research, giving gifts for knowledge is a legitimate form of exchange, but I never felt right about it. I wondered whether it destroyed honest exchange from the outset.

However, in spite of my misgivings, gradually a pattern emerged. I provided transportation for the women's errands, and they answered questions during the drive. I often bought meals and gifts for the women who were struggling. In time they came to expect this system of payment; but we also became closer, and gifts and lunches were part of sharing friendship as well. Although I wanted our friendships to be equal, I never allowed the women to pay for me because I knew that they did not have the resources. They gave me small gifts when they could and sent cards and thank-you notes when I did something for them. The women were not hesitant to let me know if I transgressed privacy boundaries; and thus, if I was manipulating them (which I'm not sure I was), it did not work very well. In fact, I often felt quite powerless.

Although Mable Jackson and the Lakes welcomed gifts and lunches, the Jones family members were clear that they would be insulted if I paid for their help in any way. When I interviewed them I brought snacks so that we could have something to eat while we visited or so that the family could eat while they waited for a delayed meal. I drew up a formal kinship chart for the Jones family for Betty's birthday, and the family happily accepted it and had the chart framed for Betty.

Gift giving probably had a different meaning to each of us due to differences in social class. Molly seemed to accept this exchange system of sharing information for small resources most easily. She talked freely to me about her beliefs and her life, and she took advantage of the meals, my babysitting offers, the gifts, and the handed-down clothes for her children. At times her mother, Mahalia, or Sister Kent chastised her for "using" me. But Molly was pragmatic and, unlike her mother and Sister Kent, she did not feel she could afford to refuse favors, especially when she needed things for her children. She often stated, "You're here, and I need, and you have."

Writing

I had one primary rule that I tried to follow in my writing. This rule was taped above my desk: "Write this story for the people at Morning Sun Church to read and you won't have any trouble." Thus, I tried to write so that all readers could readily understand and use the material. In addition, as I wrote the women's stories, I tried to maintain the primacy of the women as subjects and agents. I kept in mind that whatever I wrote could be used for political purposes, both to help black women and to harm them. Thus, I attempted to examine my words from every possible angle to see whether they might be used to support efforts for liberation or employed to maintain oppression. In the end I was not sure that I had any control over how a reader might choose to interpret and use this content.

In writing the women's stories and my interpretations, I tried to keep judgment out of the discussion. Hancock (1989) has suggested that continually asking the question "How?" instead of "Why?" assists this process. Knowing that the stories were to be returned to the women for reading helped in this regard—I never wanted to say anything that might hurt someone.

Other minor issues of writing style needed to be resolved in the presentation of this research. I have used the term *black* interchangeably with *African American* because *black* was the preferred term of the people of Morning Sun Church. In the research literature, *black* has been alternately capitalized and not capitalized, depending on the writer, and I have not used capitals for any terms referring to specific groups unless they are proper names.

Interpretation and Analysis

I began my analysis by studying the women's life stories to firmly orient my interpretation in the women's voices. Their spoken life histories were not neat and tidy stories: they flowed quickly between past and present and future and back again. Scattered throughout the women's stories were the theories, principles, or belief systems by which they lived their lives.

In presenting these life histories I tried to refrain from discussing and analyzing material, preferring as much as possible to let the women speak for themselves. In general I organized each woman's story into a readable form, and I sometimes summarized lengthy episodes without sacrificing essential content. In addition to the interviews, some of the story content evolved from my written records of day-to-day interactions with the women. Each woman read and approved her story.

Interviewing members of the same family at different stages in their lives vastly enriched the stories. It became possible to see how beliefs and values were passed from generation to generation through historical, environmental, and social changes. Different vantage points regarding the same experiences lent depth to particular stories and demonstrated how family members developed separately and together, and how they influenced one another's growth.

A World of Contrast

Moving between my world and theirs on a daily basis forced me to continually juxtapose the two, comparing and contrasting. However, I found that the most traumatic times of encounter occurred not in the black world of the women of Morning Sun, but in my own white world. In my relationships with the women, I struggled to build a bridge, and in the meantime I was suspended over a chasm. I was surprised and angry to find that I was no longer comfortable and sure of finding a landing place in my own world. hooks (2004) notes:

> The meaning of "home" changes with . . . radicalization. At times, home is nowhere. . . . Home is that place which enables and promotes varied and ever changing perspectives, a place where one discovers new ways of seeing reality . . . reveals where we are, who we can become, an order that does not demand forgetting. (155)

It took me some time after completing the research to redefine and reclaim the meaning of "home," but several years later I move easily between both worlds. I am very cognizant of the fact that sadly, there are two separate worlds—one for poor women/people of color and one for primarily white middle-class people. The churchwomen, other women of color, and some white professors in academia are allies as I continue to work on these issues through my teaching and writing.

Social and health statistics and the women's stories help students to understand both the macro picture and the everyday impact of poverty. Stories especially help students to see the unique individuals who share some, but not all, experiences related to race, class, and gender. Each portrait removes a brick in the wall of stereotypes and generalizations, and learners begin to understand the extraordinary depth and breadth of the wall. As students grapple with questions of difference and sameness, they find hope in the promise of these words—"We are all of one blood." Some students take this promise to heart, become motivated to help others to understand what they have learned, and begin to tackle the problems of oppression in their personal and health-care work environments. In this and in other small ways, I know that I am "moving the rock."

There is one more important lesson that I learned from the members of Morning Sun Church. It would be an injustice to them and to myself if I failed to mention it. From the churchmen and women, I learned how to pray.

RESEARCH QUESTION, THEORIES, AND METHODS

The research study for *Moving the Rock* took place with African American women who live across town from me in Seattle, Washington. It is only twenty to thirty minutes by car from my house in Northeast Seattle by the University of Washington to their homes and church in the Central District, but the distance between us is relative and relates to poverty and race. Sometimes it is much greater than the seven miles; sometimes there is no distance at all.

It was not the job of the participants to instruct me in the complexity of the social world that we all inhabit, and prior to beginning my research I tried to learn everything that I could about how the intersection of race, class, and gender creates oppression. I studied the history and social conditions of poor people of color; obtained a solid knowledge foundation in social justice, oppression, and resistance theories; and immersed myself in the stories and experiences of black people through works of literature, poetry, and nonfiction.

However, for the churchwomen in this book, experience represents the difference between intelligence and education. Although they respected education, they felt that it was meaningless without the intelligence gained through experience (Abrums 2000b). Similarly, Collins (1991) notes that "book learning" without experience can create an "educated fool" without the "mother wit" a person needs to make his or her way in the world (190). In the black community, experience is a necessary "criterion for credibility" (Collins 2000, 257).

Although I possessed "book learning" and clinical knowledge from working with black clients in health care, I lacked experience with the "everyday" of the black community. As I drove those seven miles over and over again during the eighteen months of my research, I wondered many times—would the women ever willingly share their perspectives with me? And, even more importantly, if they did, would I truly listen and understand?

These critical questions were gradually answered over time and with patience and persistence on all our parts. The research process also required dedication and follow-up. Many studies with oppressed groups have been used (or misused) in harmful ways and/or have gone nowhere. But people who agree to participate in research deserve to see how their valuable time and energy will make things better for themselves and for others.

As I gained experience, I learned to be flexible in adapting to the women's wisdom and insights. In addition to this hard-earned knowledge, I found that "book learning" was invaluable in laying the groundwork for the project. In the following sections, I discuss the evolution of the research question and the theories and methods that supported the research process.

What Was the Question Anyway?

As a nurse and an anthropologist, I was initially interested in doing ethnographic research to learn more about African American women, racism, and meaning systems related to health and health care. I was familiar with the statistics and stereotypes about African American women's health, and I wanted to learn the women's points of view. As a nurse, I knew what good health and health care looked like, and I was sensitive to its absence—and it *was* absent. Elsewhere I have written about the women's health and how they made meaning from their experiences. This work is not reiterated in *Moving the Rock*, but interested readers are referred to prior analyses (Abrums 1995, 2000a, 2000b, 2004).

When I began the research, I found that every time I asked the women about their health, they wanted to talk about gospel music or their families or everyday life. It took me awhile to "get it," but finally I realized that this *meant* something. Thus the question changed over the course of the fieldwork. I did learn about meanings and health, but my deepest learning came from the realization that health could not be taken out of context. Therefore, I learned about the complex tapestry of the women's lives, including the accompanying values and beliefs that helped them create meaning. It was only when I stopped selectively listening for health-related information that I could hear what the women thought it was important for me to learn. I spent many months doing what they advised me to do—mostly going to Morning Sun Church, visiting their homes, and running errands with them.

Observing the women's experiences gave me the broad context that eventually helped me to adapt my original research question. My first interview instrument contained about thirty specific health-related questions. By the time I was finally granted interviews, I had developed a more flexible tool with a few open-ended questions that encouraged the women to guide the interview process. The interview included statements and questions such as, "Tell me about your life. How do you cope? What makes you feel good/bad?" (refer to figure 1 in chapter 12, p. 172). It was only after changing my interview approach that I was able to move into the space where they wanted me to go, the space where they lived out their lives.

In the women's interviews, they spoke about experiences that supported my observations when I was with them: they experienced discrimination in grocery stores, when driving or riding on the bus, when applying for jobs or home loans, when going to the clinic, when asking to use the restroom, when advocating for their children at school, and so on. Some stories highlighted individual acts of discrimination; some told of systems-level or institutional barriers. The particularities of these experiences have been described in *Moving the Rock* so that readers can see the patterns of daily discrimination and oppressive circumstances that the women faced. Other story vignettes illustrated how family and friends supported them and brought joy to their lives. On a daily basis and in the interviews, the women emphasized the importance of their religious faith—how it helped them find meaning and gave them the resilience to cope with the challenges they faced.

Theory

The research question changed because the women took me where they wanted me to go, but I also knew I had to follow. I found I had to live out the philosophies that provided the original groundwork for the research study. (Surprise, surprise—the academic knowledge and theories needed to be applied!) Three interrelated theories/perspectives grounded this study and its specific approaches: feminist and black feminist theories and critical reflexive feminist anthropological theory/method. These theories all lent support to an essential component of this project—the relationships between the women and myself. Feminist theory states that the research relationship is an equal one between two subjects engaged in the process. Participants are not objects of study, but actively influence both the research process and their world. Black feminist theory notes that black women value the "self in relationship" and that a dialogical relationship means to "give witness" to another's testimony (hooks 2004, 158). Critical reflexive feminist anthropology recognizes that the researcher brings a subjective self to the research encounter and is part of the story. Thus the researcher must continuously examine how his or her biases and beliefs may be influencing the interaction.

Feminist Theory

The choice of a theory "provides the kind of map we need to get us where we want to go" (Harding 1998, 163). Feminist theory supports the study by integrating the following ideas: that the research relationship is one between two equal subjects; that the study of "gendered activity," that is, "the lived realities of women's lives," has value in and of itself; that oppression influences these realities; that women can be "subjects of knowledge" about their own oppression; that this knowledge has the potential to create change and lead to improved conditions for women and for all oppressed groups; and that research with oppressed groups mandates action to address the circumstances of oppression (Harding 1986, 141,146; Harding 2004b; Hartsock 2004).

Feminist theory holds that certain aspects of race, class, and gender relationships are disguised in the social world because the dominant ideology prevents clear awareness about conditions of inequality. Meticulous study of gendered activity helps to explicate these conditions. Through the study of women's experiences, certain aspects of a common worldview related to the oppression of women (and others) can be identified and articulated. However, there is no "one true story." Each individual's knowledge is based on her own experiences and is partial and unfinished.

Knowledge from all individuals and groups must be considered in order to come closer to a collective understanding of the meaning of oppression for women (Collins 1991, 193; Collins 2000; Harding 1986, 191–193). In *Moving the Rock* we see that each woman describes different experiences, yet similar themes resonate in many (but not all) of the stories.

Even though the study of gendered activity can teach us much about oppression, researchers from many fields assume that black women, sometimes uneducated, always from the margins, and often poor, cannot create the knowledge that asks the important questions and produces the answers related to oppressive circumstances. However, Collins (2000, 2004), a black feminist theorist, argues that women of color have the ability to recognize and interpret their experiences within social relationships and contexts. Pratt (1986) agrees, stating, "Subjective experience is spoken from a moving position already within or down in the middle of things, looking and being looked at, talking and being talked at" (32). The women of Morning Sun clearly ask questions about and have their own interpretations for experiences of personal and institutional oppression. Their knowledge is "socially situated," and they readily identify the influences of history and social relations (Harding 1998, 154; Harding 2004b, 4).

Jaggar (2004) notes that "oppressed groups suffer directly from the system that oppresses them. . . . Their pain provides them with a motivation for finding out what is wrong, for criticizing accepted interpretations of reality, and for developing new and less distorted ways of understanding the world" (56); but she also sees that while members of oppressed groups know that they are suffering, they might not necessarily recognize the underlying causes of their oppression (60). Comaroff (1985) agrees, seeing that people may be simultaneously knowing and unknowing about the forces that oppress them. In *Moving the Rock*, the middle-aged or elderly women understand and articulate personal meanings of oppression and resilience. However, the younger women often seem to search for alternative explanations to discriminatory experiences and feel that they will overcome their circumstances. Mahalia Lake supports this hopefulness in her young granddaughters by often telling them, "Having a dream, that's what it's all about." But Mahalia is more discouraging when her forty-one-year-old daughter, Molly, yearns for a home of her own, flatly stating, "You were born in the wrong family." The older women all describe times of acute grief or despair, when they went "back to [their] faith" to find the resilience and comfort they needed. These perspectives reflect the complexity of both knowing and unknowing, as well as the dialectic of acceptance and hope for future generations.

In contrast to the knowing recognition of oppressed groups, members of the dominant group are often convinced by their own beliefs and "fail to perceive the suffering of the oppressed or . . . believe it is freely chosen, deserved or inevitable. . . . Many members of the ruling class are likely to be convinced by their own ideology . . ." (Jaggar 2004, 56). This is as true in research as it is in society. Feminist analysis reveals that the "objective science" of research is not really objective at all. Instead, research is often immersed in the dominant discourse and thus is never neutral (Harding 2004b, 4). Rather, the questions, methods, and analyses are embedded in the political, cultural, and historical moment and in the discourse of dominant social relations. Social science research often transposes the realities of the lives of subjugated peoples into analysis about how "they should change." This discourse is then used to support policies that are deeply flawed. This "cultural imperialism" operates in a circular effect, es-tablishing the boundaries of inquiry and then engendering more research and policies that reflect the beliefs of the dominant group rather than the experiences of the people that the research professes to serve (Smith 2004, 23–24). In order to break this cycle, feminist scholars believe that researchers must hold an "engaged" or liberatory vision that will hopefully reveal and ultimately change oppressive structures (Hartsock 2004, 37). Thus a social justice philosophy that includes an action mandate is es-sential in feminist scholarship.

Black Feminist Theory

Black feminists note that feminist theory developed primarily by white middle-class academic women often suppresses and minimizes the experiences of women of color. The stories in *Moving the Rock* bring the experiences of a small group of black women to the front and center of our awareness. The women offer wisdom from the margins, not only about gender oppression, but also about how the intersection of race, class, and gender creates oppressive structures in their lives (Collins 2000, 2004). Their necessary labor, like that of other black women in white institu-tions (and historically in white homes), has helped the churchwomen to develop what Collins (2000) describes as an "outsider within" stance (11). This social location engenders a unique critique of oppression based on the women's "distinct views of the contradictions between the dominant groups' actions and ideology" (11).

It is within black homes, churches, organizations, and communities that black women have developed the intellectual traditions that enable them to survive and prosper in spite of the oppressive conditions that they face elsewhere. In these settings they have learned to value one another's wisdom, the wisdom that comes from experience, from "bought sense" as Molly Lander calls it.

Collins (2004) notes that these traditions are seen in both black women's activism and in their expressions of creativity. They can be found in religious and social justice theories; in literature, the arts, music, and prayer; in oral narratives, poems, and songs; and in dialogical encounters with family, friends, and extended kin. There is a "long and rich tradition of black feminist thought"; and much of it "has been produced by ordinary black women in their roles as mothers, teachers, musicians and preachers" (105). As seen in *Moving the Rock*, contributions to black feminist theory come from women from all walks of life and take on different forms, but they are consistently "both tied to black women's lived experiences and aim to better those experiences" (Collins 2000, 31). It is from within black women's social locations and through these intellectual traditions that African American women have created their own ideas about the many meanings of oppression and black womanhood (Collins, 2000, 2004).

Black feminist scholars stress that people from all walks of life must be able to understand theories of oppression so they can have the knowledge that supports action. When theory is understood only by academics, that is, the "elite," it becomes meaningless and "cannot be used to educate the public." Instead, it is used to silence, "to divide, separate, exclude, and keep at a distance" (hooks 1994, 65). When black women share their experiences of pain and struggle, they act as teachers and guides in the development of liberatory theory; and they challenge academic theorists and others to commit to making the pain go away (hooks 1994; Walker 1967/1983).

Collins's (2004) theory identifies three common themes that speak to black women's shared experiences: the meaning of self-definition and self-valuation, the interlocking nature of oppression, and the importance of African American women's culture (105–115). These themes appear often in the stories of the women from Morning Sun, but there are "different expressions" of these themes based on differences in age, class, and education (105).

In the first theme, self-definition involves "challenging . . . externally defined, stereotypical images of Afro-American womanhood." Self-valuation requires "replacing these images with authentic black female images" (106). When Molly Lander from Morning Sun says with strength and pride, "I am somebody because I am the child of a King!" she is giving a strong message that she values herself, is resisting objectification, and is claiming the power of being God's child (Abrums 1995, 2004). Through this "humanizing speech," she chooses survival, pride, peace, and joy (hooks 1989, 131).

The women of Morning Sun experience and readily articulate the second theme—the interlocking nature of race, class, and gender in oppression. The women tell stories of hardship related to their race, their poverty, and their relationships with black men (who, they note, also struggle because of racism and poverty). In response to this oppression, they proclaim common humanity—"We all bleed the same"—and ascribe to both Christian and civil rights views of social justice that demand equality for all.

Collins's final theme, the importance of African American women's culture, is integral to the stories and lives described in *Moving the Rock*. In the women's narratives, they define themselves and express their self-value within the context of home, family, and church. They describe how they find and express creativity in gospel music, in prayer, in the blues tradition, and in poetry. It is particularly striking how gospel music functions to "create a sphere of freedom" that nurtures and sustains Molly Lander and Mahalia Lake, the poorest women in the church (Collins 2000, 98). There is a similar freedom and escape from suffering in the poetic devotional prayers of Mable Jackson and Mahalia Lake.

Within the women's culture in Morning Sun Church we see a place where Collins's themes have developed and are nurtured. Walker (1967/1983) explains how black women's culture engenders a specific type of activism for social justice:

The real revolution is always concerned with the least glamorous stuff. With raising a reading level from second grade to third. With simplifying history and writing it down (or reciting it) for the old folks. With helping illiterates fill out food-stamp forms—for they must eat, revolution or not. The dull, frustrating work with our people is the work of the black revolutionary artist. It means, most of all, staying close enough to them to be there whenever they need you. (135)

The theories of the women of Morning Sun relate to survival wisdom, the best ways to raise children, how to recognize and resist oppression in white systems of power such as health care systems, the meaning of "intelligence," how to "come out fighting" when necessary, how to pray, and how to find peace and justice.[1] This is their activism.

Critical Reflexive Feminist Anthropology: Theory and Method

Feminist and black feminist theories offered the background needed to understand, analyze, and communicate with the women in the community of Morning Sun. Feminist perspectives also supported and influenced the research approaches and methodology. However, the actual research design was developed from the traditions and approaches found in critical reflexive feminist anthropology. As Harding (2004b) notes, women's ethnographies are often the first step in explaining the intricacies of power relations—it is within the women's descriptions that "the very best of human knowledge" can be found (7).

Ethnographic methods of anthropology, that is, participant observation and life history interviews, were used to collect the data. These tools allowed me to portray the women's everyday lives and realities in "an ethnography of the particular" (Abu-Lughod 2006, 162). This type of ethnography is consistent with feminist and black feminist theories because it gives precedence to and respects women's stories and experiences. "Ethnographies of the particular," especially when done with a small group of people, do not allow for generalizing to others. However, larger forces (for example, the presence of few "marriageable" men in poor black communities) can be found in particular descriptions. Such forces are "embodied in the actions of individuals living in time and place . . . ethnographies of the particular capture them best" (Abu-Lughod 2006, 163).

Anthropologists have a long history of being members of the dominant group while working with people who are "on the margins," and they have modeled and advocated for self-awareness and reflexivity during the research process.[2] As Rabinow (1977) points out, all research is an interactive process, and the self is always closely involved in and changes every encounter. Anthropologists recognize that fieldwork with people of various cultural groups has "the capacity to arouse consciousness of ourselves" (Prell 1989, 251). The researcher often learns as much about herself and her own social location and culture (or even more) as she does about the people and the culture being studied. In articulating this knowledge, she acknowledges and examines the influence of her subjective self on the research process.

Thus, feminist ethnographers "give careful consideration to the extent to which their (relatively) greater power [has] shaped the fieldwork encounter and ethnographic presentation" (Lewin 2006b, 20). The researcher employs self-reflection to continually explore how her biases, beliefs, sociocultural position, education, and training (that is, her "home base") influence every exchange.[3]

In this way, feminist anthropology accepts that the observer is "part of the story" and that, ethically, "demanding visibility for women across cultures also mean[s] that the author [is] visible" (Lewin 2006b, 25). To maintain the primacy of the participants' influence, the researcher adapts her approaches in response to input from her informants. This reflective stance reflects a strong commitment to listen carefully to the participants in order to identify patterns of inequality in specific locations (and in the research itself) and to determine how the findings of the research explicate these patterns and how meaningful interventions can be created.

Life history interviews were used in this study to help illuminate the particularity of the women's experiences. The interviews became dialogues between the storyteller and researcher (Vaz 1997b, 1997c). This is consistent with the principles of both reflexive anthropology and the use of feminist theory in participatory research.

In life history interviews, the interviewer structures the process as little as possible to give the greatest freedom to the storyteller (Gluck 1996; Riessman 1993). This allows both participants in the interview the ability to respond and follow where the story leads. Back-and-forth dialogue enables the interviewer to seek clarification to better understand an experience in the way the interviewee wants her to see it (Peterson 1997). The interviewer's role within this interpretive, mediating process is to foster and protect the freedom of the storyteller to tell her own story as she desires (Anderson and Jack 1991). The focus is on process, "on the dynamic unfolding of the subject's viewpoint" (23–25). Hence, the interviewer immerses herself in the story, follows the narrator's lead, and protects the storyteller's privacy by not intruding on areas that are off limits.

The life history "retains the perspective of the subject" but is also mediated by the researcher (Wright 1989, 155). The interviewer is an active participant and interpreter in shaping the narrative (Personal Narratives Group 1989b; Prell 1989). In Myerhoff's dialogical reflexive work:

> The self accommodates to the story, possibly undermining it, but certainly developing in relationship to it. . . . This human/cultural process of . . . storymaking through stories was an example of reflexivity, the capacity to arouse consciousness of ourselves. . . . In the life history, two stories produce one. A hearer and listener ask, respond, present and edit a life. (Prell 1989, 250–251, 254)

Just as the observer is part of the story in ethnography, the "listener/interpreter is part of the text" in the life history interview (Riessman 1993, 18). Each question asked, each story/experience followed, every verbal, nonverbal encouragement, or distraction, as well as the editing process itself, determine the course of the final story. Although the interviewee constructs personal meaning as she tells the story, it is often the interviewer who brings in the broader historical and social context (Atkinson 1998; Gluck 1996).

In "African American oral traditions, storytelling is used as a tool for providing instruction, building community, nurturing the spirit, and sustaining a unique culture . . ." (Banks-Wallace 2002, 417). Scholars who participate in life history interviews with black women note that the expression of their experiences is a complex task characterized by the intersection of race, gender, and social class with language, history, and culture. The oral narrative is ideally suited to describe this "multi-layered texture of black women's lives" (Etter-Lewis 1991, 43).

Dialogue between the storyteller and the listener "has deep roots in African-based oral traditions and in African-American culture" (Collins 2000, 261). It is through dialogical encounters that "new knowledge claims are . . . developed" and ideas are "tested and validated" (261). Dialogue "is a humanizing speech, one that challenges and resists domination" (hooks 1989, 131). When using dialogue in the research interview, the interviewer becomes a "participant witness" to the women's "acts of testimony" (Taylor 1998, 59–60). The ultimate goal of witnessing is to translate the stories in a way "that is beneficial to African American women and improves their social and material conditions" (60). In *Moving the Rock*, I have tried my best to honor these intentions.

Listening

Within the women's experiences, readers will "hear the broken voice," and "the pain contained within that brokenness—a speech of suffering; often it's that sound nobody wants to hear" (hooks 2004,153). It *is* painful to learn about some of the women's particular experiences, but it is important to "bear witness" to honor and record the hard-earned knowledge that the women share. In the listening, there is respect. In the hearing and speaking, there is the potential for change and healing. In the passing on of stories and in the descriptions of the everyday, there is the possibility of creating the activism needed for social justice movements.

hooks (1989) cautions, "When we write about the experiences of a group to which we do not belong, we should think about the ethics of our action, considering whether or not our work will be used to reinforce or perpetuate domination" (43). I have worried about this extensively, but the women want their stories to be told. They have shared their lives so that others can learn from them and create change. They know that their stories have power.

In the stories of the women from Morning Sun, there is pain, but there is also wisdom about power relations and resisting oppression. There are "how-to" survival strategies; knowledge about the healing power of creative expression; and explication of how women care for one another and raise their children. Intrinsic to their lives and stories, a distinct vision of a peaceful, just, and happy world is articulated in their prayerful hopes for change that will make things better for themselves, for their children, and for others.

NOTES

Introduction

1. All quotations in the book from the church members of Morning Sun were taken from original research: Abrums, Mary E. 1995. "Jesus will fix it after awhile": A study of black Christian women and their church. PhD Diss., University of Washington.

2. Please see the following resources for additional narratives and in-depth histories of the African American experience in Seattle, the Pacific Northwest, and the West: Black Oral History Collection (2007), de Chesnay (2005), Mumford (1980), Northwest African American Museum (2008), Orleck (2005), Peterson (1990), Spratlen (2001), Seattle Civil Rights and Labor History Project (2004–2009a), Taylor (1994/2003), Taylor (2007–2008), and Taylor and Moore (2003).

3. More recently, leaders such as Seattle's first black mayor, Norman Rice, and former King County Executive, Ron Sims, appointed in 2009 as the deputy secretary for the U.S. Department of Housing and Urban Development (HUD), have worked actively for similar pressing issues in the black community and across the city as a whole (Ervin 2009; Taylor 1994/2003).

4. Schools in Seattle have become more resegregated with the end of mandatory busing in the late 1990s and the demise of voluntary busing after a 2007 Supreme Court decision banned "racial tie breakers" that had encouraged school choice. As a result, today public schools in the CD and South Seattle serve mostly poor children of color with all the corresponding problems associated with poverty, while schools in the north end are flourishing with a recent influx of white middle-class children. Meanwhile, middle-class parents in the CD often choose private schools for their children, contributing to public school segregation problems. The majority of Seattle parents seem to want diverse schools that are close

to home; but many have come to believe that children cannot be asked to resolve long-standing problems related to residential patterns based on both economics and race (Shaw 2008).

5. In addition to the references cited in the chapter, extensive historical and current studies on the black family have been done by the following scholars (see also footnote for chapter 3): Aschenbrenner (1975), Du Bois (1899/2007), Drake and Cayton (1945/1993), Hill, Murry, and Anderson (2005), and Tucker and James (2005).

6. For more in-depth scholarship on the black church in the United States, please see the following resources: Blassingame (1972/1979), Cone (1970), Cone (1989), Du Bois (1903/1989), Grant (1989), Hine and Thompson (1998), Jones (1985), Karenga (1989), Mattis (2005), and Wilmore (1989a, 1989b).

7. Grant (1989) presents an analysis of "womanist theology," that is, black women's liberation theology, that uses Alice Walker's definition of womanism:

> Womanist, from womanish. (opp. of "girlish." i.e. frivolous, irresponsible, not serious). A Black feminist or feminist of color. From the Black folk expression of mothers to female children, "You acting womanish." Usually referring to outrageous, audacious, courageous or willful behavior. Wanting to know more and in greater depth than is considered "good for one." Interest in grown-up doings. Acting grown up. Being grown up. . . . Responsible. In charge. Serious . . . (Walker 1967/1983, xi).

Chapter Two

1. For more extensive discussion related to the black extended family, please see the following references in addition to those cited in chapter 1: Billingsley (1992), Collins (2000), Dilworth-Anderson and Goodwin (2005), Jones and Shorter-Gooden (2004), McAdoo (1988), McLoyd, Hill, and Dodge (2005a, 2005b), Martin and Martin (1978), Stack (1974), and Wilson (1996).

Appendix

1. The word *theory* is deliberately chosen to refer to the women's belief systems that are based on their experiences and that they refer to on a daily basis. It is defined as follows: "an explanation based on thought; explanation based on observation and reasoning, especially one that has been tested and confirmed as a general principle explaining a large number of related facts" (Barnhart and Barn-

hart 1993). Please see Abrums (1995, 2000a, 2000b, 2004) for in-depth analyses of the women's theories on health and meaning.

2. It has been essential for me to incorporate self-reflexive activity through every step of the research process, similarly to other researchers who use the methods of ethnography and life history interviews. A personal narrative of the ethnographer's experience has traditionally been incorporated in the written ethnography, albeit often as an "aside" (Pratt 1986). This self-reflexive fieldwork account acknowledges that the researcher as participant is an integral part of the process. The following scholars (in addition to those already cited in this chapter) have modeled and advocated for self-awareness and reflexivity in research and have contributed to the approaches used in this study: Bowen (1954), Brown (1997), Clifford (1986), Ebron (2006), Gluck and Patai (1991), Hurston (1935/1963), Lewin (2006a), Martin (1987), Myerhoff (1978), Personal Narratives Group (1989a), Pratt (1986), Rabinow (1977), Shostak (1983), and Vaz (1997a).

3. Both feminist and ethnographic approaches have influenced this feminist participatory research. Feminist participatory research pushes the subjective reflexive stance further in that it aims to be nonhierarchical, acknowledges the researcher's values and emotions, is committed to the transformation of power relations, and strives to understand women's struggles in context (Kingman 1997; Thompson 1991). Because I believe that research is ultimately political from the initial stages of conceptualization through the final stages of application, I have tried to be as aware as possible of the influence of my intentions, my feelings, and my biases on the research and writing processes. Harding (2004a), Haraway (2004), hooks (1981), Martin (1987), Phillips and McCaskill (2006), and Rose (2004), in addition to the feminist theorists referred to in this chapter, have shaped my thinking about the politics of research and science.

REFERENCES

Abrums, Mary. 2000a. Death and meaning in a storefront church. *Public Health Nursing* 17 (2): 132–142.

———. 2000b. "Jesus will fix it afterwhile": Meanings and health. *Social Science and Medicine* 50: 89–105.

———. 2000c. The meaning of racism when the "field" is the other side of town. *Journal of Cutural Diversity* 7 (4): 99–107.

———. 2004. Faith and feminism: How African American women from a storefront church resist oppression in healthcare. *Advances in Nursing Sciences* 27 (3):187–201.

Abrums, Mary E. 1995. "Jesus will fix it after awhile": A study of black Christian women and their church. PhD Diss., University of Washington.

Abu-Lughod, Lila. 2006. Writing against culture. In Lewin 2006a, 153–169.

Andersen, Margaret L., and Patricia Hill Collins, eds. 2007. *Race, class, & gender: An anthology.* 6th ed. Belmont, Calif.: Wadsworth-Thomson.

Anderson, Kathryn, and Dana C. Jack. 1991. Learning to listen: Interview techniques and analyses. In Gluck and Patai 1991, 11–26.

Aschenbrenner, Joyce. 1975. *Lifelines: Black families in Chicago.* New York: Holt, Rinehart and Winston.

Atkinson, Robert. 1998. *The life story interview.* Qualitative Research Methods Series 44. Thousand Oaks: Sage Publications.

Banks-Wallace, JoAnne. 2002. Talk that talk: Storytelling and analysis rooted in African American oral tradition. *Qualitative Health Research* 12: 410.

Banks-Wallace, J., and Ama Saran. 1992. Sisters in session. Paper presented at the Women's Health Research Group. University of Washington, Seattle.

REFERENCES

Barnhart, Clarence, and Robert K. Barnhart, eds. 1993. *The world book dictionary*. Chicago: World Book, Inc.

Billingsley, Andrew. 1992. *Climbing Jacob's ladder: The enduring legacy of African-American families*. New York: Touchstone.

Black Oral History Collection. 2007. Washington State University Libraries. www.wsulibs.wsu.edu/holland/masc/xblackoralhistory.html (accessed 4 April 2009).

Blassingame, John W. 1972/1979. *The slave community: Plantation life in the antebellum South*. New York: Oxford University Press.

Bowen, Elenor. 1954. *Return to laughter*. New York: Harper & Row.

Braman, Donald. 2004/2007. *Doing time on the outside: Incarceration and family life in urban America*. Ann Arbor: University of Michigan Press.

Brown, Georgia W. 1997. Oral history: Louisiana black women's memoirs. In Vaz 1997a, 83–95.

Burnham, Linda. 2007. Welfare reform, family hardship, and women of color. In Andersen and Collins 2007, 413–422.

Burton, Linda M., and Sherri Lawson Clark. 2005. Homeplace and housing in the lives of low-income urban African American families. In McLoyd, Hill, and Dodge 2005a, 166–188.

City of Seattle. 2000. Seattle poverty rates vary widely. *Demographic snapshots*. Prepared by Diana Corneluis, Department of Planning and Development. Seattle. www.seattle.gov/dpd/cms/groups/pan/@pan/documents/web_infor mational/dpds_006763.pdf (accessed 15 May 2009).

———. 2004. Population by race and neighborhood district. *Census 2000 (Summary file 1)*. Prepared by Department of Neighborhoods, Department of Planning and Development, Seattle, www.seattle.gov/dpd/cms/groups/pan/@pan/documents/ web_informational/dpds_007745.pdf (accessed 15 May 2009).

———. 2006. Central neighborhood district map. *Populations and demographics: Neighborhood districts*. Prepared by Department of Planning and Development. Seattle. www.seattle.gov/dpd/cms/groups/pan/@pan/documents/web_informa tional/dpds_007726.pdf (accessed 15 May 2009).

Clifford, James. 1986. Introduction: Partial truths. In *Writing culture: The poetics and politics of ethnography*, ed. James Clifford and George E. Marcus, 1–26. Berkeley: University of California Press.

Collins, Patricia Hill. 1991. *Black feminist thought: Knowledge, consciousness, and the politics of empowerment*. New York: Routledge.

———. 2000. *Black feminist thought: Knowledge, consciousness and the politics of empowerment*. 2nd ed. New York: Routledge.

———. 2004. Learning from the outsider within: The sociological significance of black feminist thought. In Harding 2004a, 103–126.

Comaroff, Jean. 1985. *Body of power, spirit of resistance.* Chicago: University of Chicago Press.

Cone, James H. 1970. *A black theology of liberation.* Philadelphia: Lippincott.

———. 1989. Black theology as liberation theology. In Wilmore1989a, 177–207.

Cross, Charles R. 2005. Beyond a broken boyhood, Jimi Hendrix lived to play. [Excerpted and condensed from *Room full of mirrors: A biography of Jimi Hendrix.* 2006. Hyperion Books]. *Seattle Times Pacific Northwest,* August 7, 16–22, 24–26.

Davila, Florangela, and Justin Mayo. 2001. The Central Area: Seattle's changing heart. *Seattle Times and Seattle Post-Intelligencer,* July 22, A1, A 16–17.

de Barros, Paul. 1993. *Jackson Street after hours: The roots of jazz in Seattle.* Seattle: Sasquatch Books.

de Chesnay, Mary. 2005. "Can't keep me down": Life histories of successful African Americans. In *Caring for the vulnerable: Perspectives in nursing theory, practice, and research,* ed. Mary de Chesnay, 221–231. Boston: Jones and Bartlett.

Dilworth-Anderson, Peggy, and Paula Y. Goodwin. 2005. A model of extended family support: Care of the elderly in African American families. In McLoyd, Hill, and Dodge 2005a, 211–223.

Douglas, Susan J., and Meredith W. Michaels. 2004. *The mommy myth: The idealization of motherhood and how it has undermined all women.* New York: Free Press.

Drake, St. Clair, and Horace A. Cayton. 1945/1993. *Black metropolis: A study of Negro life in a northern city.* Chicago: University of Chicago Press.

———. 1899/2007. *The Philadelphia Negro.* New York: Cosimo.

Du Bois, W. E. B. 1903/1989. *The souls of black folk.* New York: Bantam Press.

Ebron, Paulla A. 2006. Contingent stories of anthropology, race, and feminism. In Lewin 2006a, 203–215.

Ervin, Keith. 2009. Ron Sims leaves legacy of change as he heads for HUD. *Seattle Times,* Feb. 3. http://seattletimes.nwsource.com/html/politics/2008700732_simsmainbar03m.html (accessed 15 May 2009).

Etter-Lewis, Gwendolyn. 1991. Black women's life stories: Reclaiming self in narrative texts. In Gluck and Patai 1991, 43–58.

Frye, Marilyn. 2008. Oppression. In *The meaning of difference: American constructions of race, sex and gender, social class, and sexual orientation.* 5th ed., ed. Karen E. Rosenblum and Toni-Michelle C. Travis, 363–368. New York: McGraw-Hill.

Gifted with hope: Five religious women talk about their changing roles. 1985. An interview with Majorie Tuite, Melinda Roper, Luanne Schinzel, Joan Chittister, and Rosemary Radford Ruether by the editors. *Sojourners: Faith, politics, culture,* April: 12–22.

Gluck, Sherna. 1996. What's so special about women? Women's oral history. In *Oral history: An interdisciplinary anthology*. 2nd ed., ed. David K. Dunaway and Willa K. Baum, 215–230. Walnut Creek, Calif.: AltaMira Press.

Gluck, Sherna Berger, and Daphne Patai, eds. 1991. *Women's words: The feminist practice of oral history*. New York: Routledge.

Grant, Jacquelyn. 1989. Womanist theology: Black women's experience as a source for doing theology with special reference to Christology. In Wilmore 1989a, 208–227.

Gregory, James N. 2005. *The southern diaspora: How the great migrations of black and white southerners transformed America*. Chapel Hill: University of North Carolina Press.

Gutman, Herbert. 1976. *The black family in slavery & freedom 1750–1925*. New York: Vintage Books.

Hancock, Emily. 1989. *The girl within*. New York: Faucett Columbine.

Haraway, Donna. 2004. Situated knowledges: The science question in feminism and the privilege of partial perspective. In Harding 2004a, 81–101.

Harding, Sandra. 1986. *The science question in feminism*. Ithaca: Cornell University Press.

———. 1998. *Is science multicultural? Postcolonialisms, feminisms, and epistemologies*. Bloomington: Indiana University Press.

———, ed. 2004a. *The feminist standpoint theory reader: Intellectual & political controversies*. New York: Routledge.

———. 2004b. Introduction: Standpoint theory as a site of political, philosophic, and scientific debate. In Harding 2004a, 1–15.

Hartsock, Nancy C. M. 2004. The feminist standpoint: Developing the ground for a specifically feminist historical materialism. In Harding 2004a, 35–53.

Henry, Mary. 2007. Brown, Odessa (1920–1969). In *BlackPast.org: Remembered and reclaimed*, ed. Quintard Taylor, 2007–2008. www.blackpast.org/?q=aaw/brown-odessa-1920-1969 (accessed 15 May 2009).

Hill, Nancy E., Velma McBride Murry, and Valerie D. Anderson. 2005. Sociocultural contexts of African American families. In McLoyd, Hill, and Dodge 2005a, 21–44.

Hine, Darlene Clark, and Kathleen Thompson. 1998. *A shining thread of hope*. New York: Broadway Books.

hooks, bell. 1981. *Ain't I a woman: Black women and feminism*. Boston: South End Press.

———. 1989. *Talking back*. Boston: South End Press.

———. 1994. *Teaching to transgress: Education as the practice of freedom*. New York: Routledge.

———. 1995. *Killing rage: Ending racism*. New York: Henry Holt & Company.

———. 2004. Choosing the margin as a space of radical openness. In Harding 2004a, 153–159.

How to use the Bible in everyday life. n.d. *Portals to Bible study in ways to health and happiness*, 65.

Hurston, Zora Neale. 1935/1963. *Mules and men*. Bloomington: Indiana University Press.

Jaggar, Alison M. 2004. Feminist politics and epistemology: The standpoint of women. In Harding 2004a, 55–66.

Jones, Charisse, and Kumea Shorter-Gooden. 2004. *Shifting: The double lives of black women in America*. New York: Perennial.

Jones, Jacqueline. 1985. *Labor of love, labor of sorrow: Black women, work and the family, from slavery to the present*. New York: Vintage Books.

Karenga, Maulana. 1989. Black religion. In Wilmore 1989a, 271–300.

Kingman, Leslie Ann. 1997. European American and African American men and women's valuations of feminist and natural science research methods in psychology. In Vaz 1997a, 250–259.

Lewin, Ellen, ed. 2006a. *Feminist anthropology: A reader*. Malden, Mass.: Blackwell.

———. 2006b. Introduction. In Lewin 2006a, 1–38.

Marger, Martin N. 2003. *Race and ethnic relations: American and global perspectives*. Belmont, Calif.: Wadsworth-Thomson.

Martin, Elmer P., and Joanne Mitchell Martin. 1978. *The black extended family*. Chicago: University of Chicago Press.

Martin, Emily. 1987. *The woman in the body*. Boston: Beacon Press.

Mattis, Jacqueline S. 2005. Religion in African American life. In McLoyd, Hill, and Dodge 2005a, 189–210.

McAdoo, Harriette Pipes, ed. 1988. *Black families*. 2nd ed. Newbury Park: Sage Publications.

McLoyd, Vonnie C., Nancy E. Hill, and Kenneth A. Dodge, eds. 2005a. *African American family life: Ecological and cultural diversity*. New York: Guilford Press.

———. 2005b. Introduction: Ecological and cultural diversity in African American family life. In McLoyd, Hill, and Dodge 2005a, 3–20.

Minister, Kristina. 1991. A feminist frame for the oral history interview. In *Women's words: The feminist practice of oral history*, ed. Sherna Berger and Daphne Patai, 27–41. New York: Routledge.

Mumford, Esther Hall. 1980. *Seattle's black Victorians 1852–1901*. Seattle: Ananse Press.

Myerhoff, Barbara. 1978. *Number our days*. New York: Simon & Schuster.

Newman, Katherine S. 2007. The invisible poor. In Andersen and Collins 2007, 303–312.

REFERENCES

Northwest African American Museum. 2008. Seattle, Washington. http://naamnw.org/ (accessed 4 April 2009).

Oliver, Melvin L., and Thomas M. Shapiro. 2006. Wealth and racial stratification. In *Race and ethnicity in society: The changing landscape*, ed. Elizabeth Higginbotham and Margaret L. Andersen, 240–246. Belmont, Calif.: Wadsworth-Thomson.

Orleck, Annelise. 2005. *Storming Caesar's palace: How black mothers fought their own war on poverty*. Boston: Beacon Press.

Painter, Nell Irvin. 1976/1986. *Exodusters: Black migration to Kansas after reconstruction*. New York: W.W. Norton.

Patillo-McCoy, Mary. 2007. Black picket fences: Privilege and peril among the black middle class. In Andersen and Collins 2007, 136–143.

Personal Narratives Group, eds. 1989a. *Interpreting women's lives: Feminist theory and personal narratives*. Bloomington: Indiana University Press.

———. 1989b. Whose Voice? In Personal Narratives Group 1989a, 201–203.

Petersilia, Joan. 2003. *When prisoners come home: Parole and prisoner reentry*. Oxford: Oxford University Press.

Peterson, Elizabeth A. 1997. African American women and the emergence of self-will: The use of phenomenological research. In Vaz 1997a, 156–173.

Peterson, Jane W. 1990. Age of wisdom: Elderly black women in family and church. In *The cultural context of aging worldwide perspectives*, ed. Jay Sokolovsky, 213–227. New York: Begin & Garvey.

Phillips, Layli, and Barbara McCaskill. 2006. Daughters and sons: The birth of womanist identity. In *The womanist reader*, ed. Layli Phillips, 85–113. New York: Routledge.

Pratt, Mary. 1986. Fieldwork in common places. In *Writing culture: The poetics and politics of ethnography*, ed. James Clifford and George Marcus, 27–50. Berkeley: University of California Press.

Prell, Riv-Ellen. 1989. The double frame of life history in the work of Barbara Myerhoff. In Personal Narratives Group 1989a, 241–258.

Rabinow, Paul. 1977. *Reflections on fieldwork in Morocco*. Berkeley: University of California Press.

Riessman, Catherine Kohler. 1993. *Narrative analysis*. Qualitative Research Methods Series 30. Newbury Park: Sage Publications.

Riley, Glenda. 2003. African American women in western history: Past and prospect. In *African American women confront the West 1600–2000*, ed. Quintard Taylor and Shirley Anne Wilson Moore, 22–27. Norman: University of Oklahoma Press.

Rose, Hilary. 2004. Hands, brain, and heart: A feminist epistemology for the natural sciences. In Harding 2004a, 67–80.

Seattle Civil Rights and Labor History Project. 2004-2009a. University of Washington. http://depts.washington.edu/civilr/ (accessed 15 May 2009).

———. 2004–2009b. Segregated Seattle. University of Washington. http://depts.washington.edu/civilr/segregated.htm (accessed 15 May 2009).

Shaw, Linda. 2008. The resegregation of Seattle's schools. *Seattle Times*, June 1. http://seattletimes.nwsource.com/html/education/2004450677_reseg01m.html (accessed 4 April 2009).

Shostak, Marjorie. 1983. *Nisa: The life and words of a Kung woman.* New York: Vintage Books.

Smith, Dorothy E. 2004. Women's perspective as a radical critique of sociology. In Harding 2004a, 21–33.

Spratlen, Lois Price. 2001. *Registered nurses in Seattle: The struggle for opportunity and success.* Seattle: Peanut Butter Press.

Stack, Carol B. 1974. *All our kin.* New York: Harper & Row.

———. 1996. *A call to home: African Americans reclaim the rural south.* New York: Basic Books.

Taylor, Janette Y. 1998. Womanism: A methodological framework for African American women. *Advances in Nursing Science* 21 (1): 53–64.

Taylor, Quintard. 1994/2003. *The forging of a black community: Seattle's Central District from 1870 through the Civil Rights era.* Seattle: University of Washington Press.

———, ed. 2007–2008. *BlackPast.org: Remembered and reclaimed.* An online reference guide to African American history. www.blackpast.org (accessed 14 May 2009).

Taylor, Quintard, and Shirley Ann Wilson Moore, eds. 2003. *African American women confront the West 1600–2000.* Norman: University of Oklahoma Press.

Thompson, Janice L. 1991. Exploring gender and culture with Khmer refugee women: Reflections on participatory feminist research. *Advances in Nursing Science* 13 (3): 30–48.

Travis, Jeremy, and Michelle Waul, eds. 2003. *Prisoners once removed: The impact of incarceration and reentry on children, families, and communities.* Washington, D.C.: Urban Institute Press.

Tucker, M. Belinda, and Angela D. James. 2005. New families, new functions: Postmodern African American families in context. In McLoyd, Hill, and Dodge 2005a, 86–108.

U.S. Census Bureau. 2000. Department of Commerce. *The black population 2000.* C2KBR/01-5. Prepared by J. McKinnon. Washington, D.C. www.census.gov/population/www/cen2000/briefs.html (accessed 15 May 2009).

———. 2005. Department of Commerce. *Income, poverty, and health insurance coverage in the United States: 2005.* Prepared by C. DeNavas-Wait, B. Proctor, and C. Hill Lee. Washington, D.C. www.census.gov/prod/2006pubs/p60-231 .pdf (accessed 15 May 2009).

U.S. Department of Labor. 2002. Bureau of Labor Statistics. *A profile of the working poor, 2000*. Report 957. Washington, D.C. www.bls.gov/cps/cpswp2000. htm (accessed 15 May 2009).

Vaz, Kim Marie, ed. 1997a. *Oral narrative research with black women*. Thousand Oaks: Sage Publications.

———. 1997b. Introduction: Oral narrative research with black women. In Vaz 1997a, 1–3.

———. 1997c. Social conformity and social resistance: Women's perspectives on "women's place." In Vaz 1997a, 223–249.

Walker, Alice. 1967/1983. *In search of our mothers' gardens*. San Diego: Harcourt Brace Jovanovich.

Waller, Maureen R., and Raymond Swisher. 2006. Fathers' risk factors in fragile families: Implications for "health" relationships and father involvement. *Social Problems* 53 (3): 392–420.

Warren, Gwendolin Sims. 1997. *Ev'ry time I feel the Spirit*. New York: Henry Holt & Co.

Wehler, Cheryl. 1995. Quoted in Colin Greer. Something is robbing our children of their future. *Seattle Times Parade Magazine*, March 5: 4–6.

Wiggins, Daphne C. 2005. *Righteous content: Black women's perspectives of church and faith*. New York: New York University Press.

Wilmore, Gayraud S., ed. 1989a. *African American religious studies: An interdisciplinary anthology*. Durham and London: Duke University Press.

———. 1989b. General Introduction. In Wilmore 1989a, xi–xxii.

Wilson, William Julius. 1996. *When work disappears: The world of the new urban poor*. New York: Vintage Books.

Wright, Marcia. 1989. Personal narratives, dynasties, and women's campaigns: Two examples from Africa. In Personal Narratives Group 1989a, 155–171.

Zwerin, Mike. 1994. Before grunge rock: Seattle's jazz roots. *International Herald Tribune*, April 15. www.iht.com/bin/print_ipub.php?file=articles/1994/04/ 15/cald.php (accessed 31 July 2007).

INDEX

ABOUT THE AUTHOR

Mary Abrums is an associate professor and sociocultural anthropologist in the Nursing Department at the University of Washington, Bothell. Dr. Abrums earned her nursing degree from the University of Colorado Medical Center, a masters degree in parent and child nursing, and masters and PhD degrees in sociocultural anthropology from the University of Washington in Seattle. She specializes in culture and diversity, community health, and national and international health disparities. She is the author of several articles on health in the African American community. She lives in Seattle, Washington, with her family.